Globalization and Women in Academia

Sociocultural, Political, and Historical Studies in Education

Joel Spring, Editor

Globalization and Women in Academia
North/West–South/East

Carmen Luke
University of Queensland

LAWRENCE ERLBAUM ASSOCIATES, PUBLISHERS
2001   **Mahwah, New Jersey**   **London**

Lawrence Erlbaum Associates, Inc., Publishers
10 Industrial Avenue
Mahwah, NJ 07430

Cover design by Kathryn Houghtaling Lacey

Library of Congress Cataloging-in-Publication Data

Luke, Carmen
Globalization and women in academia : North/West-South/East
  Carmen Luke.
      p. cm.
    Includes bibliographical references and index.
  ISBN 0-8058-3668-3 (cloth : alk. paper)
  ISBN 0-8058-3669-1 (pbk. : alk. paper)
  1. Women—Education (Higher—Cross-cultural studies. 2. Women in ed-
    ucation—Cross-cultural studies. 3. Women college teachers—
    Cross-cultural studies. 4. Women college students—Cross-cultural
    studies. 5. Comparative education. I. Title. II. Series.
  LC1567 .L85   2001
  378′.0082 —dc21   2001018805
                                                          CIP

Books published by Lawrence Erlbaum Associates are printed on acid-free
paper, and their bindings are chosen for strength and durability.

Printed in the United States of America
10 9 8 7 6 5 4 3 2 1

Contents

Preface

Western research on women in higher education has produced a substantial volume of scholarship on women's progress in the last 25 years. A range of structural-institutional, social, and cultural factors and ideologies have been identified as glass-ceiling barriers to women's academic career advancements. In response, numerous intervention strategies to support women in academics have been developed and implemented under equity and affirmative action banners. But in the last 25 years, the relatively stable modernist model of the university has been transformed into a corporate, postmodern university forced to look beyond the campus perimeter at global student markets, product diversification, and electronic delivery of courses. The university is both educational institution and workplace, and it has long been characterized as an international enterprise. More recently, the accelerated pace of people and information flows, global marketing, and increasing standardization across the sector have reshaped its institutional practices and discourses into what is now commonly termed the "globalization of higher education." In such an environment, how women fare globally in higher education, whether as staff or students, should matter. Feminism has long argued for the importance of local, situated analyses, yet there is hardly any research on the cultural politics of dis/advantage mediating women's academic career paths in higher education in nonwestern countries.

Feminist research on women in higher education has paid little attention to globalization theory or the globalization of higher education, other than to point out that women are the first and biggest casualty in organizational restructuring and the casualization of academic labor. I agree that this is an important and devastating consequence for women of a larger global drift toward institutional downsizing and financial belt tightening. But there is more to globalization than economic rationalist and reductionist agendas. One such issue is the lack of educational scholarship on how women might factor into new times and new conditions.

In this book, I focus on women in higher education in four Southeast Asian countries: Thailand, Singapore, Hong Kong, and Malaysia. In a series of case studies, I bring the insights of a group of Southeast Asian academic women to light in dialogues about the extent to which feminism, local cultural politics, equity and affirmative action agendas, and accountability mechanisms of quality assurance discourses have supported or failed women. As western academics, we can only speculate—unless we ask women to explain in their own terms—how local cultural and political ideologies and social histories circumscribe gender hierarchies and women's educational and employment opportunities. I hope that this book, then, goes part of the way to bridge some of the knowledge gaps among women differently situated but nonetheless engaged in globalized forms of academic labor conducted in the increasingly isomorphic workplace of the postmodern 21st century university.

OVERVIEW

This book is divided into two parts. Part I investigates northern and western research, current debate, and theoretical and political issues related to globalization, education, equity, and women in higher education. Part II presents views on education, equity, and women in higher education from the south and east, including four case studies of women in higher-education management in Thailand, Singapore, Hong Kong, and Malaysia. Location markers such as south, east, north, and west are geographic signposts and modernist conceptual metaphors that have divided the world into abstract sectors and innumerable hierarchies of development authored in the north and west. These terms are bracketed here to situate perspectives, vantage points, and speaking positions. I am mindful of the conceptual traps of totalizing complexity and heterogeneity within a spatial category, a geographic marker such as west or east. I use these terms cautiously—not as object-level descriptors—and am fully cognizant of the political and conceptual risk of using modernist, industrial-era labels, especially in a feminist-postmodernist debate about globalization.

Chapter 1 provides an overview and analysis of feminist research on women in western higher education and concludes with an overview of current debates about the globalization of education. Chapter 2 takes a closer look at globalization theory. I examine student, knowledge, and capital flows, the globalization of educational principles and visions through global discourses and organizations, and I analyze the changing nature of academic work as a consequence of educational globalization.

Chapter 3 provides a case study of the implementation of quality assurance mechanisms at one university and its effects on academic women. Quality assurance is one aspect of the global proliferation of economic rationalist and new managerialist discourses sweeping across higher-education sectors on a global scale. I argue that quality assurance mechanisms of accountability, transparency, and quality now pervading the higher-education sector can be used to women's advantage.

Chapter 4 bridges Part I and II by exploring how we might reconcile the globalism of western feminism, even in its third world and postcolonial variants, with locally situated theorizing, practices, and identities. I argue that research and intellectual labor are always situated and embodied, and always reflect a "centric" view from somewhere. Yet local standpoints, whether those of the western-trained or western-based postcolonial or feminist intellectual, are also infused with global and cosmopolitan orientations, linked into global networks through class-based affinities, and global communities through adherence to globalized western models of scholarly inquiry, publishing, and knowledge dissemination regimes. This chapter raises questions about cultural and local authenticity of postcolonial and third-world feminist theorizing, and about the role of cosmopolitan intellectuals in cultural translations and the politics of local knowledge production.

In Chapter 5, which introduces Part II, I present views on education, development, and gender from the south and east. This chapter draws on a broad range of Southeast Asian postcolonial, feminist, and educational scholarship to set the conceptual framework for the remaining case study chapters. Chapters 6, 7, 8, and 9 present the case studies on women in senior academic management in Thailand, Singapore, Hong Kong, and Malaysia. Aware of the difficulty of representing women's experiences and voices in the linear logic of print and the academic genre and protocol of analysis and interpretation, I nonetheless attempt to let women do most of the talking.

I argue throughout this book that the local-global dynamics are not as simple and straightforward as they may seem in the standard binarist logic offered to us in most globalization literature. Throughout the chapters, I illustrate my discussion with reference to the experiences and interpretations of the women in this study, my own academic experience and history, and my teaching and research in the region. I hope to be able to convey some of the complexity of global sweeps and trends in education and feminist discourses as they intersect with local cultural variations but also dovetail into patterns of regional similarities.

ACKNOWLEDGMENTS

Research for parts of this book was supported by grants from the University of Queensland and the Graduate School of Education. My thanks to Ravinder Sidhu for her insightful editorial help and Naomi Silverman at Lawrence Erlbaum for her support and encouragement. Special thanks to Frances A. Maher of Wheaton College and Denise Murray of San Jose State University for their instructive comments and suggestions on my initial manuscript. I thank all the women who participated in this research. My special thanks to Molly Lee, Sali Zaliha Mustapha, and Saisamorn Srisukphrasert for their help, support, and cultural translations. Most of all, I am grateful for the guidance and advice, the hours of talk and years of enduring friendship of Anneliese Krämer-Dahl, Phyllis Chew, and Audrey Ambrose-Yeoh.

I wish to thank the following for permission to reproduce parts of previously published articles: With kind permission from Kluwer Academic Publishers for "Quality Assurance and Women in Higher Education," *Higher Education*, 1997, 33(4), 433–451, ISBN 0018-1560; Asian Center for Women's Studies, Korean Women's Institute, Ewha Womans University, Korea, for "Women in Higher Education Management in Thailand," *Asian Journal of Women's Studies*, 1997, 3(4), 98–130, ISSN 1225-9276 74; Carfax Publishers for "Cultural Politics and Women in Singapore Higher Education Management," *Gender & Education*, 1998, 10(3),

245–63, ISSN 0954–0253; Hong Kong Institute of Educational Research, Chinese University of Hong Kong, for "'I got to where I am by my own strength': Women in Hong Kong Higher Education Management," *Education Journal*, 1998, 26(1), 31–58, ISSN 1025-1936.

—*Carmen Luke*

Introduction

"Women in higher education" is not my topic of choice for research and writing. Rather, it is a lived reality, a long-term project in which I have been subject and object, participant and observer, in charge and out of control of my life project. It is a personal map that frames the issues I raise in this book. The often circuitous pathways of a woman's academic career, the geographical locations and institutional contexts of her educational and work histories, her generation, family circumstances, and personal "identikit" shape her experiences in higher education, her theoretical and methodological choices, and her political take on the life around her in the academy.

My identikit is probably just another immigrant's story. I am German-born of German-Jewish ancestry. My family immigrated to Canada in the early 1950s when I was 7, and I received all my schooling there. My partner of some 25 years is second-generation Chinese American. We have one daughter, we are both in academics, in the same discipline, and have always worked in the same institutions. There is another story to be told here of academic couples, of interracial couples, and of the unpredictable cultural politics that value, devalue, and hierarchize the mix of race and gender differently in different social and academic contexts.

I have only been in academics since 1985. But this has been long enough to write volumes about women's experiences of the good, the bad, and the ugly. Unlike other professions, reaching the senior professorial levels involves decades of academic competition. I started late, beginning my undergraduate degree in Communications at the age of 28 at Simon Fraser University in Canada. A four-year BA was followed by a two-year research MA and a three-year full-time Ph.D. Halfway through my BA, I enrolled in a one-year teacher certification program so I could substitute teach on days I didn't have classes. Teaching was never a career move for me, but in the days of hefty fees, substitute teaching for nearly C$75 a day was a windfall. In the early 1980s, academic jobs were tight in Canada. Many of us ended up in temporary jobs as teachers, waiting for the market to open up. Others turned into "freeway profs," holding down several contract lecturer jobs at community colleges, substitute teaching positions in local schools, and perhaps a temporary teaching or research assistantship at a university.

My graduate days had already taught me a lifetime of lessons about gendered academic hierarchy, the silencing tactics of male classmates or professors. I had spent a decade learning and reproducing the canon, what we then called "male-stream thought." Getting ripped off by professors for authorship was one important lesson. It didn't take long to figure out that influential grant, conference, and publishing contacts circulated among the boys and that rites of passage and induction into the academy happened at the pub or on the basketball court.

In 1983, my partner and I applied for academic positions in Canada, the United Kingdom, and Australia. Our daughter was 12 years old. A lecturing position for my partner in a regional university in northern Australia came through first, and we moved there in 1984. We both went through a profound culture shock. We were unprepared for the prevailing racial attitudes, the shift from North American metropolis to small-town Australia: little things like the heat, a phone system with no direct long-distance dialing, Christmas in the scorching heat and humidity of summer, three TV stations that transmitted only from 10 a.m. to midnight, an accent that I found difficult to understand. Stranger yet was the university: some 2,000 predominantly white Australian students, an all-male professoriate, and only a few women lecturers who were clued into the gender equity and education debate. I learned later that well-known feminist Dale Spender had taught in the department but had left a few years prior to my arrival. Dale's legacy was twofold: bad jokes among the men about feminist radicalism and a dedication among some of the women to the intellectual and political pursuit of gender equity. She and I have since reminisced about our time in "the north."

When I left Simon Fraser University in 1983, administration was fully computerized, the library was partially electronic, staff had computers on their desks, and graduate students had mainframe log-in access. I had written my master's thesis on a computer. At my new university, library research was conducted on card catalogs housed in little wooden drawers, and the thump of an ink stamp validated book check-in and check-out. There wasn't a computer in anyone's office, and academic life was conducted on a paper trail, on rotary dial phones through old-style switchboards. The IT revolution evident elsewhere was still a long way off.

I came to Australia in late 1984 with no job but managed to secure a six-month contract at the university in early 1985. Although I had a book under contract and had published my master's thesis with SUNY Press, I was appointed at the lowest level in the lowest lecturer classification. For the next two years, I went through consecutive 6-month contracts, followed by two years of 10-month contracts, all of which were just short enough to disqualify me from accumulating tenure track and sabbatical leave, from university contributions to a pension fund, from accruing holiday leave and pay, and from serving on a range of faculty and university committees. Important for us, however, was the lack of income during the summer months when I was between contracts. As a new recruit, I had no choice over my teaching and was thrown into classes nobody else seemingly wanted to teach: large first-year sociology of education classes and the special intake stream of Aboriginal and Torres Strait Islander students. My Canadian training had not prepared me for either mainstream Australian or indigenous educational issues. The teaching of indigenous students and research on indigenous education was at the time the exclusive domain of white Australians. I felt totally out of my depth and out of place.

For two years, my department head refused to call me by my name, referring to me instead as the "Smith replacement," in deference to the person I had replaced. I don't recall ever being addressed as Dr. Luke in those years, but I do recall the belligerent twist the department head and his mates would put on pronouncing Foucault (Foo-coll) or poststructuralism in reference to the work I was publishing out of my thesis. This was a big joke: so French and continental, so totally unrelated to education! Those who got ahead seemed to have insider access to an endless supply of departmental research or travel funds, and secured tenure and promotions with no Ph.D. and less than modest publication records. Some of them golfed together on Fridays or belonged to the same church. It wasn't until some years later, with a starter package of academic capital under my belt, that I started heading out to conferences at urban universities. Those early forays into the academic mainstream confirmed my sense of the colonial outpost mentality and culture of my own university.

In 1989, a new department head was appointed who changed my life. I was relieved of my heavy teaching load to write and publish and was supported for promotion and tenure. I was networked into grant applications, committees, conference and publication opportunities, and this department head never failed to introduce me as "Dr. Luke, she writes the books here." After years of intellectual marginalization and structural impediments thrown at me principally by men, the new department head proved the exception to what I had experienced as seamless patriarchal collusion in the enactment of the rules, routines, and structures of the university.

Tenure qualified me to apply for sabbatical, and my first trip back to North America was in 1992. Tenure had given me security of employment as well as a speaking position. I gradually began publishing more feminist scholarship, no longer worried that the politics of this intellectual direction would incur ridicule or undermine future promotional prospects.

I spent part of my sabbatical at the University of Madison in Wisconsin and basked in the vibrant intellectual environment I had missed for so long. I returned to Australia committed to pursuing the establishment of a Women's Studies Centre at my university, among the last in the country not to have a dedicated degree program. A lot of hard work, lobbying, and devastating setbacks filled the next few years as I and a group of women tried to establish the Centre. In 1994, I was promoted to associate professor, and the Centre was formally established. As foundation director I became a member of all university committees on which heads and deans sit. In other words, I gained access to senior information circuits and policy decision-making levels. I had to learn new strategies and tactics to get a voice, get heard, and maintain the floor.

The time had come to move on. Having arrived in Australia a decade earlier with only a handful of book review publications and a contract to publish my master's thesis, I finally had enough academic capital to feel confident about moving from the academic margins to the center. As is probably the case elsewhere, moving from a regional university to what in Australia are called the "sandstones" (equivalent to American ivy league universities) is a lot more difficult than shifting the other way. A greater dilemma, however, was securing two senior positions in the same discipline, in the same city, at the same time. Spousal positions are not negotiable in the Australian system. Neither my partner nor I were willing to relocate on one position and expect the other to take whatever would come along. We had come too far individually to let either career slip into uncertainty for the benefit of the other. Eventually, in 1996, we secured two senior positions in the Graduate School of Education at the university where I now work.

The long wait has been worth it. After nearly 15 years in this country, I have been able to move beyond the bitter experiences that colored my early years as an academic. Yet the Australian higher-education sector has changed dramatically since then, with institutional downsizing, changing funding formulas, and the push to internationalize, all of which has generated a climate of insecurity and change fatigue among staff. Drastic federal funding cutbacks and the move toward full-fee-paying students has pushed universities to seek educational dollars overseas. In the spirit of internationalization, Australian universities have sent staff scurrying on recruitment missions and program delivery across Southeast Asia. Part of my workload in the last few years has been to teach graduate subjects, to recruit, and to offer seminar and short-course components in several countries in the region. This has sparked an unexpected new intellectual lease on what I thought had become a somewhat sedentary and mundane academic life.

My work in Asia has reshaped how and what I teach in attempts to blend the western models and knowledge for which students seek credentials with local knowledge, cultural norms, and contexts, and students' variable English competencies. I have branched into new disciplinary fields to teach myself the histories, politics, cultures, economics, and social demography of the region. I have learned a tremendous amount about local postcolonial histories and their links with nationalist discourses, with human capital and development theories, and women's conceptual locations within those discourses.

The economic fallout from the 1997 regional economic crisis has been particularly significant for the Australian higher-education sector as the Asian educational dollar evaporated almost overnight. Our institution retained its commitment to completing programs already under way, especially in Thailand, the first and worst hit country in 1997. Korean and Indonesian students were recalled from our campuses, Malaysia followed suit, and Thailand legislated overseas travel restrictions for all civil servants. In our case, many of our students are civil servants teaching in colleges, polytechnics, and universities. In short, my department's postcrisis strategy was to maintain "good faith" commitments to programs and people, despite the drop in revenue. During these last few years, then, I have had opportunities to work in Thailand, Malaysia, Hong Kong, and Singapore. I have been able to teach about and research changing economic and political fortunes that have affected schooling and higher-education, women's roles and opportunities within the higher-education sector and across labor markets, and women's roles within rapid economic and social change and in relation to nationalist discourses. Most rewarding, personally, have been opportunities to develop new relationships with many academic women in these countries.

My theoretical understandings of feminism have been challenged and reworked over the years through my experiences with other academic women and women students, with senior antifeminist and profeminist women, with community activist women, and with anti- and profeminist men. However, those experiences have been located in the western cultural context of the academy. I have learned the lessons of both impenetrable and cracked glass ceilings, and I know the formal texts and subtexts of male academic culture well. But as a consequence of my work in the region over the last few years, I have rethought many of the feminist theoretical and political assumptions I had taken for granted. I am still learning, but I have developed a more comprehensive understanding of the complexity of a whole range of cultural differences within and among Asian countries, particularly as these relate to women and the larger project of feminism and discourses of equality. First, in terms of women's culture-specific attitudes toward and applications of feminist or gender agendas; second, in terms of women's status and interpretations of their experiences within higher education in local sites; and third, in terms of nation-state and cultural differences that frame larger societal discourses on gender and, in turn, mark the cultures of the academy.

What I had understood from the western literature about the politics of structural and cultural career impediments for women, about masculinist discourses pervading the university sector, has been reframed as I have gained insights, albeit partial, into diverse regional-cultural variations on an essentially European model of university education. Governance structures, academic program or job classification structures, disciplinary divisions and groupings, and so on are similar across the globe, especially in postcolonial states where British legacies are palpable even after decades of local reworkings and adaptations. More recent drifts toward international standardization of education as a consequence of globalization have created even greater isomorphism across the sector in different nation-states. And yet women's localized experiences and opportunities, their explanatory and analytic templates in accounting for women's social roles and status within this increasingly internationalized sector, do not fit neatly within the conceptual and theoretical frameworks developed by western feminism. Although western feminism has long insisted on the need for analytic sensitivity to the situatedness of experience, context, and identity, very little research is available on the cultural specificities of women's experiences and career pathways in higher education in non-western countries. This, then, has been the focus of my work over the last few years and it is the focus of this book.

Any analysis or discussion of higher education today has to contend with globalization. The marketing of education, the commodification of knowledge, degrees and students, staff and student mobility are the hall-marks of what is variously called internationalization or globalization of education. The north and west is said to be in the business of educational product and service delivery to the south and east. Generally overlooked in such explanations of center-to–margin currents are countercurrents that emanate from the so-called peripheries. Australia, for instance, is currently a cheap educational alternative to the United States or Europe. The United States, the United Kingdom, and Australia are often default choices for students unable to gain entry, for a variety of scholastic or political reasons, into prestige universities in the region, such as the University of Tokyo, the University of Malaya, the National University of Singapore, or the University of Jakarta. These universities are high-status magnets in the region, drawing students from across the eastern to western Asian basin and the Asia-Pacific region. Japanese universities, particularly Tokyo and Keio, are accorded greater status and social capital by the Japanese than are American or British universities. By contrast, Malaysian, Hong Kong, and Singaporean business, political, and professional elites have always sent their children to study in Europe or the United States. There are many centers on the so-called peripheries, and flows of culture, capital, educational products, and consumers are multidirectional and uneven. Moreover, whether we look at regionalization, internationalization, or globalization of education, the actual delivery and consumption of education remain situated in local sites embedded in local cultures, nation-state formulated rules and regulations, and localized intersubjective relations among and between staff and students. Even "virtual" degrees are consumed by subjects in a place and produced and assessed by subjects in yet another place.

The point is that analysis of education cannot ignore theoretical debates about and influences of globalization, nor can engagement with globalization issues and discourses ignore local uptakes, local contexts, resistances, and appropriations. My task here, then, is to counterpose both local and global to write a different narrative about women in higher education, one that does not rehearse the same perpetrator arguments and generalizations about a universal patriarchy and oppressed women. My aim is to analyze local and global conditions that situate women on interlocking grids of local histories, nation-state ideologies, and cultural politics, and show how those situated differences nonetheless are infused with aspects of globalism, and dovetail into universal patterns of similarity that characterize the academy. I argue that under new globalizing conditions that today permeate higher education, academics in Southeast Asia and no doubt elsewhere have become relay points or cultural conduits through which global *and* local discourses and practices flow.

Globalization theory has tended toward abstraction, even when concrete, by now clichéd examples such as "McDonaldization" or "Coca-Colazation" are invoked. My intent here is to provide concrete illustrations, both from my own experiences and the women in this study, of how "glocalization" is actualized in specific discourses, institutional practices, and nation-state and cultural contexts. My empirical focus in the second half of this book is on women in higher-education management in Southeast Asia. This necessarily requires analytic links to countries' educational provision, girls' and women's educational opportunities, and local cultural constructs of gender, femininity, and gender relations. These are further set against precursor genealogies of colonial and postcolonial legacies embedded in nationalist and cultural agendas that shape women's educational opportunities and academic careers. To map the local in the context of the global, I look at current globalization theory and research on the globalization of education. Contrary to a generally pessimistic view espoused by western (and primarily male) globilization theorists, I argue that some aspects of globalization have "productive" consequences for women that have been largely overlooked. World organizations such as UNESCO, the World Bank, or NGOs, for example, have globalized principles of gender equity in education, reporting, and accountability mechanisms, and are now expanding the gender equity agenda to include women in higher-education management.

The university has long been characterized as an international enterprise in terms of research and the international, indeed global, dissemination of scholarship (and scholars) through publication systems and conference circuits. Globalization, some argue, has accelerated the pace of information and people flows enabled by electronic communication and post-jet-age travel. Academic business in the age of globalization is as much about increased pressure for more research output as it is about electronic content delivery, marketing, and strategic research alliances with business and industry. The ivory tower has become a marketing machine, and the armchair academic is being pried out of old comfort zones and pushed into public debates and accountability. Some label this new class of academic-cultural workers as cosmopolitan intellectuals. These globally mobile intellectuals and cultural "translators" are as likely to be on university recruitment jaunts in China or South America as working with the World Bank on development projects or on TV discussing ecotourism and environmental impact issues, AIDS education, or the politics of development and local heritage listings. Academic women have become part of this new intellectual elite in the west and in Southeast Asia. As such, current debates about cosmopolitanism are germane to any discussion of women in academics in a globalized educational economy.

Typical of globalization arguments generally, educational accounts of globalization of higher education tend to engage economistic approaches that obsess over facts and figures, the dollars and cents of state expenditures, international marketing budgets, student intakes, academic productivity and accountability, and so forth. And because that research and its authors are of a particular generation trained and embedded in an ostensibly more "gentlemanly" culture of the academy, there is a fair bit of lamenting over old times: the golden era of "academic freedom," "authentic" face-to-face teaching, pastoral and informal management rather than the "new" accountability, the certainty of print knowledge and culture rather than the new digital frontier. For many of us, those good old days never existed. What that research has missed altogether is that the old culture did not have to account for its exclusionary practices of ruling women and other "not white and male" academics out of bounds. So-called globalization and its traveling companions, economic rationalism and the new corporatism, have in many cases actually opened up opportunities for previously marginalized groups to stand up and be counted and get speaking positions.

There is a huge gap in what we know about globalization. There is no identifiable corpus of feminist scholarship on globalization, and virtually no feminist work on educational globalization, particularly as it relates to women. Moreover, in a globalized educational economy where increasing standardization and sameness is said to characterize academic labor, we know very little about women in academics in nonwestern contexts. And yet education is a major Australian export earner, we export and in-service academic management models to the region, and half of our international students are women, many of whom in fact work in higher education. It seems to me that there is not a whole lot of feminist interest in tackling theoretical, economic, or cultural issues of globalization.

Perhaps not surprisingly, the lack of research funding for, or publishers' interest in, feminist studies of globalization, women, and Southeast Asia doesn't exactly encourage scholarly pursuits into these areas of inquiry. Indeed, my efforts to secure federal grants to study Southeast Asian higher education and, particularly, Southeast Asian women in academics, have been repeatedly rejected on grounds that research on women in Southeast Asian higher education does not fall within current Australian research priorities. Why study women in higher education? Why Southeast Asian women? Who cares? My attempts to secure a book contract met with similar disinterest until Joel Spring and my editor Naomi Silverman at Lawrence Erlbaum had the political insights to support and stand behind this project.

In an increasingly global economic, cultural, and educational environment, the "far east" is no longer far or east in traditional modernist terms. Most of the women in this study are not on the outer fringes of global circuits of intellectual exchange or institutional networking but very much a part of the "new" local and regional cosmopolitanism. And yet, like all things social and cultural, their location and trajectories on regional and global flows are ultimately gendered and shaped by emergent and residual cultural, political, and patriarchal discourses. I hope that the partial snapshots provided by the women in this study will convey some of the intricacies and complexities of the "glocalization" of cultural politics that circumscribe women's professional career opportunities in academia.

I

Women, Education, and Equity:
North/West

Women in Academics: Views From the North/West

This chapter provides an overview of western feminist explorations of gender equity in educational contexts. I trace the conceptual and political pathways that feminism has traveled in efforts to analyze and redress the "gender imbalance problem" in education. After a sketch of the historical trajectory of western feminist debates on women in higher education, I discuss the implications for women of current shifts in the academy toward internationalization and globalization. I begin with the 1970s equal opportunity and sex discrimination policy interventions of the 1970s and conclude with discourses of globalization of the 1990s. I argue that, for academic women in the north and west, globalization has changed academic work and enabled the formation of new communities and relationships among women worldwide.

Yet any effects of globalization can be made intelligible only by analysis of local sites where "glocalization" is actualized, experienced, appropriated, or contested. In an increasingly globalized educational economy, the impediments identified by western feminism to women's academic career mobility, and solutions formulated to remove those barriers, require situated analyses that identify women's "place" on local circuits within the push-pull dynamics of global flows. This chapter locates western perspectives on women in higher education and also introduces the conceptual terms of debate for subsequent chapters.

THE CONTEXT

In a landmark report titled "Women in Higher Education Management," published in 1993 by UNESCO , editor Elizabeth Dines commented that "with hardly any exception the global picture is one of men outnumbering women at about five to one at middle management level and at about twenty or more to one at senior management level" (p. 11). Nearly a decade later, this observation remains accurate, as evidenced in the significant body of scholarship and case study research published in the last 10 years.

Numerically, women's participation has increased across the sector and position classifications in western and some newly industrializing countries. However, the largest increases for women have been in more junior, untenured, and part-time positions, where they often outnumber men. In a study of academic women in the United Kingdom, Ann Brooks (1997) notes a substantial increase of 143% in women's professorial appointments over the decade 1981–91, but the actual "numbers of academic women compared to academic men remain small" (p. 27). Certainly, a proportional change from 89 women vs. 3,689 men in 1981 to 217 women vs. 4,189 men in 1991 is not exactly dramatic. Elaine El-Khawas, vice president for policy analysis and research of the American Council on Education, notes that although American women have made significant gains since the 1960s in higher-education participation, both as students and faculty, women remain underrepresented at the most senior levels of academic management. She writes: "Today women hold 16 percent of chief executive positions in U.S. colleges and universities. A decade ago, women held 10 percent of these positions; two decades, ago women held 5 percent" (in Eggins, 1997, p. *xii*). A similar picture emerges for Australia: In 1998, women accounted for 14% of full-time tenured professors and associate professors, up from 13% in 1996 (DETYA, 1999) and 9% in 1990 (Burton, 1997). Because senior management positions are usually drawn from internal and national pools of professorial staff, women's low numbers at professorial levels reduce the chances of a female flow into top-level management.

Two decades of feminist research, most of it emanating from northern and western countries, has asked: What is the problem? Why are there so few women in senior academic management? What are the many-leveled and intersecting, visible and invisible barriers that impede academic women's access to the most senior ranks in higher education? By now, we are familiar with some of the answers. "Pipeline theories" are often invoked to explain women's underrepresentation, arguing that not enough women have come up through the system to form a kind of critical mass of qualified candidates for senior positions. Glass-ceiling explanations have highlighted the many overt and covert cultural and structural barriers that impede women's career paths. These include male managerial styles; discourse and language that shut women out; informal organizational cultures (also referred to as the old boys' club); lack of transparency and accountability in hiring and promotion procedures, whereby male managers are free to reproduce institutions in their own image (men are more comfortable with and appoint others like them, namely other men); women's reluctance to self-promote their achievements and capabilities, making them institutionally invisible; and the persistence of cultural values and attitudes that still prioritize women's child-care, family, and domestic responsibilities above career aspirations.

Moreover, given what many scholars have called this "chilly climate" for women in universities, women often self-select out of an untenable situation of working the double-day of professional commitments plus domestic and child care duties, maintaining a competitive research and publication record, sustaining an often unreasonable teaching load, counseling and supervising students, and putting in the 14-hour day plus weekends that their administrative posts often demand. Under such conditions, women's career aspirations erode, guilt mounts over the inability to "do it all," family tensions and breakups are not uncommon, and finally, if women pull out of the race, they confirm patriarchy's self-fulfilling prophecy that women don't have what it takes to stay the course for the long haul. This, then, can make women seem like unreliable candidates for the most highly coveted academic positions.

Nonetheless, in the United States, Australia, Canada, England, and many other Commonwealth and non-Commonwealth countries, a range of initiatives have been established to thaw the chilly climate of cultural and structural impediments and to help women overcome many of the barriers that result from their structural disadvantage at point of entry. That is to say, women's initial appointments at lower classification levels put them at a structural disadvantage by increasing the time needed to claw up academic ladders and by reducing their access to influential committees, to senior researchers with whom they might network and co-apply for prestigious grants or consultancies, and to other senior women who might support them in role-modeling or mentoring capacities. In many cases, part-time faculty, tutors, or lecturers are considered inappropriate to represent a department on faculty or university committees, and "weak" service records, in turn, can diminish promotional prospects.

Too often, new female recruits end up ghettoized in a department's contract mill of tutors, course developers or technicians, and junior lecturers. Moreover, finishing a Ph.D. and beginning a first academic job often coincides with women's biological age where they are likely to start a family. A junior position coupled with the time- and labor-intensive tasks of rearing young children makes research productivity and the building of a sustained and uninterrupted research profile more difficult for women and can also make part-time work more attractive. In most cases, entry-level positions demand big teaching loads and, often, a fair amount of lower-level "administrivia" that middle-rung and senior academics pass off to new staff. In a time of work intensification, a "more-for-less" ethos has swept across the sector. It is junior-level staff who absorb the bulk of hours in jobs that do not necessarily yield into the kind of productivity valued on a CV, let alone lead to a promotion.

INTERVENTIONS

Although sex discrimination and equal employment acts were passed in Australia in 1984 and in the United States and the United Kingdom in 1972, the rate at which women have ascended academic career ladders in these countries is maddeningly slow. And despite the many strategies implemented sectorwide over the last 20 years to enhance women's opportunities, feminist research as well as government and nongovernment reports repeatedly show the persistence of a profound gender imbalance at senior levels, where women are few, and at junior levels, where women far outnumber men.

Systemic change has been implemented by various means. In Australia, mandatory reporting mechanisms of equity programs, targets, and outcomes have been tied to resource allocation. Embedding equity into national policy frameworks has forced local change at institutional levels through the establishment of a range of programs. To encourage "pipeline flows," programs at the undergraduate level have occurred in nontraditional areas (e.g., engineering and computer science) to increase women's enrollment, maintain retention rates, and increase completion rates. Examples of such changes are curricular and pedagogical reform towards more inclusive knowledge content and teaching, and special bridging or tutorial programs for women. However, special add-on initiatives designed for women easily lead to the reproduction of deficit ideologies.

Affirmative action programs, established in Australia in 1986, have resulted in the establishment of equal opportunity offices or units in universities and the requirement that equal opportunity officers sit on appointment, hiring, and promotions committees. If an equal opportunity officer had been present at my first interview for a six-month contract position, I probably would not have been asked by a panel of eight men if I planned to have any more children. Federally mandated planning for equity indicators has forced universities to set proportional targets for female representation on university committees, increase women's enrollments in nontraditional areas, and improve promotional and tenure rates. Categories of "early career" or "interrupted career" that consider women's reentry or late start in academics have filtered into hiring, promotion, tenure, and grant and scholarship applications. Universities and higher-education statutory and government bodies have implemented a range of training and networking initiatives, such as executive development and leadership programs and conferences for women, national registers of senior women, and policy-drafting subcommittees.

Networking can play a crucial role in facilitating women's opportunities. Given the isolation women can experience, networking with other academic women is seen as socially supportive as well as a source of building influential contacts and gaining access to important information circuits. Mentoring by senior women can serve an important role-modeling function and provides opportunities to gain insights and entry into more senior ranks.

In more recent years, universities have trialed initiatives that provide child on-campus and allow time off or reduce teaching loads for women to complete higher degrees and/or improve their research and publications profiles. In addition, strategies have been developed to encourage women to apply for tenure and/or promotions, familiarize women with the normative expectations for promotion, and provide career planning or time management advice.

However, within the prescriptions of government equity policies, local implementation of specific interventions remains uneven and sporadic (Burton, 1997). Moreover, more courses for women and increased female participation on committees do not in themselves change the masculinist culture of the academy; masculinist organizational norms, structures, and procedures endemic to bureaucracies; or the fundamental social division of labor that cements women into primary child care and domestic responsibilities. As innumerable studies have demonstrated, and as I have found in the case studies I have discuss later in the book, women with children take longer to complete higher degrees, and many women defer having children until they have completed their Ph.D.'s and have secured permanent positions (Lie & O'Leary, 1990; Sutherland, 1985). Time out for childbearing and childrearing means interrupted careers and fewer years of continuous service, and thus less seniority. Women in senior management, unlike their male counterparts, are more likely to be single and not to have children. These facts are well known, and no training courses or special provisions for "interrupted careers" or "reentry candidates" are likely to change the fundamental cultural value systems and social organization of gender in this or any other society. That said, the argument of socialist feminists in the 1980s that the total demolition of capitalist-patriarchal structures is the only way to eliminate all forms of oppression and discrimination remains politically and theoretically valid, but its realization is unlikely.

In the meantime, while we wait for that improbable mother of all revolutions, women have struggled on in efforts to change the rules of the academic game at several levels. On one level, the proliferation of support mechanisms and augmentative programs has continued unabated, and these have been conceptualized and lobbied for by women. Governments may have provided the green light for equity, but it is women's research and scholarship that has identified where the impediments and flashpoints of resistance are and how they can be eliminated. On another level, women have taken on the more difficult task of challenging and redefining the insidious assumptions underlying the very criteria, standards, and definitions of what counts as merit, success, productivity, career, disciplinary authority, academic rigor, and so on (Clark, Garner, Higonnet, & Katrak, 1996). In so-called liberal democracies, the myth of meritocracy is so fundamental to and embedded in the "first principles" of androgynous individualism or natural rights (Young, 1990) that the masculinist bias underlying the genesis and continuing legitimacy of such core concepts as merit masquerade as natural, neutral, and beyond reproach. Feminist challenges to liberalism's most cherished conceptual templates are all the more astounding in light of the changes in discourse and practices that women have indeed been able to effect.

However limited the gains may seem in retrospect, gender equity has been placed on many national and global educational agendas; myths of merit have been exposed as masculinist fictions; concepts of career have been subtly altered to include women's different life and career trajectories; and hiring, tenure, appointment, and promotion policies, criteria, and processes have been retooled to account for women's differently situated realities. The importance of hard-won gains should not be underestimated. But we cannot afford complacency in light of massive workplace restructuring across the sector that has had a profoundly negative effect on women, and, not least, in light of the stubborn persistence of shifting glass ceilings and chilly climates in the academy.

GLASS CEILINGS AND CHILLY CLIMATES

The conceptual metaphors developed by feminist scholars over the last two decades to identify and theorize women's complex positioning within the profession of academics and the workplace of higher education conjure up images of pyramidal ice palaces or dungeons with cold "stone floors." Metaphors of a glass or cellophane ceiling, "greasy pole" (Hede, 1994), "protective shield" (Still, 1993), "brick wall" (Bacchi, 1993), "sticky floor" (Poole, 1995), or "stone floor" (Heward, 1994; Heward, Taylor, & Vickers, 1997) have been widely used in feminist analyses of women's career trajectories and opportunities. The term *glass ceiling* generally refers to transparent cultural, organizational, and attitudinal barriers that maintain relatively rigid sex segregation in organizations. The politics of glass ceilings are commonly attributed to the closed-ranks mentality and fraternity of a generalized male bureaucratic and organizational culture. Glass ceilings are usually invisible to both women and men: Women look up the occupational ladder and get a clear vision of the top rungs, but they can't always clearly see where they will encounter obstacles. Men, on the other hand, "can look down and ask why women are not achieving and, seeing no barrier, can only surmise a lack of talent, commitment or energy" (King, 1997b, p. 94).

The analytic and explanatory validity of the pipeline theory depends on the quantification of female educational participation and outcomes.

By contrast, the concept of glass ceiling lends itself more to qualitative analyses of occupational and cultural variation. That is, the particularities of glass-ceiling politics are specific to informal workplace cultures and professional milieus within occupations and organizations, and are always specific to a society's cultural values and attitudes. More recently, the metaphor of glass walls has emerged to complement glass ceilings. Together, walls and ceilings construct a conceptual imagery of both vertical and horizontal impediments to women's career trajectories.

Unlike private or other public sector industries (e.g., law, engineering, business, mining, health, public education), universities are fertile ground for horizontal sex segregation because they credential a wide range of professions. Moreover, as both a workplace and a research, training, and credentialing institution, the university is a hotbed of both vertical and horizontal sex segregation. Women are vertically clustered in low-level, low-pay, low-status positions as academic and general staff, and are concentrated horizontally in traditionally female areas of study that generally lead to low-prestige, low-pay professions (e.g., in social work, education, nursing, arts, and the humanities). Although women have broken into what used to be exclusively male areas of study, such as veterinary science, law, business, and medicine, the general pattern of sex-segregation in disciplinary fields remains dispersed in what Becher (1989) termed academic tribes and territories.

One might argue that the new market values, which have swept the higher-education sector on an international scale, have led to the standardization of educational delivery and the administration of students, staff, policy, and processes, thereby eroding tribes and territories, disciplinary and departmental fiefdoms. That is, forcing uniformity across the sector through the new managerialism of total quality management discourses, performance indicators and measurable outcomes, and transparency and accountability principles, has the potential not only to enforce and standardize equity principles on a systemwide basis but also to dislodge established patterns of occupational and disciplinary sex segregation. However, the marketization of education has also profoundly undermined the relatively limited gains women had made under the equity legislation of the 1970s that increased access and participation for women and "minorities." Deregulation and marketization have hit women particularly hard through increased part time and contract labor, the devaluing of tenure, and the ease with which masculinist criteria and principles slip back into definitions of quality, productivity, and performance. But, like any discourse, deregulation, marketization, and quality discourses and practices have contradictory and unanticipated outcomes, some that disadvantage women and others that can be harnessed to promote women's interests and career opportunities. I discuss this further in Chapter 3.

TRANSITIONS

The conceptual metaphors widely used in analyses of women in academics arose historically out of first-wave equality of opportunity discourses. These were based on unitary concepts of femininity, oppression, and patriarchy. Throughout the 1980s, the conceptual singularity of *woman* was transformed to the plurality of *women* as increasingly sophisticated feminist concepts of subjectivity emerged. In many disciplinary quarters, essentialist thinking of first-wave, experience-based, consciousness-raising feminism was rejected in favor of constructivist epistemologies and theoretical models. The fervor with which many feminists embraced poststructuralist theory throughout the late 1980s and 1990s, coupled with emergent feminist postcolonial theorizing, saw a sea change in feminism's theoretical orientation. The essentialist, totalizing construct of feminine subjectivity gave way to one celebrating identity politics based on kaleidoscopic difference and diversity, hybridity and multiplicity.

In many ways, feminist thought—even among those who would reject the naming of their work as postmodern—was part and parcel of the larger postmodern turn toward epistemological uncertainty, the rejection of metanarratives and universalisms, including feminism's foundational texts and assumptions. This turn was paralleled by rapid and dramatic changes in economic organization and capitalist alignments, in technological and cultural changes now termed *globalization*. We witnessed these changes in our universities and classrooms as workplace restructuring, quality assurance discourses, the push to incorporate technology into teaching and learning, and new funding formulas swept through the sector. In many, but not all, institutions and disciplines, the postmodern moment had arrived. Established theoretical templates in the humanities and social sciences were increasingly considered inadequate investigative tools for analyzing and explaining "new times." Scholarship and research on women in academics changed in tandem.

The introduction of equal opportunity legislation across western countries around the mid-1970s put equality at the forefront of educational and workplace legislation. In part a spillover of the civil rights and first-wave women's liberation movement, equality of opportunity in workplace and educational access had become relatively widely institutionalized on paper, albeit contentiously, by the late 1970s. In Australia, for instance, equal pay legislation was passed in 1972, and in the United States, the Equal Employment Opportunity Act was passed in 1972. Job advertisements carried the obligatory "equal opportunity employer" policy position, equal opportunity offices sprang up in universities, and women began to take employers to antidiscrimination boards or tribunals for equal pay breaches or sexual harassment charges. Equality, equity, parity, and affirmative action were the new legislative slogans aimed to reverse the gender imbalance "problem." At the time, the primary aim was equality of access rather than outcomes.

Although feminists did not consider it a problem at the time, liberal theory provided the political and theoretical framework from which to argue against undemocratic and socially unjust restrictions on access that, in turn, led to unequal participation and, subsequently, unequal outcomes. The argument was that once access barriers were removed, then classes of people such as minority groups and women would have equal chances to participate and compete within the system. This rationale lowered the bar at entry points but left the system unchanged. Moreover, it took for granted that groups classed as disadvantaged were equally situated and shared single-factor characteristics that accounted for institutional discrimination against them (Young, 1990). In the United States, affirmative action legislation set progressive quota systems in place to ensure female and minority entry into workplaces and higher education. The aim was to compensate previously disadvantaged groups and to seek proportional representation for women and minorities. To reverse historical injustices, affirmative action initially sought a short-term remedial solution; once disadvantaged groups were in the pipeline, the marketplace of merit would promote and distribute talent in the natural and neutral dynamics of a liberal meritocracy. In Canada and Australia, antidiscrimination legislation sought the same ends of equal opportunity by breaking down access barriers. Under the banner of equal opportunity, workplaces and the professions were under siege as women lobbied, often through the courts, to gain access to jobs previously closed to them, such as underground mining, commercial aircraft piloting, and the military. But throughout the 1970s, universities for the first time opened their exclusive gates to huge numbers of women and minority students.

Throughout the decade, women were starting the long march through the academic ranks, graduating with Ph.D.'s in increasing (albeit still small) numbers, getting jobs, getting published, and moving up. As more women achieved promotion and tenure, which do provide some security of employment as well as speaking positions, feminist scholarship started to roll off the presses in earnest. Women academics started to question and critique, reflect on, and write about their own career paths in the academy. For many, especially publicly avowed feminists or women choosing women's issues as a research focus, being perceived as a feminist put them in double jeopardy. On one hand, women were seen as an alien infiltration into the most hallowed bastion of male authority, historically privileged and empowered to speak the word, the truth, the canon. On the other hand, women marked as feminist were readily stereotyped as humorless, man-hating separatists: radical, disruptive, unfeminine, and noncompliant. As women experienced the consequences of their marginalization and invisibility, and watched their male colleagues nimbly pass them on the promotional and tenure ladder, feminist analyses of the discourses, structures, and processes of gender and cultural politics in the academy mushroomed.

Feminist scholars in education had already led the way in the late 1970s and 1980s with works on gender equity related to girls and schooling (e.g., Arnot & Weiner, 1987; Walkerdine, 1989). This body of work focused on curriculum reform (particularly in mathematics and science curricula) and new forms of pedagogy designed as more "girl friendly." Feminist educators also began to look at teachers' work and subsequently on the politics of women's work in higher education. In the early 1980s, American feminist educators (e.g., Bunch & Pollack, 1983; Culley & Portuges, 1985) focused critical attention on the ideological and political structures and processes that construct gender identities in pedagogical relations from grade school to graduate school. The theoretical focus of much feminist work of that era sought to expose patriarchy: its normative constructs and practices defining the entire educational enterprise. At the same time, feminists were theorizing more collaborative, pastoral, "ethics of care" approaches to teaching and learning relations, and challenging masculinist knowledges across the school and university curriculum (e.g., Gilligan, 1982; Lewis & Simon, 1986; Maher, 1985; Noddings, 1984; Schniedewind & Maher, 1987).

Analytic approaches to gender equity had settled roughly into three theoretical camps throughout the late 1970s and 1980s. Liberal feminists argued for equality of natural rights and privileges within existing systems of the liberal meritocracy. Radical feminists rejected the possibility of women's equal rights and opportunities within existing patriarchal systems and argued instead for alternative systems that would value and accommodate women's qualities, which were seen as fundamentally (and essentially) different from men's. Separate spheres were proposed. Socialist feminism also saw no immediate or substantive hope for women's equitable access and participation within capitalist-patriarchal systems that, at their core, can only flourish on the backs of deeply embedded class-based systems of inequality and oppression. Class-based inequalities are gendered, and only the complete elimination of all forms of prejudice, oppression, and exploitation within capitalist, liberal democracies can, in principle, ensure women's fair and equal participation in public and private life. Radical and socialist feminists proposed larger long-term agendas for reversing the gender imbalance: Building separate women's communities and infrastructures or dismantling the capitalist apparatus were generational projects, although women-only institutions (e.g., banks, publishers, Internet sites), networks, and communities have continued to flourish over the decades. Liberal feminism, by contrast, had more immediate, short-term solutions that have remained the mainstay of gender equity legislation and institutional interventions.

Starting in the mid-1980s, poststructuralism surged through a range of social science and humanities disciplines. Analytic and theoretical attention moved away from macrostructures and processes to what Foucault called "the little habitat": to local sites of power/knowledge, to subjectivity, to the making of the self and the self constructed in discourse. By the early to mid-1990s, a substantial amount of scholarship had emerged, much of it loosely informed by a poststructuralist orientation that focused on the feminist classroom and feminist pedagogy (e.g., Acker, 1994; Bannerji, Carty, Dehli, Heald, & McKenna, 1991; Gore, 1993; Lather, 1991; Maher & Tetreault, 1994; Weiner, 1994). However, feminist scholars working in education were not alone in their quest to challenge and retheorize the politics of authority, knowledge, and power implicit in the pedagogical relations of the academy. Feminist scholars in philosophy (Bartky, 1990) and literature (Chow, 1993; Fuss, 1989; Gallop, 1995; Spivak, 1993) were moving toward a feminist reworking of Foucauldian poststructuralism, and their work, although not specifically focused on educational equity debates, began to retheorize and de-essentialize feminine subjectivity, often with specific reference to the context of the university classroom.

By the 1990s, feminist appropriations of Foucauldian poststructuralism had taken root in pockets across the arts, humanities, and social sciences, and formed an influential base on which research on women in higher education was scaffolded. Moving away from a unitary and essentialist concept of woman, generalized notions of universal regimes of oppression, and a conceptually totalized patriarchy, feminism turned analyses to the social constructions of feminine differences. Differences of identity and experience bound to differences of class, race and ethnicity, sexuality, and ability were factored into the "gendered disadvantage" equation, not as essential or demographic characteristics but as discursive constructs. What emerged were previously silenced voices that contested mainstream feminist analyses of women in higher education. Women of color, older women, lesbians, married and single women with children, women with disabilities began to speak about their institutionalized marginalization, their absences in policy or curriculum discourses, and their exclusion from systems of privilege not only accorded to male academics but that had also been claimed by white, middle-class heterosexual women in the academy (Acker, 1994; Bannerji et al., 1991; Davies, Lubelska, & Quinn, 1994). Cracks in the armor of "sisterhood" built around gender equity crusades over the last decade were becoming evident. In retrospect, this move formed part of the larger backlash against "white, bourgeois feminism" mounted by academic women whose experiences and identities had been ignored by mainstream feminism.

What has been labeled postmodern feminism in the United States and poststructuralist feminism in Canada, the United Kingdom, and Australia had arrived. Feminist scholarship was now deconstructing intersections between knowledge and power, embedded in discourses that construct identities, opportunities, experiences. The operations of power and knowledge that constitute profoundly gendered epistemologies, social structures, and identities in a range of discourses were subject to the clinical "digs" of archeological excavations: in canonical scientific knowledge (e.g., Haraway, 1992), in legal discourse (e.g., Z. Eisenstein, 1988; 1994), in policy discourse (e.g., Blackmore & Kenway, 1988; H. Eisenstein, 1991; 1996; Marshall, 1994), in pedagogical relations and classroom discourse structures (Gore, 1993), and research models (Lather, 1991). This work revealed the persistence and not-so-hidden hand of masculinist culture clubs in defining and enacting the rules of the academic game, despite some two decades of legislated "equity" interventions. Accompanying these larger top-down macroanalyses, feminist work loosely informed by poststructuralism also produced a volume of microanalyses of women's interpretations of their experiences in higher education. Throughout the 1990s, life history and case study research flourished and revealed the diversity of women's generational and institutionally situated experiences (e.g., Brooks, 1997; Davies et al., 1994; Glazer-Raymo, 1999; Lewis,

1993; Middleton, 1993; Morley & Walsh, 1996; Oerton, 1996). In broad terms, then, feminist analysis moved from single-factor explanations (gender) in the 1970s and dual disadvantage (gender and race) in the 1980s to investigations in the 1990s of multilayered structural and cultural barriers that interact throughout the life cycle of women's professional careers.

Although western feminists came to learn about the complex differences among women, and learned to exercise caution in speaking for "all" or "the other," issues of cultural difference remained analytically and theoretically tied to subjectivity and institutionally and socially produced identity markers of difference. Other research on culture focused on differences in organizational cultures emanating out of the women and management literature. In education, British and Australian feminists were documenting cultural differences between traditional Ivy League or "sandstone" universities and lower-ranked post-1968 polytechnic and technology institutes recently amalgamated into the university sector. Other forms of cultural differences were noted in regards to dominant ideological assumptions about academic "women of color" and the impact of such racist ideologies on the treatment and opportunities of African American, Caribbean, or Hispanic women in the academy (Henry, 1994; Narain, 1997; Ross, 1996). However, comparative analyses of higher education across culturally distinct nation-states were few (Lie & O'Leary, 1990; Malik & Lie, 1994; Wilson, 1997). Feminist theory and research was seen to drift toward generalized "broad" explanations at the expense of analyses of specific institutional systems in specific countries. As educational sociologist Sandra Acker (1994) points out, "While feminist theory gives broad reasons for inequalities of gender, focused studies in specific countries and educational systems are necessary to fill in the detail" (p. 147).

The lack in comparative international research on women in higher education shifted in the 1990s as increasing numbers of women from around the globe began raising issues about women in higher education. Women were speaking up at local and international conferences, on the Internet, in dialogues enabled through a proliferation of feminist journals, and at newly created special "women's days" and "gender sessions" at conferences. The Association for Commonwealth Universities (ACU) is another global conduit of student, academic, and knowledge flows in which women have been able to build networks and alliances and discuss equity issues (Gibbons, 1998; Singh, 1997). In 1990, the ACU inaugurated the Commonwealth Higher Education Support Scheme (CHESS), which in turn manages the ACU-CHESS Women Managers in Higher Education Program. The aim of this program is to "enhance the participation of senior women managers in higher education" through publications, management and leadership training programs, and conferences that rotate among the 53 member-countries representing "about a quarter of the human race" (Singh, 1997, p. 27).

Such forums bring large numbers of women together from different cultural and religious backgrounds and political systems. They enable opportunities for cross-cultural exchanges of ideas and strategies, for expressing different kinds of feminist interventions or viewpoints, for establishing and consolidating networks. Aspects of globalization infiltrated the academy unevenly within and across different systems and countries. However, since universities have tended to be among the first sectors to computerize and go online, electronic networking was perhaps the first encounter with globalization for many academic women in the west and elsewhere.

INTERNATIONALIZATION

Other emerging connections and community formations among women have developed as a consequence of the rapid expansion in the 1990s of the globalization of higher education (Scott, 1998). As internationalization pushed western universities to seek market share overseas, increasing numbers of overseas students became part of our teaching and supervision load abroad and on campus. The changes brought about by deregulation and sector rationalization, marketization and internationalization altered the contours and colors of student populations, mobilized curriculum and staff into "offshore delivery" on site or online and also enabled new cross-cultural contacts, interactions, and networks among women on an international scale. Arguably, a significant influence that helped shape a broader international dialogue among women was the advent of digital and networked information technologies, albeit uneven across newly industrializing countries. Throughout the 1990s, women from around the world logged onto to the Internet, e-mail, electronic bulletin boards, or chat groups by the millions. We might recall how much planning, administration, and political activism leading up to the 1995 United Nations Conference on Women in Beijing was conducted electronically. In short, our "little backyard" of local and national networks and frames of reference has gradually expanded to what we might characterize as a global village of women debating and talking up a storm.

The university is both workplace and educational institution. As I will argue in more detail in the next chapter, the global proliferation of an essentially European model of the university, coupled with a drift toward increasing standardization of educational content, delivery, and credentialing wrought by educational globalization, suggests an increasingly standardized and universal institutional structure. Yet despite the global reach of western models of higher education, scientific paradigms, knowledge dissemination networks, and English as the global language of scholarly production and exchange, universities are locally adapted in different nation-states with different cultural inflections and political agendas. Gender politics and glass ceilings, likewise, may reveal global patterns of disadvantage but they are regionally and nationally inflected with local cultural and political ideologies.

Given the increasing fluidity of global movements of intellectual capital, educational credentials, students, and academics, I believe that the variables that constitute glass ceilings or chilly climates for women in nonwestern contexts require the same kinds of fine-grained analyses feminists have undertaken of their own local western universities. We cannot assume the efficacy of a generalized patriarchy or male academic culture as a uniform and universal source of women's marginalization in higher education.

New global flows of people and information have formed new communities and networks across societal borders. Higher education is one such globalized knowledge community in which new patterns of knowledge, accreditation, research alliances, and social relationships are emerging. Although higher education remains under the bureaucratic control of a male managerial elite, academic women too are circulating along international educational currents in new configurations that enable new contacts, relationships, and opportunities for knowledge exchange. Analysis of how aspects of educational globalization affect academic women at local levels in western and nonwestern universities is key to understanding how our work is changing as a consequence of changing student compositions, how equity issues writ large into global policy discourses translate into concrete opportunities at the local level, or how women variously mobilize local equity initiatives in the context of greater global dialogue and support schemes among women.

Globalization theorists talk about "glocalization": the nexus or inter-sections of global forces with local sites, uptakes, and historical contexts (Robertson, 1995). Globalism is identifiable in demographic or statistical quantifications of trade and migratory labor flows, information flows through media and technologies, and consumer flows through "McDonaldization" and "Coca-Colonization." But whatever concept of the new global citizen or the new cosmopolitanism is constructed in the-ory, the lived experience and "consciousness" of globalization is localized (Featherstone, 1996). That is, the so-called compression of space and time, the new informationalism or global consumerism of the same cul-tural icons are apprehensible and materialized in the local site of embod-ied social subjects, in the local site of home, village, supermarket, or school. The global citizen is in the first and last instance socially sited in a material body situated in a local space, social network, and historical con-text. These are material, bodily sites where surfers surf, networkers net-work, traders trade, and consumers consume. As Robertson (1995) argues, the issue is not about the local versus the global, or the global voraciously eroding the local: "it is not a question of *either* homogenization or hetero-genization, but rather of the ways in which both of these two tendencies have become features of life across much of the late-twentieth-century world."

The analytic challenge, then, is to explicate how so-called global compression or cultural homogenization are experienced in local sites; how emergent forms of "hybrid" social, intercultural, or multicultural relations are constructed in local sites; how old boundaries and distinc-tions (of class, ethnicity, or nation) erode and yet others are erected; and how recessive differentiation through emergent nationalisms interact with forms of globalization. Global awareness, or "global consciousness" (Robertson, 1992; Waters, 1995), is said to characterize cultural globaliza-tion, whereby individual or national points of reference are increasingly linked to global concerns and issues. Discourses of one planet and sus-tainable development, of human rights, of global environmental, food pro-duction, and population issues, or of gender, development, and education issues integrate localized individuals and collectives of nation-states into a "global field"—a supranational consciousness.

Few governments would deny that education is a human right, regard-less of class, race, or gender. Yet while such global ideologies have an "inexorable logic of their own" (Waters, 1995, p. 43), they are articulated in local sites by governments, policy makers, institutions, organizations, and the individual women and men who populate governments, universities, NGOs, think tanks, or international congresses, and so forth. How is what we now call globalization, internationalization, or the new world order articulated and experienced in situated localities, from village to metropolis, village school to urban university? How does the local reposition or redefine itself in terms of new kinds of global networks, transnational and regional alliances, emergent nationalisms, power dynamics, or new global communities of information-knowledge exchanges?

Education has become a global trade. Technologies have enabled new forms of community and knowledge exchange. Old boundaries and sovereignties, whether of nation, class, or paradigm communities, are eroding as new formations take shape. In that regard, the influences of globalization on women in higher education in industrialized and newly industrializing countries warrant scrutiny in terms of global discourses and local interpretations, changes in academic work and their effects on women. The case studies of academic women in Southeast Asia presented in Part II, for instance, show that all the women were familiar with concepts of glass ceilings, affirmative action, gender equity in education, quality assurance, and lifelong learning. These are global discourses saturating UNESCO policy and briefing papers, academic debate, journals and conferences. Yet local applications and interpretations are very different among and within countries.

Women in higher-education management, although still few in number everywhere, are also a privileged class everywhere. In any country, they are among the minority of a society's most highly educated sector, which links them into networks of social and cultural capital. The social fields in which cultural capital has symbolic and material exchange values are culture specific but, in almost all industrialized countries and many newly industrializing countries, the most highly educated also constitute the upper echelons of social class hierarchies, with all the class-based connections, resources, and privileges accrued by elites. Globalization, some argue, has changed the profile of class elites. This, I suspect, has far-reaching implications for women in higher education.

Part of the development of post-industrial capitalism in tandem with the emergence of what Appadurai (1990) has termed global mediascapes, ethnoscapes, technoscapes, and finanscapes, is the formation of a new bourgeoisie, a new middle class of information and service managers, political elites and knowledge brokers (e.g., Robison & Goodman, 1996). This new elite includes knowledge experts—often academics—who constitute a new class of professional nonpartisan politicians serving on international organizations, regional government and nongovernment associations, and regional branches of the World Bank, UNESCO, or NGO development and aid agencies. Granted, in Southeast Asia at least, they coexist in various alliances and collaborations with "old-style" modernist political and corporate dynasties (Rodan, 1996). Nonetheless, the cultural frames of reference, lifestyle, and attitudinal, aspirational, and professional similarities among this new global middle class suggests that class and ideological differences are more marked and evident today within societies than between societies. These new cultural formations, according to King (1997a), are "both material, social and symbolic" and

> enable an increasing number of scientists, academics, artists, and other elites . . . of widely different nationalities, languages, ethnicities and races to communicate more easily with each other than with others of their own ethnic or national background in the less globalized regions of their society . . . such a "global" culture could also be called another form of localism. (p. 152)

Arguably, women have become part of this new middle-class, professional elite. The women in the case studies presented in Part II, those working in cosmopolitan Hong Kong, Singapore, Bangkok, and Kuala Lumpur, are all western trained, constantly on the go between countries on university and/or government business, and pursuing an endless round of conferences in the United Kingdom and the United States. They are world experts on tropical medicine, aquaculture, educational administration, Chinese literature, cardiology, and so forth. They publish in international English-language journals and presses, some have property in the United States and England or Australia, and they send their children to elite North American or British universities. I met many in their homes, or was offered transport in their cars, and was often astounded at the level of affluence in which these women lived that far exceeded my own solidly middle-class existence. Other women, however, primarily in rural Thailand, lived in less affluent circumstances and, on my interpretation, seemed less a part of the cosmopolitan elite of academic knowledge workers in the so-called global information society.

In all four countries, I sensed a lack of "solidarity" or dialogue among women across different higher-education sectors. University deans all knew one another, often recommending other women for my interviews. They knew deans in their disciplinary fields in Australia, the United Kingdom and the United States, but they didn't know other deans in their own second-tier, lower-prestige universities or polytechnics. In Thailand, too, deans in Rajabhat Institutes (similar to polytechnics) knew few women in the university sector and vice versa. In Malaysia, different divisions among women emerged, pivoting principally around race and religion. Arguably, there is a new global elite of academic knowledge workers of which women are a part—mobile, westernized, relatively affluent, and part of the international currents of higher education and the corporate heavyweights of NGOs, UNESCO, or the World Bank. Arguably we are a new species of nomadic yet situated intellectuals, a new type of shop managers. But there are also large numbers of women in higher-education management who, for a range of political reasons, are relatively isolated and excluded from access to agenda-setting elites. Not all academics are part of the global network of the cosmopolitan intellectual elite.

Globalization is here and it's here to stay. Its variable impact on higher education, specifically on women in higher education, can be made intelligible only by analysis of local sites and practices, gender and political ideologies. In this last part of the chapter, I have tried to argue that the local and global are co-constitutive and mutually inclusive—neither exists without the other. Reciprocity and synthesis characterize local-global links and articulations but always within local sites of competing discourses (around, for example, race or religion), unequal exchange, and class relations (Abou-El-Haj, 1997; Dirlik, 1996; Featherstone, 1996; Hannerz, 1997; Pieterse, 1995). Higher education has become part of and subject to the positional and relativization dynamics by which sectors and nation-states position themselves in regional alliances and, in turn, within global policy, or aid and trade networks and organizations. Within the local arena, whatever *globalization* means by the time it filters to the grassroots of village, kitchen, or factory floor, it is lived on the backs and in the minds of human subjects, differently situated within local regimes of power, differential access, race and gender ideologies, and so forth. In short, then, to get an empirical or theoretical handle on what it is about globalization that makes the local seem different today than even a few decades ago, or what has shaped and is implied by slogans like "think global, act local," we need to look at the particularities of local expressions of global community, of global information and knowledge networks, or globalized education.

New times are evident. Academic work everywhere is changing as neoliberal restructuring, total quality management, and reduced state funding sweep the sector globally. Electronic globalization has not only connected women everywhere but has also brought them into the fold of "global-speak" about global issues and about globalization itself. Western feminism has identified a plethora of barriers that impede women's academic career mobility and has formulated a range of solutions and interventions to enhance women's opportunities. Yet such strategies must invariably adapt to diverse cultural and political contexts.

Western feminist explanations of women's educational disadvantages have been founded on a specific concept of individualism, and by extension of gender relations, based in liberal theory, and derived from research conducted principally in western, self-defined, liberal democratic states. Hence, theories of the politics of disadvantage have accounted for culture, the individual, public and private spheres, equality, femininity, or gender politics through distinctly western epistemological lenses. Although the patterns of disadvantage in higher education across the four countries that I describe in Part II seem universal and appear to parallel research findings of women in western universities, women's interpretations of those disadvantages are not consistent, nor are the strategies they propose to eliminate them. Cultural ideologies and institutional and political constraints shape women's educational and career opportunities in profoundly distinctive and variable ways from those identified and theorized by western feminist research. Indeed, the women in this study are divided on the usefulness of western feminist theory and research for Southeast Asian contexts, on western postcolonial and their own local postcolonial interpretations of problems and solutions.

2

Globalization

The concept of globalization, like postmodernism, is contested, overused and trapped in dangerous dualisms. It is a western and masculinist construct that, once again, has pulled a macrodeterminist blanket over the heads of many feminist and postcolonial scholars who have only just succeeded at tabling the political importance and theoretical relevance of microanalyses at the level of the subject, local sites, local problems, and solutions.

Postmodern theory claimed deferral and ambivalence, the end of "man," and the death of the author at a time when exscribed voices and identities were seizing political and epistemological ground on which to stake identities and standpoints. Perhaps not coincidentally, globalization theory has emerged at the very moment when the local is only just beginning to argue its case and claim a space. I do not wish here to track the various economic, cultural, and philosophical strands within globalization theory. Rather, I want to consider both sides of the local/global debate with specific reference to my own regional "backyard" of Southeast Asia, and then look at some emerging changes in higher education in the context of internationalization. To expand the context, I will then map how globalization impacts locally on women's work in the academy with specific reference to my own institutional context, mindful that my experience does not reflect all academic women's encounters with aspects of globalization or all university contexts.

Globalization is more than theory. There *is* something fundamentally different about economic and cultural life today. We are caught up in new information, consumer, and people circuits that shape new experiences, construct new relationships and hybrid identities, and move us bodily and electronically through time and space in ways radically different from even a few decades ago. However, the push-pull of globalization, of capital, culture, and commodities, flows in many overlapping and countervailing directions in what Appadurai (1990) calls a complex, overlapping, "disjunctive order" that consists of uneven flows of technology and communications, information and ideas, people, finance and capital, and media and cultural images.

It may be analytically tempting and rhetorically powerful to describe the practices and consequences of globalization principally around the metaphor of the Golden Arches (Watson, 1997). Yet there is more than meets the western eye to globalization. Questions of globalization are at least in part questions of optics and standpoints. Most globalization scholarship has emanated from the west and north, which, I would argue, has reproduced a particular Euro-American optic of inside-out theorizing, a way of viewing the world from the west to the rest. In that regard, the current intellectual take on globalization is itself local and localized— "another form of localism" (King, 1997, p. 152).

If anything, we ought to resist the pull of grand narrativizing, of totalizing the other yet once again from the perspective of western us and them epistemology that, in effect, globalizes the discourses of globalization and globalizes claims about effects and processes of globalization (Robertson & Khondker, 1998). Yet we should not fall prey to valorizations of "pure" local spaces by reproducing victim narratives of local corruption and contamination by the predatory tactics and optics of western capital and culture. In Abou-El-Haj's (1997) view, "the periphery is by no means a defenseless victim; rather it has powerfully shaped the centre" (p. 142). The position I wish to pursue here follows Hannerz's (1992, 1997), Robertson's (1992, 1995, 1997), and Featherstone's (1995, 1996) arguments about multidirectional and mutually constituting global-local dynamics. Nonetheless, the directions or force of globalizing flows are always apprehended, made intelligible, or theorized from a location, from a point of view. I begin with examples to illustrate local optics and multidirectional flows.

COUNTERVAILING
FLOWS IN A DISJUNCTIVE ORDER

Australia and New Zealand consider themselves part of the intellectual, cultural, and geopolitical west, yet their relatively isolated location on the globe in the far south and far east situates us very much on the geopolitical and cultural margins. We are part of the region, although geographically on its southeastern periphery. We are economically tied to the region but culturally the most distinct from any of our neighbors. Yet countries that the north and west has marked out as Pacific Rim peripheries—Asia, Australasia, and others—consider their histories and futures very much at the center. Neither existentially, economically, nor politically are these histories and futures taken by locals, including cosmopolitan locals, as mere footnotes in an inexorable or unproblematic process of globalization and homogenization driven by New York or London, EU, or NAFTA power blocs.

Whatever we read into the relational dynamics between local and global, it is at least as much about local optics and "place" of view as it is about western narratives of center hegemony and marginalized peripheries, of global sweeps and alleged local victims.

In remote towns on the Myanmar-Thai border, kids wear Chicago Bulls hats back to front, pirated copies of Hong Kong videos and CDs are available, and Thai-made Toyota pickup trucks rule the road. The signs and wrappers of American McCulture have spread across Asia and indeed the globe. Yet "Asian" ethnic dress, the new "oriental" make-up palette, and styles created in the "rich brocades" of Asia or on the gossamer wings of Asian butterfly hair clips and brooches parade across international fashion magazines and on the catwalks of Europe and New York. Today it is "them" visiting "us," as "Asian" tourists throng Disneyworld in Paris and Florida and European tourist meccas (Beauregard, 1999; Rojek & Urry, 1997). The Japanese yen, despite the current downturn, remains a global currency benchmark. MTV Asia pipes Pavarotti crooning with the Spice Girls across the Asian subcontinent. Malaysian women in *tudung* (headscarf) and *baju kurung* (long-sleeved and high-necked tunic over a long skirt) sport Chanel and Dior purses, and the Malaysian island of Langkawi or islands off the Thai coast are the latest must-see exclusive resort destinations for the well-heeled throughout Southeast Asia.

In the last decade, Thai and Vietnamese restaurants have mushroomed across Australia, alongside the century-old establishment of Chinese restaurants in every town and city. The shelves of Australian bookstores are packed with regional cookbooks, and culinary tours of Southeast Asia (especially Thailand) are the latest spin on cultural tourism. Video rental stores, especially larger chains such as Blockbuster, offer entire sections of Hindi and Hong Kong videos. Walk into any urban supermarket, and aisles of Southeast Asian specialty and staple foods are available. The big-brand megadepartment stores throughout Southeast Asia are not American chains but Japan's Isetan and Sogo and (formerly) Hong Kong's Robinson's and Metro, where Southeast Asian, European, and American designer goods from apparel to furniture and household goods are available. Gap, Armani, Kentucky Fried Chicken, and McDonald's are sprinkled within the landscape of megamalls, most of which are barely distinguishable from Asia's upscale palatial hotel genre.

The twin Petronas Towers in Kuala Lumpur—the world's tallest building until 2002 when Shanghai will topple Malaysia's controversial postindustrial statement—is widely acknowledged as a culturally and politically significant semiotic marker of postmodernity as well as regional economic muscle. It is anchor-tenanted by Japan's Isetan department store. These are the haunts of an emerging well-heeled middle class that increasingly displays images of self-identity and a structure of wants that, indeed, can be said to characterize global consumption patterns and middle-class lifestyle aspirations (Chua, 2000; Pinches, 1999b; Robison & Goodman, 1996). And, although a global middle class can only be made intelligible by reference to local and cultural value systems and appropriations of style and taste, there is a commonality evident that, despite regional differences, can often look more homogeneous than nationally diverse.

What shared characteristics distinguish the new Asian bourgeoisie? Exclusive golf and country club memberships; international cuisine and international travel; high-security, walled compounds or apartments; top-of-the-line European cars with drivers are just a sampling. In Singapore, the saying is that a good education will guarantee the five Cs: cash, credit card, car, condominium, and country club membership. Markers of class status and privilege also include the less tangible positional goods of education qualifications. Overseas credentials from the best universities or private schools have long been coveted cultural capital for the children of affluent parents. Such aspirational material and symbolic goods, social power and position, may well characterize the new rich in Asia. But they are not a homogenous group regardless of how global and cosmopolitan their orientations, lifestyle, and social-professional networks may be, or how flexible their capital and credentials. The middle-class car dealer in a provincial capital has different economic networks and access to social power or cultural influence than the local retailer or schoolteacher. The rural or provincial middle class must further be differentiated from the urban professional middle class: owners of capital, mid-level bureaucrats, and those with managerial and technical skills or directors of regional conglomerates (Kahn, 1995; Robison & Goodman, 1996). Yet they may all harbor the same aspirations of sending their kids overseas for an education, planning a holiday in Europe, getting a better satellite dish on the roof, or upgrading to a new car or larger apartment.

The flow of capital, ideas, and people is no longer exclusively west to east, north to south, and "no longer a narrative of the history of Europe" (Dirlik, 1996, p. 30). Few would deny the west's obsession with "Made in Japan" electronic goods or automobiles equated in the public imaginary with quality high-end commodities. Since the 1980s, Japanese automobile and electronics manufacturing and research and development laboratories and partnerships have been established in the United States and elsewhere (Angel & Savage, 1997). The east-to-west flow of Japanese company models and quality assurance systems into American assembly line production reshaped shop floor and management relationships (Sadler, 1997). At the same time, the proliferation of Japanese branch plants in the United States and elsewhere met with strong local resistance alongside support for foreign job-creation initiatives. In Australia, the "Asianisation" on the honeymoon strip of the Gold Coast—a less flamboyant equivalent of Florida's South Beach—has generated similar resistance by locals. Yet millions are spent on promoting Australia's sunshine state to the Asian tourism market, tourism is Australia's second largest export industry drawing heavily on the Asian market and, not surprisingly, Asia remains the primary holiday destination among Australians, with Bali a perennial favorite.

Foreign direct investment (FDI) by Japanese and Southeast Asian transnational corporations has been described as both a regionalizing and globalizing strategy (Dicken & Yeung, 1999). For example, "until the collapse of Japan's bubble economy in the early 1990s," FDI in North America (U.S.$9.6 billion) and Europe (U.S.$3.6 billion) exceeded investment in Southeast Asia (U.S.$2.1 billion) (Dicken & Yeung, 1999, p. 112).

Thailand's outward investment into developed, principally western European countries increased from 24% in 1988 to 33% in 1991. Nonetheless, regionalization of both FDI and transnational corporations (TNCs) is the dominant pattern in Southeast Asia. This is due, on the one hand, to the massive size and depth of the regional consumer market and, on the other, to the ease with which production networks can be organized because of geographic proximity and the loosely shared social, cultural, and institutional contexts of the Asian regional economy (Dicken & Yeung, 1999, p. 122). And yet, despite the regional meltdown, TNCs such as Korea's Samsung, LG, Hyundai, and Daewoo and Taiwan's Acer are maintaining "ambitious globalizing route[s]." Korea and Taiwain particularly show evidence of a "small 'wave'" of pursuing "the Japanese example in establishing a globalizing strategy and locating operations in North America and Europe" (p. 127). These are just snapshots of what are much more intricate and historically variable patterns of multidirectional flows of commodities, people, images, and ideas that manifest in uneven and contradictory ways in local sites. Capital and commodity flows and the political and economic strategies made operational by nation-states to achieve a mix of globalizing, internationalizing, and regionalizing strategies are not uniform even within the proximity of geography. However, what unifies local, national, and regional diversity on a global scale is the intensification and deepening of cross-border integration of political-economic activity, social processes, and cultural frames of reference, engineered through national and regional bloc mix-and-match strategies that combine regionalization, internationalization, and globalization.

Population mobility is a further hallmark of globalization often "dubbed the age of migration" (Vervoorn, 1998, p. 220). Travel, displacement, and border crossing are often cited as indicative aspects of globalization, with mass and niche tourism from and to all corners of the globe, and population movements across national borders in search of work and improved quality of life. In Southeast Asia, such movement predates late 20th century globalization and late 19th century industrialization. Chinese migration, in fact, is integral to the historical development of almost all Southeast Asian nations before, during, and after various regimes of colonization, including Laos, Cambodia, Vietnam, Indonesia, the Philippines, peninsular Malaysia, and what would in the 1960s become the independent nation-state of Singapore (Cheng & Katz, 1998). In fact, most western explanations of globalization do not consider the constitutive role of diasporic Chinese in the economic and cultural formation of countries in Asia and the Pacific Rim (Dicken & Yeung, 1999; Kong, 1999), a pattern that has shaped Asian and Pacific nation-states, economies, and cultures for centuries (e.g., Ong, 1998).

Since the early 1980s, during the economic take-off decades that saw the emergence of the Asian Tiger and Cub economies, countries like Thailand, Malaysia, and Singapore have built their economic success stories using migrant labor from Myanmar, Indonesia, Laos, and Bangladesh. Steady streams of Southeast Asian workers are drawn to Arab and Persian Gulf states, and Singapore and Hong Kong are magnets for Filipina and Indonesian domestic workers (Bulbeck, 1998; Castles, 1998). Maids and servants (e.g., gardeners, drivers) provide a "source of consumer status" for the new rich and also "symbol[s] of collective ethnonationalist achievements vis-à-vis the Philippines and Indonesia which, in turn, contributes to a 'counter-quest' for prosperity [and] regional honour" among countries that supply domestic labor (Pinches, 1999a, p. 31). In the mid-1990s, some 15% of the Philippine labor force was estimated to work overseas in approximately 120 countries. Between 1990 and 1991 remittances from about 1 million overseas contract workers supported 10% of the Philippine population and totaled U.S.$2 billion, or 5% of the gross national product (Pinches, 1996). Remittances back home from overseas earnings contribute to national economies and "play a critical role in the economic survival of their countries as well as their families" (Vervoorn, 1998, p. 222). Flows of capital and people are multidirectional within regions and on a global scale.

Among the hallmarks of globalization are assumptions of western "capitalocentrism" (Gibson-Graham, 1996, 1997)—presuppositions of the unilinear outward and downward flow of capital, power, and empire. Yet these flows do not necessarily begin from or end in the west. Asian capitalisms, economic power, and regional control within local social and economic fields are as pervasive and distinctive in their characteristic configurations and aspirations, hybrid values (e.g., "Confucian" capitalism), identities, and practices as western capitalism (Robison, Beeson, Jayasuriya, Kim, 2000). Abou-El-Haj (1997) reminds us that

> because the nation-state has been the political form under which international capital expanded, it does not follow that this political form and its cultural expression arise only from the center nor that it would have achieved its massive success without a corresponding local formation of merchant capital to receive global industrial and financial capital. Similarly cultural forms which help to shape capitalist social relations arise also on the periphery. (p. 142)

Capital flows east to west, south to north. These are not periphery victim narratives, not stories of economic brute force exerted by Wall Street, General Motors, or News Corporation. Globalization is as much about regional and national agency and capital, class and cultural interests, as it is about an extension of American or western hegemony. Indeed, Robertson (1992) and others have argued, that globalization is less about center-deployed hegemonies of the margins than it is about a global repositioning, a "relativization" of all social arrangements, political and economic organization in relation to the capitalist west. In short, "in increasing sectors of the world this relativization process involves a positive preference for western and capitalist possibilities" (Waters, 1995, p. 4). Certainly that is the case with higher education where countries increasingly seek to position themselves in strategic alliances to ensure educational advantages both as consumers and providers of educational "goods." As consumers, the aim is to invest in local human capital to maximize labor force productivity and economic competitiveness and, in turn, to crank up the gross national product. As providers, the aim is to transform the traditional model of offshore educational provision from aid to trade.

Providers and consumers thus seek different but similar strategic educational and economic ends that create positional advantages vis-à-vis each other. Australia competes with the United Kingdom and the United States in educational product delivery. Southeast Asian countries compete with each other to provide the most educated, skilled, and flexible labor force as an economic asset, as fundamental to global and regional competitiveness and, not least, to invite foreign investment in the form of regional branch plants or company headquarters. The information- or knowledge-based economy of the moment incorporates education in its ensemble of competitive advantages, making educational goods part of relational assets alongside stocks of material or infrastructural assets. Collaborations between providers and consumers are achieved through twinning programs or institutional agreements that enhance global student and staff mobility, a push for greater standardization of degree programs and accreditation and, as I will discuss shortly, membership in and compliance with the global benchmarking discourses proposed by UNESCO or the OECD.

Standardization and differentiation are *the* defining features of globalization, but current intellectual discourse and media popularizations of globalization too often overdetermine standardization, which clouds conceptual and analytic clarity. Robertson and Khondker (1998) rightly note that globalization has become a slogan, a sound bite, that has "rapidly become a scapegoat for a wide range of ecological, economic, psychological, medical, political, social and cultural problems" (p. 32). On one hand, the literature on globalization *has* made gestures to complexity to uneven, ambiguous, and heterogeneous effects. But on the other hand, it has also tended to overemphasize homogeneity (of the flows and organization of capital and local economic activity) and uniformity (of identities, cultural experiences, consumer desires, and behaviors). So while we might accept that greater educational standardization is part of the globalization and massification of higher education, educational provision in fact looks very different on the ground where it is culturally, locally, and regionally differentiated. This, despite what may appear as a seamless "global-speak" policy document or UNESCO country briefing paper on educational targets, systems, and benchmarks.

Globalization is not a one-way street, a monolithic force voraciously gobbling up the margins, eroding local cultures, and leaving a global footprint of McWorld across nation-state and cultural differences. Robertson (1992, 1995, 1997), King (1995, 1997), and other globalization theorists (Abu-Lughod, 1997; Beyer, 1998; Pieterse, 1995) have repeatedly argued that global forces, trends, or systems are only manifest, intelligible, and materialized in local sites by situated human subjects. And yet rejections of the "myth of globalization" (Leyshon, 1997) must not fall prey to romanticizing the local. For the local is never purely local—an untainted, pristine, and authentic community, social structure, or cultural practice—but is always already embedded in historical sediments of extralocal influences and practices. Moreover, globalizing processes overlay differently in different nation-states, they often pull in different directions and are locally taken up and translated in ways not always guaranteed or predictable by the "imagineers" of the center accused of masterminding that "brakeless train wreaking havoc" (Harvey, 1995, p. 8).

HIGHER EDUCATION: WORLD DISCOURSES

Book-based education has long been global in the sense that its expansion out of medieval Europe followed the trade routes of European imperialism and colonialism. But even before ventures into the New World, the notion of itinerant scholars, the structure of knowledge organized in seven liberal arts disciplines, and the use of Latin as an international language of scholarly and scientific exchange were the foundations of the international character of scholarship and the academy (Altbach, 1989; Scott, 1998b). The advent of the book in the late 15th century accelerated both standardization and the international exchange of knowledge. Printing presses and book publishing sprang up along cities on the communication and trade pathways of Europe's river systems (E. Eisenstein, 1980; Febvre & Martin, 1976; Luke, 1989). The legacies of the British Empire, the Dutch East India Company, and the Spanish Conquistadors included the building of European model schools and "higher" education institutions in which to train local elites for the colonial bureaucracies from Buenos Aires to Bombay, Jakarta to Manila. Scott (1998b) quite rightly observes that the contemporary university is very much the product of the modernist nation state that developed between the end of the Renaissance and the advent of the Industrial Revolution. During this period, the university "took on many of its present functions, servicing the professional needs and ideological requirements of the new nation state of Europe and later, of the world" (p. 123). This model was reshaped again during the 19th and 20th centuries as universities became identified with science and technology that, although centered in Europe and America, were transposed and adapted around the world. As such, New World copies of European models of higher education formed a modernist precursor to post–World War II "postmodern" globalization trends in higher education.

This century has seen an extraordinary global expansion of education systems. Regional and individual nation-state differences have become increasingly eroded as world ideologies, structures, and practices operate across nation-state systems. Comparative studies of education have found that educational policies and practices and organizational forms reflect increasing isomorphism across nation-state systems in response to global ideologies about human rights to education (McNeely & Cha, 1994; Spring, 1998). Importantly, compliance with these imperatives and ideologies is an important source of internal state legitimacy as well as exogenous legitimacy in terms of funding and aid opportunities. Compliance and accountability, then, in the form of being signatories to, members of, and responsive to the accountability and reporting mechanisms of international organizations is a positional, relational advantage. Such an advantage, in turn, is reinforced and rewarded by organizations like the International Monetary Fund and Asian Development Bank.

International organizations such as the OECD, UNESCO, the Asian Development Bank, and the World Bank have been instrumental steering mechanisms in the promotion and management of a global and standardized educational apparatus based on cultural claims that are allegedly shared globally. Principal among these is the claim in the 1948 UN adoption of the Universal Declaration of Human Rights for global human rights to education, which were seen as fundamental to economic development. Part of the sweep of standardization and uniformity enacted by global organizations is their mandate to formulate definitions, criteria, and standards, and in the spirit of providing support and guidance, to develop normative benchmarks, policy drafts, and information collection mechanisms. A kind of global quality assurance surveillance is thus self-enacted at the grassroots level of individual member countries under the aegis of international organizations through systematic reporting mechanisms (e.g., of targets, national action plans, outcomes measures) on which funding for newly industrializing countries is based. "Concerns over quality assurance are an integral part of international trade in professional services . . . [it] is increasingly being defined in terms of reciprocity and international norms and standards by professional bodies, accreditation agencies, higher-education institutions and multilateral and non-governmental organizations" (Mallea, 1999, p. 11).

International megaorganizations are at the core of larger global collaborations among educational sectors and across nation-states. Individual countries thus participate in certain standardized procedures of accountability, operational and administrative processes, information sharing, and participation in shared visions of the means, outcomes, and futures of education. Country briefing papers or reports commissioned by UNESCO or the Asian Development Bank all speak one conceptual language: from preambles, indicators, NGO reports, national policies, and action plans, to aid amounts and origins, target areas, benchmarking, implementation, monitoring, evaluation, and so forth. Statistical quantification is almost always augmented by qualitative data: "in the field" testimonials whether from women in development programs, students, teachers, administrators, or local trainers and health care workers (Kojima, 1995; McDonald, 1995; Zemin, 1998). The standardization of educational discourses and practices converge with economic development goals toward participation in a global (capitalist) economy, but it also has put equity on the global educational agenda, particularly in terms of schooling for girls and women, and female participation in higher education as students and staff.

Following the 1998 UNESCO World Conference on Higher Education, a "World Declaration on Higher Education for the Twenty-First Century" and a "Framework for Priority Action for Change and Development in Higher Education" were developed to put substantial emphasis on the participation and role of women in higher education. Fourth among the declaration's 17 missions and functions of higher education is gender equity. Article 4, "Enhancing participation and promoting the role of women," encourages the inclusion of "gender studies (women's studies)" as "a field of knowledge, strategic for the transformation of higher education and society." The elimination of all gender stereotyping in higher education is encouraged, as is the need to "consolidate women's participation at all levels and in all disciplines in which they are underrepresented, to enhance their active involvement in decision-making". Finally, "efforts should be made to eliminate political and social barriers whereby women are under-represented and in particular to enhance their active involvement at policy and decision-making levels within higher education and society" (UNESCO, 1998b).

Priority actions at national levels include the need to establish legislative, political, and financial frameworks to eradicate any form of educational discrimination on the basis of *inter alia*, gender, and the development and "implementation of national policies to eliminate all gender stereotyping in higher education." Priority actions at the level of systems and institutions include the removal of "gender inequalities and biases in curricula and research and . . . appropriate measure to ensure balanced representation of both men and women among students and teachers, at all levels of management." Resolutions and action plans are no guarantee of worldwide or systemwide implementation. However, they do position gender equity as an ongoing global priority, not only in terms of the removal of discriminatory barriers to women's participation in higher education but also, importantly, by placing equal emphasis on enhancing academic women's participation and roles in higher-education management and administration. Moreover, these are collaboratively authored discourses that delegates and representatives of member countries have agreed on following the 1998 World Conference and that were predated by extensive global collaborations through regional consultations from 1996 to 1997 in Havana, Dakar, Tokyo, Palermo, and Beirut.

International organizations are knowledge industries in their own right, producing what Hacking (1982) called an "avalanche of numbers"—in the spirit of what Foucault (1980) called bio-power or the disciplinary regime of the examination. Countries account for their bodies in production and submit that data on the OECD, UNESCO, or World Trade Organization (WTO) "examination" form. Bodies in production are quantifiable on two levels. First, the raw material of the educable child is processed through schooling and produced as a quantifiable skilled and literate worker. Second, productive bodies in the labor force are quantifiable as human capital investments in gross national product and development indices. Results are collated into massive data banks that become truths in their own right to which individual countries, in turn, appeal as normative definitions and benchmarks in their subsequent accounts of progress towards targets and/or requests for aid. This text too is complicit in the reproduction of those facts.

The massive data banks amassed by world steering organizations, thus, position nation-states on comparative development grids (e.g., the UN Human Development Index) that function as global benchmarks to which nations are encouraged to aspire. But such statistical quantification also makes visible women's variable positions in public life on a global scale. As such, women as a category have become part of nation-states' and global accountability. For example, the UN Human Development Index provides a subset Gender Empowerment Measure. This measure ranks countries on a composite index of the percentage of seats held by women in parliament; the percentage of administrative, managerial, professional, and technical positions held by women; and women's share of earned income. The 1998 UN ranking of 178 countries put the United States 11th, Australia 12th, the United Kingdom 20th, and Canada 7th. Singapore ranked 42nd, Malaysia 45th, Thailand 60th, and no indicator was provided for Hong Kong on the 1998 Index (United Nations, 1998).

Globalization of the kind administered by nonpartisan governmental world organizations can erode nation-state isolationism and enable information sharing and benchmarking across countries, albeit information conceptualized collaboratively among member-states within the ideological frameworks of the UN, the OECD, or the World Bank. The public and global circulation of information and accountability through tightly networked international organizations can make it more difficult for countries to hide social justice abuses or fail to ameliorate systemic inequalities, particularly since highly coveted aid is the carrot that guides the reporting and accountability stick.

And it is not only organizations like UNESCO with a high recognition factor that are forcing and monitoring global educational change and convergence. The World Bank is the single largest external financial source for education, allocating some $1.7 billion annually between 1992 and 1997, of which 23% was lent to nonvocational higher-education sectors. Its educational commitment and mission states, "The World Bank is working with Governments on a country by country basis to identify the next strategic step in education that is right for that country. All within the context of international targets and good practice" (World Bank, 1998). These "international targets and good practice" include quality of learning, employability, and gender equity:

- Greater concern for results: Instead of focussing so heavily on the supply of education, more attention should be given to the quality of learning and its impact on preparing people for employment and society.
- Greater attention to equity: More needs to be done to increase the enrollment of girls, the rural poor, linguistic minorities, and street children (n.p.).

Many other international governmental and nongovernmental organizations are systemically linked within umbrella organizations like the World Bank, the OECD, the UN High Commission for Refugees, UNESCO, or UNICEF. The International Development Association (IDA), the World Health Organization (WHO), the WTO, the UN Development Program, the International Labor Organization (ILO), the Asian Development Bank, and many more all function in tandem through consultative and collaborative processes that appeal to the same definitions and visions of educational provision and outcomes, development processes and goals, human rights principles and/or violations (McNeely & Cha, 1994). The WHO demands literacy for women's health and self-management of reproductive rights, and the WTO demands compliance with human rights as entrée into the global community of trade flows. The Asian Development Bank's development strategy is to help women transition into market economies, which again requires a reduction in women's illiteracy so that they may participate in and benefit from emergent market opportunities.

While curricular content remains under nation-state control, increasingly generic principles and skills such as information technology literacy, critical and creative thinking, or lifelong learning become embedded in local content. In terms of higher education, the global mobility of students (and future workers) requires agreement on notions of "transfer credit," or global transferability of the knowledge and skills implicit in credentials (Lenn & Campos, 1998; OECD, 1998). Regulatory reform of professional accreditation means convergence of international standards, but also the creation and mobilization of intellectual capital, which is increasingly seen as an investment in "knowledge-based economies" another global economic value and aspiration. From the point of view of economic trade, "international trade in education and training services [is] a category that forms an important part of the international trade in the professional serv-ices, and is itself a major growth area" (Mallea, 1999, p. 11).

Professional bodies within global and regional trade blocks such as NAFTA, the Association of Southeast Asian Nations (ASEAN), or WTO's Working Party on Professional Services organize themselves within UNESCO and OECD guidelines to collaborate on standardizing interna-tional qualifications in, for example, accounting, architecture, engineer-ing, and law (Mallea, 1999). UNESCO's 1998 "World Declaration on Higher Education for the Twenty-First Century" and "Framework for Pri-ority Action for Change and Development in Higher Education" acknowl-edge the importance of "regional conventions on the recognition of degrees and diplomas in higher education . . .. Regional and international normative instruments for the recognition of studies should be ratified and implemented, including certification of skills, competencies, and abilities of graduates" (UNESCO, 1998a, p. 22).

Standardization of educational qualifications is not new. A Ph.D., for instance, embodies a set of criteria a candidate has achieved and panels of experts have judged according to scholarly standards and definitions rec-ognized worldwide. An undergraduate education fulfills similar globally recognized and agreed-on criteria. And so, an MBA or BS looks pretty much the same the world over, as does the lecturer-to-professor progres-sion of position classifications and university mission statements. Educa-tional standardization and convergence, then, operate at multiple levels. And it is on the various organizational grids and operational levels that equity of educational access and participation can be mandated alongside accountability and literacy mandated alongside human capital develop-ment theory.

Educational globalization has wrought a sharp increase in the last two decades in the changing composition, mobility, and volume of interna-tional student flows. The direction of flows is principally south to north and east to west and to English-speaking countries. The total global popu-lation of students enrolled in higher education has increased from 51 mil-lion in 1980 to 82 million in 1995. This increase of some 31 million students has been supported by an increase in tertiary teaching staff of only 2 million: from 4 million in 1980 to 6 million in 1995 (UNESCO, 1998b). UNESCO statistics do not provide a gender breakdown of teach-ing staff, but the 1995 Commonwealth Universities Yearbook (Common-wealth Higher Education Management, 1998) summary of countries' self-reports on gender distribution of academic staff notes that the per-centage of women employed in full-time academic positions ranges from

9.5% (Ghana) to 50% (Jamaica). However, the survey does not disaggregate for position levels, some countries report on only one university level institution, many of the academies are agricultural institutions where women are few, and countries with less than a total of 90 male and female academic staff were excluded. The numerical extent to which women are engaged in teaching some 82 million students worldwide and how women have fared in the 2 million increase in academic staff over the 15-year period from 1980 to 1995 are not known.

National reporting on international student out- and inflow is sporadic and even data collected in the past few years by the OECD and UNESCO is often outdated and does not provide consistent data of country of origin, gender, or ethnic background of overseas students enrolled in OECD countries. A common lament among researchers is that the "examination of the nature, size and scope of the international market in education and training is in its infancy. The sector lacks definition and statistical data are hard to come by" (Mallea, 1999, p. 11). Nonetheless, summing up export revenue for all levels of education for each country, UNESCO reports that "each year students bring in $7 billion to the U.S. economy, between $1.7 and $2 billion to the United Kingdom, and $750 million to Australia and $730 million to Canada" (Boukhari, 1998, p. 31). The Australian federal government in 1998 put the figures higher, estimating a 39% revenue increase from AU$3.22 billion in 1997 to AU$4.49 billion in 2001. To support continued growth of this export industry, the government has committed AU$21 million over four years (1998 to 2002) for international marketing campaigns. Overseas student enrollment figures for all levels of education were 151,464 in 1997 and expected to rise to 181,000 by 2001 (DETYA, 1999).

UNESCO estimates that approximately 900,000 young people studied abroad in 1980 compared to 1.6 million at the end of the 1990s. Almost all the women in the case studies I present in Part II had received one or more overseas postgraduate degrees during the last two decades. Australia, Canada, the United Kingdom, and the United States are among the top 10 provider countries with the highest number of overseas students in higher-education institutions (UNESCO, 1998b).

United States	1995	453,787
United Kingdom	1995	197,188
Australia*	1999	93,400
Canada	1995	31,435

*IDP Australia, 1999

Although these UNESCO figures predate the 1997 Asian economic crisis, which saw a drop in overseas student enrollments, Australia's "aggressive policy for attracting foreign students, especially Asians" (Boukhari, 1998, p. 33) has managed to reverse the one-off revenue dip in 1997. Devalued regional currencies have made tuition and general cost of living expenses for study in the United Kingdom or the United States prohibitive, and Australia provides an attractive alternative (IDP Australia, 1999).

As I have argued so far, some of the consequences of "new times" and global flows in education are greater standardization across the sector, increasing diversity of student populations, and greater international mobilization and exchange of knowledge that generate new intercultural contexts for learning. These new contexts for learning apply to students and academics. Exchanges of knowledge, viewpoints, and understandings transpire in graduate classes and study groups, in corridor talk and over coffee, where international students teach each other and resident staff a tremendous amount about the cultural, academic, and professional contexts from which they come and to which most return. For example, before I began my fieldwork, I received extensive insider advice from the international students in my department about cultural protocol, the administrative structure of higher education, and the cultural politics surrounding various education and employment policies.

Many overseas graduate students are professionals and/or academics in their home countries. In the course of several years of residency in a university abroad, many become part of departmental cultures. As student representatives on departmental or faculty committees, or team members on large-scale research projects, they are often exposed to a range of financial or project management issues and administrative procedures that can include budgetary accountability, equity and access issues, target setting or forward planning, and so forth. Some of our own students, professionals in their own countries, claim that student access to committees and the transparency of processes they are witness to are unheard of in their own universities. Many of the women I interviewed for my case studies made similar observations but from the vantage point of hindsight. Many claimed that they had in fact attempted to implement gender equity initiatives but with variable success. What I am suggesting here is that alongside the perpetuation of what some see as knowledge and cultural imperialism enabled by globalization (Urry, 1998), international students are also embodiments of mobile intellectual capital who, as professionals in their home countries, have the potential to become social change agents but on their own terms.

LOCAL CIRCUITS ON GLOBAL FLOWS:
CHANGING ACADEMIC WORK

I now turn to a discussion of changes in academic work and social relations, particularly as they relate to women, consequent of educational internationalization. I illustrate my points with references to my own and colleagues' experiences. In Australia, new ethnicities and demographics of on-campus student composition are perhaps the most visible and widely publicized indicators of educational globalization. Look on any university Web site, and cheery Asian students are positioned alongside white Australian students, signifying a multicultural and harmonious learning environment. Students study abroad to gain western credentials and western knowledge that are seen to have greater cultural capital and market value than local knowledge and degrees (Rizvi, 2000). Prospective students (and their families) value European and American credentials—"that's where you find the most four-star programmes"—and "the use of English as a world language" (Boukhari, 1998, p. 32). Students want a western education, western expertise, theoretical models, and skills because in a global occupational marketplace, the transnational marketing of western credentials and expertise enable greater workplace flexibility and geographical mobility. However, not all students buy into the "west is best" model. Students' uptake and reworking of the knowledge options we provide can challenge our own ways of seeing.

A doctoral study group that operated in our department over the last three years consisted of men and women from Indonesia, Vietnam, Fiji, India, Hong Kong, mainland China, Korea, Malaysia, and the Philippines. The students were professionals in their home countries, holding posts in the World Bank, education ministries, colleges, and universities. Our postcolonial readings, mostly authored by western academics of color (e.g., Anzaldua, 1987; Bhabha, 1991; Brah, 1996; Mohanty, Russo, & Torres, 1991; Spivak, 1993), failed to provide the kind of location and context-specific explanatory model these students were seeking. In short, the epistemological position of most of this work, based on center-margin, north-south, east-west, insider-outsider dualisms, failed to provide answers for students' questions about the politics and reproduction of dominant centers at the so-called margins—whether in terms of patriarchal and

racialized dominant curricular narratives, forms of authoritarian government, or the uniformity and persistence of gender and race-based hierarchies and inequalities across religious and culturally different nation-states
and postcolonial histories.

Singaporeans, mainland Chinese, Indonesians, Malaysians, and pre-
1997 Hong Kong Chinese do not see themselves at the margins, as victims
of western expansionism and globalization. They see their own countries
as regional power brokers, as world financial centers and, invariably, as
culturally superior to each other and certainly to the west. They reject victim narratives of silenced postcolonial voices and western feminist constructs of women in the developing world. Feminism, including what has
been termed postcolonial or third world feminism, comes under similar
scrutiny and challenge from students. In Chapters 4 and 5, I explore in
more detail the political and epistemological problems raised by postcolonial theorists, whether authored by western-based or locally based but
western-trained intellectuals. What I am suggesting here is that the globalized educational marketplace has irrevocably changed student compositions on our campuses, and it is changing us in the process. More
culturally diverse student mixes open up new cross-cultural learning
opportunities among students, and challenges intellectual complacency on
our parts. Although not everyone can be pried out of the comfort zone of
old ways and old models, it is fair to say that academic work—how and
what we teach, and, not least, what we research—is being transformed as
a consequence of globalization.

Overseas travel for course delivery has become part of the workload
reality for many academics and is increasingly valued as a performance
indicator on the academic CV. Travel opportunities can enable new cultural experiences, new social relationships, and new challenges to academics' established knowledge base and teaching repertoires. My
teaching-related travels have enabled me to make contacts with many academic women who networked me into further contacts that subsequently
became a core sample for my research on women in higher education. As
academics, my students are also my colleagues, and on visits to their institutions, I have spent many hours in the company of women over lunch or
dinner, in their classes and offices. We have discussed workloads and
office politics, the silk weave of their office curtains, or the orchid collec-
tions on their patio gardens. Globalization has made an impact on my university and academic work by opening up new connections and
friendships with many women in diverse cultural and academic contexts.

Overseas teaching always requires a substantial amount of effort and time to prepare reading materials, overhead transparencies, Power-Point presentations, and so on. In countries where resources are scarce, many of us usually haul an extra suitcase of books for student access during our visits. Time away from the office always translates into accumulated paperwork and the interminable e-mail pile-up that awaits us upon return. These are workload issues for both men and women academics, but some aspects take on different dimensions for women. Extra medicines, inoculations, and a course of malarials are essential for anyone traveling into nonurban regions during malarial seasons. But for several women I know, especially women taking oral contraceptives and chronic migraine sufferers, medicating one's teaching is not a happy or healthy choice. Travel overseas for a week or more at a time can be difficult for married or single women who leave school-aged children behind since the organization of children's lives is still principally women's work. Many women do not feel entirely comfortable traveling alone in many countries, including relatively "safe" urban and English-speaking metropolitan centers such as Singapore, Kuala Lumpur, or Hong Kong. Even basic and routine events such as catching airport transfers, hotel check-ins, room security, ordering food, finding bottled water, or managing one's health can be stressful for women traveling on their own.

Our supervisory practices have also changed as a consequence of increased and diverse student populations. The cultural and gendered nuances of intercultural supervision are generally not taken up in the literature beyond commonplace assertions, such as the need for cultural sensitive pedagogies, stereotypes of Asian students' preference for rote learning, deference to teacher authority, and so on. The literature provides few guidelines on cross-cultural, cross-gender supervision (Holbrook & Johnston, 1999; Zuber-Skerrit & Ryan, 1994). Many students who arrive on our campuses from overseas experience a range of cultural adjustment issues (Aspland, 1999; Aspland & O'Donoghue, 1994). Supervision of overseas students requires sensitivities to issues that are not always apparent to the supervisor. This can often mean long transition periods of homesickness and cultural estrangements when more time is spent by a supervisor on support and nurture rather than getting on with the job of structuring the thesis argument, making theoretical and methodological choices, and so forth.

Further, when women students' supervisory relationships with male academics deteriorate, women often seek out other women for advice, guidance, and support. What little research is available on cross-cultural and cross-gender supervision has found that women supervisors show greater propensity than do men to alter their supervisory styles to accommodate culturally diverse student expectations, learning styles, and attitudes toward the teacher-authority (Acker & Feuerverger, 1996). Women's apparent tendency to assume caring and nurturing approaches within pedagogical relationships, including supervision—what Tierney and Bensimon (1996) call "mom work" or "smile work"—often means an open door policy and more time spent with students, compared to men down the hall whose doors are shut while they get on with their research. In my experience, supervision of international students can often intensify personal relationships, mentoring and nurturing, and the sheer volume of time devoted to getting students through.

Increasing diversity and numbers of overseas students not only bring different cultural groups in contact with each other but also can lead us to new knowledge and understanding, new pedagogical models, and new social relations and networks with other women. In one decade, the rules in higher education have changed dramatically. Academic work everywhere has undergone radical shifts. There is no question that downsizing, restructuring, and marketization have led to workload intensification and job insecurity. Today, fee-paying students demand value-for-money "service," and contract part-time work is the norm for new graduates seeking entry into academics. The research process has changed from library intensive book-based research to online resources "import, cut, and paste" scholarship. Teaching and academics' day-to-day administrivia have been technologized—there is no escape from e-mail! Research grant panels look for industry links and funding matches or cross-university collaborations that, in turn, eliminate the lone scholar, a whole range of feminist research, and any critical theoretical work that cannot demonstrate "applied" outcomes. Peer review, annual, or biannual performance portfolios and self-appraisals, student evaluations, grant applications, and so forth push our work life along in a *faux* seasonal rhythm. We know what time of year it is not only by semester teaching loads but also by the endless stream of institutional due dates that pop up on e-mail reminders with hotlinks to documents that can be downloaded, filled out, then uploaded. Accountability and transparency may be the buzzwords of quality assurance discourses that have forced us to front up with the evidence of student satisfaction, every research dollar spent, every student supervised, and every course taught. However, as I show in Chapter 3, it has also reduced the kind of rampant nepotism typical of many departmental fiefdoms in some institutions where academic business was conducted among suits behind closed doors. These *are* new times with new rules that require new tools.

The issues I have raised regarding globalization and higher education, and its implications for women, are more complex than I have been able to pursue and explicate here. Nonetheless, I have tried to flag several issues to indicate that the multiple effects of globalization are both uniform and contradictory, and always uneven. Rather than taking a unilinear and determinist view of globalization as world hegemony that is co-opting the so-called margins, I have argued that many discourses and practices of a globalized educational economy have enabled productive discourses in which women have been able to get a voice and write themselves into the mainstream. But that is only a start. There are many more questions that need to be asked. I will briefly raise three such issues in the following section.

WOMEN ON GLOBAL CIRCUITS

First, while we might agree that there are qualities that characterize what we might call a global patriarchal system, patriarchy takes on dramatically different cultural hues in different nation-states and religious systems. Women's identity, experience, and life chances are embedded within these cultural variants. Women in academics throughout the world, working in what I earlier described as a more or less universal model of the university coupled with the current trend toward even greater standardization, are often culturally caught in competing discourses. Nations' commitments in principle to social justice and accountability on the one hand can, on the other hand, be countered by political, customary, or religious-cultural prescriptions prohibiting women from holding senior public office. What solutions, then, should be formulated at global and local levels to promote equity, social justice, and those enshrined human rights dedicated to the elimination of gender discrimination? Western feminism has been instrumental in exposing a whole range of barriers to women's academic careers and has formulated a host of institutional and legal interventions to eliminate them. Australia, for example, exports women and leadership and management courses to the region, and so the question becomes how culturally appropriate these strategies are.

Second, scholarly research on globalization and the internationalization of education has been absolutely gender blind (e.g., King, 1997; Scott, 1998a; Spring, 1998). Feminist scholarship on women in higher education has just begun to look at the changing nature of women's work in the academy in terms of internationalization (Cohen, Lee, Newman, Payne, Scheeres, Shoemark, & Tiffin, 1998). It has ignored issues related to how overseas women, studying on western campuses or studying in distance mode, factor into the formation of women's alliances, new intercultural networks, and knowledge communities. There is very little research on the social and cultural issues that women face during their studies abroad. There is no research on how academic women in "host" countries teach, supervise, support, and form relationships with overseas women. This, in my experience and by way of anecdotal reports from colleagues, is a new challenge many academic women are facing, some with certainty, others with ambivalence.

Third, academic work is changing as a consequence of globalization, not the least of which is the electronic nature of our work—from day-to-day memo traffic or running e-tutorials, to online course design and research. Cybereducation, virtual course delivery, teleconferencing, and even telecommuting are becoming part of academic work for staff everywhere, and women everywhere are part of it. Research on the technologizing of academic work, knowledge production and transmission, or academic women's place in the cyberage is scant (Kaplan, 1997), yet the IT revolution is clearly the most evident and highly popularized aspect of globalization. In the cyberzones women create for themselves, there are no mediating hierarchies or silencing authorities that shut women down. Here scholarly, political, and institutional information scurries around the Internet among women who are no longer isolated in their institutions or little offices, cut off from global debates about inequalities, social justice, or the myriad issues women discuss online over and above their disciplinary interests. Access to information about equity initiatives in other universities worldwide, OECD or UNESCO statistics on staff or student gender distribution, or innumerable international and national policy frameworks on equity in higher education are only a click away.

Without overestimating the "empowerment" factor of online communications, I do believe that the electronic global village has made it much easier for women to come together, break their institutional isolation, and "go public" on issues that they might not publish in print or that might be politically risky to raise in their own institutional contexts. But that political freedom is still not always and everywhere guaranteed. Shortly after the release of a summary report of my research on women in higher education in Singapore, Hong Kong, Thailand, and Malaysia (Luke, 1999), e-mails trickled in from around the world from women. The paper was published in the Association for Commonwealth Universities' research bulletin that all Commonwealth universities receive. Here are two shortened pieces that represent the gist and spirit of all the e-mails I received, and that illustrate the point about academic women in new times on global electronic circuits.

Dear Carmen:

Someone who received your feature article on career mobility through the SAWISE E-mailing list shared it with me. Just wanted to thank you for highlighting important issues that affect us—women in academia—with such articulation. I'm a senior lecturer in the faculty of law at Makerere University, Kampala, Uganda, and could relate to most of the issues that women from S.E. Asia shared with you. I also noted that the problems we face are very similar to those that other women in "high" offices, e.g., politics, face. As you rightly point out, patriarchy is not going to voluntarily give up power and authority. One of the ways that women can "help themselves" is to strategize and network at the international level, and that's why I was particularly excited to read your wonderful article. The struggle continues!

Dear Dr. Luke,

I read your paper. It is very interesting. I want to work on similar lines. Would you like to send me your interview questions? I am a Professor of Educational Administration & Dean. I am working in the area of women managers. I am at M.S. University of Baroda in Baroda, India. This project will throw light on some more issues women face in India.

Clearly, the possibilities for women to connect globally, opportunities for greater student and academic mobility through credential standardization, and the ongoing rhetorical but global push for gender equity as a human rights principle cannot be written off as among the countless negative aspects of globalization.

INHUMAN GLOBALIZATION?

In this last section, I briefly raise some questions to challenge common claims about globalization's negative consequences, particularly in relation to credential standardization and the contamination of the local. My aim in these closing comments is not to defend globalization or critique its detractors. At the risk of stating the obvious, I think we need to heed Foucault's caution about falling prey to narrativizations of progressive History (instead of histories) and "global totalitarian theories" that write over "particular, local, regional knowledge . . . which is opposed by everything surrounding it" (Foucault & Gordon, 1980, p. 80, 82). It seems to me that globalization theorists have taken analytic interest in the local only to demonstrate the brute force of the global, the "inhuman globalization" (Urry, 1998), without paying much attention to what I might provisionally call "productive effects," along the lines of Foucault's notion of productive power. Following Foucault, we ought to remain committed to reading theory, history, or the historical present as messy and discontinuous, crisscrossed with both globalizing trends and local appropriations and resistances. This requires an archeological sensitivity to configurations of intersecting or overlapping nodes and countercurrents that may not be obvious through globalization's "surrounding" normative lenses and discourses. It also requires contextual analyses: genealogical analyses of "the little habitat," of local knowledge and practices that are "masked within the smooth functionalism of global theory and its history" (Dean, 1994, p. 33).

With few exceptions (Burbules & Torres, 2000), the bulk of educational, culturalist, and social science discourse on globalization has produced volumes of scholarship that argue largely for unmediated negative effects. Among these are the obliteration of local cultures, the demise of nation-states, the erosion of cultural identity and tradition, the loss of sense of place and home, the technologizing of everyday life and concomitant compression of space and time and loss of "authentic" communications, a global sameness of desires and consumption patterns, and a dramatic blowout of social inequalities and unequal capital accumulation. Complaints about the incursions of technologies that are dehumanizing social relationships and reshaping work and traditional orientations to time are as old as technology itself. The printing press, the humble typewriter, the washing machine, the car—all changed everyday life, the sense of time, and the organization of labor—whether book making, letter writing, doing the wash or getting from A to B in mechanized transport. Social inequalities based on wealth accumulation, gender, or race or other "caste systems" are as old as civil organization itself, predating the secular state, capitalism, mercantilism, feudalism, and rife in European as in Asian antiquity. Indeed, romanticizing the past or the local by "insist[ing] on local 'purity' may well serve as excuses for a reactionary revival of older forms of oppression as women in particular have been quick to point out" (Dirlik, 1996, p. 37).

In terms of education, it would be hard to argue that global electronic dialogues among women of the kind I noted above are disempowering or culturally eroding. The massive global increase of student enrollments over the last two decades at all levels of education has meant a huge influx into higher education worldwide, including newly industrializing countries. Despite continuing inequalities of access to higher education in some countries, more education for more students at primary, secondary, and tertiary levels can hardly be argued as a negative outcome. Increasingly, industrialized countries are setting up local campuses and colleges or establishing twinning programs to franchise the early years of a degree to local providers, meaning that "international students may be able to take courses in universities on the other side of the world without ever leaving home" (Scott, 1998b, p. 118). Local provision enables greater access, particularly among those who cannot afford to study abroad. Granted, educational branch plants are just that: feeder links along which the educational dollar still flows south to north, east to west. But, the desire for and valuation of overseas credentials are locally embedded in cultural ideologies that sustain (and indeed finance) beliefs in the greater cultural capital, market value, and global flexibility of a western education.

Whereas research has long been a global enterprise, more recently student and staff mobility have become keywords in debates and policy on the globalization of higher education. Very few globalization studies acknowledge the productive nature—interculturally, socially, and intellectually—of the possibilities of forging new academic networks with colleagues from around the world. Student mobility is another issue. Why should the notion of standardization and cross-accreditation of degrees been seen as yet another negative consequence of globalization? For example, what is the point of banishing immigrants with professional accreditation (often from first-rate universities in Europe, Asia, or South America) and years of experience from other countries to part-time work as cab drivers or waiters? Thousands of professional immigrants end up as provisionally registered medical, nursing, pharmacy, or psychology *locum tenens* in remote communities or on permanent night shifts in urban clinics, certified to practice only limited procedures and under the surveillance and supervision of locally credentialed practitioners (Mallea, 1999). The health sciences in particular close ranks to outsiders, forcing thousands of English-fluent and highly trained immigrant professionals to spend years repeatedly taking local exams for professional reaccreditation. Again, it seems counterproductive to oppose standardization of educational content, delivery, and assessment as the first step toward globally recognized professional accreditation. Why maintain such monopoly boundaries when their elimination would facilitate mobility opportunities as well as ease professional integration and social transition into a new country?

A short digression here to personal anecdote. When my parents with two young children arrived in Canada in the early 1950s as part of the postwar exodus, we started with a suitcase each and one crate of things from home that my mother had assembled to start a new life. For years, both my parents worked hard at menial jobs to save for the accoutrements of modern life in the new world: first the ice box, then a hi-fi, the first car and the long-awaited trip to Disneyland, and later the first black-and-white TV. After decades, they finally realized the reward of a stucco bungalow in the suburbs. This is a modernist narrative of relocation, integration, and aspirations that mixed the old with the new in ways that were often difficult for my parents and confusing for us children. Both my parents eventually became fluent, albeit unmistakably accented, English speakers, but neither ever worked in the professions for which they were trained.

Claims of globalization or postindustrial postmodernity as cause for lost traditions (Heelas, Lash, & Morris, 1996), contaminated cultures, and destabilized and hybrid identities too often argue on essentialist epistemologies that presume a pristine prior state, in which culture, tradition, and identity were whole, fixed, and unchanging (cf., Kahn, 1995). There is indeed a curious perspectival counter weight to the way western globalization theorists celebrate and conceptually attempt to freeze-frame the local. We might question why western cultural and social theorists are so appalled by (usually "third world") people's desires to get off that bicycle and buy that first car, to get rid of the radio and get a TV instead, to replace the plough or washboard with a tractor or washing machine, to save for their kid's education abroad or enrollment in English-language schools, or worse, to make a trip to McDonald's a family outing. What is it about the western standpoint that harbors wishful thinking about containment, preservation, and immobilization of all other cultures? Why this urge to fix culture and romanticize cultural tradition when tradition can often— cross-culturally and historically—mean brutal inequalities and social practices, from eugenics to prohibitions on girls' education or the maintenance of caste systems?

Robertson and Khondker (1998) have picked up an important connection between proponents of the "globalization equals western hegemony" equation and a historically shaped and culturally located intellectual position: namely, the intellectual left defense team of the subaltern, or as Featherstone puts it, the "self-appointed guardians in the West" (Featherstone, 1995, p. 186). Robertson and Khondker (1998) write

> This perspective centers on the proclamation that the West enjoys what is often called a hegemonic position in the world as a whole. In a certain sense, then, it is in the interests of those who maintain that they are representing subaltern or oppressed groups to cast the West as very dominant and thus to conceive of globalization as a form of westernisation or as imperialism or colonialism in a new guise. In this perspective many nonwestern societies are regarded as victims without agency and 'globalization' becomes simply the pejorative symbol of all things that are allegedly contaminating or disrupting these societies. (p. 32)

We might note that the concept of subaltern is a western intellectual construct and, as I noted earlier in the chapter, it is not an identity many "Asian" cultures identify with, nor do they uniformly feel particularly contaminated, disrupted, or victimized, although many political leaders in the region stand firm by this victim narrative. As I noted at the beginning of this chapter, the concepts we construct to debate the global and the local are ultimately the products of situated and perspectival optics.

I too am the product and beneficiary of the 1960s and 1970s "massification" of higher education (Scott, 1998b), when universities opened their exclusive gates to socioeconomically less privileged students, to huge numbers of women, older, and "minority" students. Scott argues that massification is linked to the development of a more local, not global, orientation among universities as they sought to redefine their responsibilities and objectives to accommodate broader student diversity. The diversity of that generation was, in part, constitutive of a new intellectual vanguard that contested elite "men and whites only" canonical knowledge, insisting instead on intellectual pursuit of local knowledge, cultural, social and class-based values and practices. Women's studies, ethnic and indigenous studies, cultural studies and, more recently, postcolonial studies emerged out of that historical shift. That is the intellectual climate in which I and hundreds of thousands of my generation were trained. Feminism, cultural studies, poststructuralism, postcolonial and postmodernist theories gave many of us a voice, a theoretical and political standpoint from which to challenge modernist social theory on its ethnocentric, masculinist, essentialist, and categorically boundaried metanarratives. "Othered" standpoints took charge of coloring in what was "masked within the smooth functionalism of global theory and its history" (Dean, 1994, p. 33), by arguing for difference and diversity, exposing discontinuities and inconsistencies, and bringing to light previously disregarded social formations, communities, and identities.

Globalization de facto and in theory is no different. Some aspects of globalization have opened up new opportunities and new social formations that are generally ignored in totalizing and reductionist accounts of globalization. Citing Rachel Kamel, Dirlik (1996) makes the point, "By understanding that every local story is part of a global "big picture," we can open up space for dialogue and sharing of experiences especially across barriers of language, nationality, gender, race and class" (p. 37).

Globalization is not one thing—a hegemonic tsunami swallowing all before it. But because it tends to reproduce the same characteristics of yet another conceptually totalizing metanarrative reminiscent of modernism's great hits, it requires robust contestation and deconstruction to reveal productive gaps and contradictions, the push and pull of counterflows and swirling eddies. Globalization is as much about setting out productive, enabling conditions in different places at different times as it is about diverse and complex human activity in "worldisation" (Chua, 1998), Disneyfication, or McDonaldization.

New Managerialism
and Women
in Higher Education

In the last decade, workplace restructuring, accountability, "new" managerialism, and "total quality management" have filtered through higher-education sectors globally. Such systems and process changes have been attributed to the global sweep of economic rationalism that has left few public and private industries untouched. Although much has been written and argued about the negative consequences for women of the new managerialism, quality assurance, and management initiatives, in this chapter I will describe some potentially positive outcomes for women. I situate the discussion in both national and local contexts and argue that the popular "repressive hypothesis" of power via governmentality masks the dialectical flip side of negative and coercive power, which Foucault (1979, 1983, 1989) characterized as "productive power."

I draw on my own and feminist colleagues' experiences at one Australian university. My intention is not to provide a formal case study; such a description would be difficult and methodologically problematic because I no longer work at that university and have no direct access to university documents or staff. Instead, I wish to develop what, in feminist methodological terms, we might describe as a "theorized narrative" (Smith, 1990) about struggle in a local context, a narrative fabric that draws from experiences, policy documents, and key events.

This narrative account reveals how a neoliberal and economic rationalist agenda such as that named in the Australian higher-education sector as "quality assurance" can be used strategically for a politics of transformation in the interests of women. That is, rather than view the economic rationalist agenda of workplace restructuring as an exclusively monolithic mechanism of patriarchal state control with little room for a feminist agenda, I propose that there are gaps and openings, however ambiguous and contradictory, available for women to work productively and politically within what Mouffe (1993) calls nodal points of shared interest and opportunity.

NATIONAL CONTEXT

In Australia, equity principles have been structured into national education and employment agendas since the establishment of equal opportunity and affirmative action legislation in the early 1980s. Since 1988, following the release of the federal "Higher Education: A Policy Statement," equity has been integrated as a central policy agenda in tertiary education. In 1992, the federal Department of Employment, Education and Training forced a focused investigation and implementation of equity policy across the university sector as part of a larger federal strategy to assure systemwide accountability and quality of performance and output through quality assurance (QA) mechanisms.

The 1992 federal Higher Education Council report, "Higher Education: Achieving Quality," recommended that universities undertake regular reviews and audits of mechanisms used to monitor and improve the quality of their outcomes. Federal quality assurance audits of all Australian universities were conducted over a three-year period from 1993 through 1995. As a consequence, many universities reportedly had become

> more systematic in the manner in which equity activities are undertaken, and this has impacted enormously on both the quantity and quality of equity programs that now operate in Australian universities. *Equity has effectively been elevated to the central policy agenda* within the tertiary sector and all institutions are now compelled to regularly review their equity performance as part of the annual educational profile process. (Bowen, 1994, p. 19) [emphasis added]

National response was initially mixed, ranging from charges of coercive federalism to legal action threatened by some universities contesting allegedly unfair national rankings following nationwide quality audits. A recurrent theme characterizing the debate took issue with the appropriateness of applying a technocratic, economic, rationalist model for change to the university sector, given its particular form of labor. In this regard, critiques of quality assurance reflected larger international skepticism toward the application of private sector principles to public sector management (*European Journal of Education,* 1994). The production of knowledge—through research, teaching, and its embodiment in students—is, after all, incomparable to the production of canned food, furniture, or cars. Quality assurance was also accused of serving the interests of external stakeholders (i.e., federal government corporations) who were accused of defining what universities are supposed to stand for in terms of their contribution to economic competitiveness in a global economy. By this account, externally defined agenda setting tied to funding mechanisms was seen, in turn, to undermine the traditional autonomy of universities, which includes the academic freedom to mount critiques of the state.

In broad terms, the academic community's general response to the imposition of corporate management systems was to argue that a cost-accounting culture would undermine "traditional structures of consensus style management and accountability. It was argued that this would effectively cut across entrenched values of institutional autonomy, academic freedom, collegiality, peer review, co-operation and support which are at the heart of both local and international [academic] communities" (Peters, 1992, p. 128). Workplace restructuring in the university, part of a more global sweep of economic rationalism, was seen by many as infringing on those values, practices, and relationships seen as "traditional" and inalienable foundations of higher learning. Particularly interesting was the degree to which skepticism toward QA and managerial technicism in universities had allied those who traditionally defended the conservative functions of the university as a cultural custodian with those who articulated a post-1960s vision of universities as sites for social criticism and social change. Both groups viewed QA as an attempt to bureaucratize university governance along private sector lines, and to begin bringing the criteria for what should count as teaching and research into alignment with private sector and state capitalist goals.

There was certainly evidence that the QA agenda, whatever its intents, had been enlisted in the services of institutional belt-tightening with the concomitant effect of work intensification in universities. Yet I would argue that there is a need to examine some of the assumptions underlying defenses of the academy against encroaching technicism, whether those defenses are based in traditional or radical visions of university work and organizational culture. We should ask which groups historically were included in "consensus style management," "collegiality," "co-operation and support," and "pastoral" pedagogies and administrative systems. Historically, in most academic institutions, these have been the informal mechanisms of patriarchal culture and rule that have long managed to rule out difference: women and feminist knowledge as well as persons and knowledge of culturally and linguistically divergent backgrounds. Indeed, was the "Golden Age of Academic Autonomy Prior to Managerialism" an epoch of access, equity, and enfranchisement for women and people of color? I think not.

THEORETICAL AND PRACTICAL CONTEXT

One indicator of what was seen to constitute quality was equity: that is, equality of opportunity, participation, and outcomes for student equity targets such as women, Aboriginal and Torres Strait Islander students, students with socioeconomic disadvantages or disabilities or from remote areas, and for female general and academic staff. Since the mid-1980s, the federally mandated affirmative action policy had already required that all Australian companies with 100 or more staff, which included all universities, generate numerical indicators to show systematic progress toward the elimination of gender discrimination at all organizational levels. Yet the ongoing gender imbalance in the academic sector of universities remained significant in comparison to other public service sectors where women's numerical representation was far greater at middle- and upper-management levels but where a more visible "femocracy" had become apparent (H. Eisenstein, 1991). In 1988, women accounted for 7% of full-time tenured professors and associate professors, which increased to 9% in 1990, to 13% in 1996, and to 14.4% in 1998 (DETYA, 1999).

Women's low representation at senior levels has been well researched and is commonly attributed to the underlying masculine culture of universities that mitigates against women's advancement through informal and hidden cultural barriers (Adler & Izraeli, 1994; Brooks, 1997; Burton, 1997; Cohen, Lee, Newman, Payne, Scheeres, Shoemark, & Tiffin, 1998; Davies, Lubelska, & Quinn, 1994; Eggins, 1997; Marshall, 1997; Morley

& Walsh, 1996; Payne & Shoemark, 1995; Probert, 1994; Still, 1993). Studies in Britain have found that equity initiatives often meet with strong resistance from males who find ways to avoid, if not subvert, equity programs and tend to deny the existence of systemic discrimination at institutional and larger societal levels (Cockburn, 1990). Masculinist values and meanings are deeply embedded in bureaucratic and disciplinary cultures of the university and are not easily dislodged. In the face of such deeply entrenched attitudes, ways of doing academic business, affirmative action, or equity legislation, as we have seen over the past two decades, do not automatically guarantee women's advancement. I would argue, therefore, that quality assurance discourses—their ideological and economic concomitants notwithstanding—can provide yet another legislated opportunity focused on implementation, evaluation, and measurable outcomes for local systemic intervention into women's employment and career advancement opportunities in one sector of the labor market. The very technicist emphasis on the actual delivery of empirical, quantitative indicators may circumvent the capacity of some universities to incorporate the discourses of gender equity without making substantive visible progress.

In some ways, the move from the naming of gender equity in policy discourses of affirmative action and equal opportunity to discourses of implementation, monitoring, and evaluation—especially as these were tied to benchmarked outcomes and funding rewards—publicly acknowledged that affirmative action and equal opportunity policies in themselves were inadequate to ensure more equitable workplace opportunities for women. QA discourse, whether localized in the Australian university audits of 1993 to 1995 or in current OECD and UNESCO policy frameworks for global quality benchmarks in educational provision, names equity as one of its core measures of excellence and quality identifiable through equity performance indicators. As such, QA can be appropriated by women as a mechanism for what Yeatman (1990) calls equity-oriented change management. Granted, such strategies risk putting women in charge of "managing equity," granting them middle management status over "traditional" feminine domains of academic work, while men retain more highly valued and privileged positions of control in academic administration and research. However, "what appears from one angle as a double bind can from another appear as a power and creative site of dynamic contradictions in the organisation" (Yeatman, 1994a, p. 21). And it is in these dynamic contradictions that women can place themselves as change agents to create opportunities previously denied women and other equity target groups. In other words, working creatively and politically within dynamic contradictions can mean rearticulating and using a managerialist discourse such as QA for social justice means and ends in the interests of women.

Particularly in light of postindustrial shifts and the multiple flows of globalization that I discussed in Chapter 2, power cannot be conceptualized as sovereign or unidirectional but as multidimensional and discursively heteroglossic. Moreover, part of the postmodern moment is the delegitimation of the center (i.e., the male and European voice of "truth," power/knowledge) with corresponding implications for the articulation of alternative power and knowledge claims, which are increasingly the voice(s) of difference. Federally institutionalized equity agendas are a case in point. The legislative and institutional implementation of QA and the consequent, albeit variable, grassroots cultural changes in universities, encouraged governmental mainstreaming of equity as a concept and strategic planning and outcomes indicator, and brought difference of historical disadvantage into the mainstream. In that regard, the systematic and legislated implementation of equity through a discourse of QA can be viewed, and indeed actualized, as one strategy, albeit a contradictory one, for structural and cultural change in the interests of women in higher education, rather than as a peripheral or compensatory add-on program for women.

It is my view that a feminist politics of intervention must remain vigilant and critical of reproductive processes of marginalization but also seize opportunities for change through contradictory and alternative readings of what has tended to be dismissed as a monolithic and seamless discourse of managerialism, corporatism, and economic rationalism. Indeed, as Mouffe (1993), Yeatman (1994a), and H. Eisenstein (1991) have argued in different ways, "toward the end of the twentieth century, it seems futile to argue that feminists should not where possible be seeking to use the political process to further our ends" (p.58).

The discourse of QA in Australian higher education functioned on both negative/reproductive and positive/productive axes in relation to women. It reproduced a host of patriarchal assumptions and processes and yet enabled the implementation of formal procedures to investigate and reverse gender imbalances that disadvantage women. Key among QA's negative consequences for equity groups, particularly women, was the drive toward standardization of teaching and research practices that are output based (performance indicators) on criteria that reflect male principles of academic knowledge production. Thus, it is argued, in the move to standardize, criteria are invoked that by and large do not take into account what some feminist scholars consider women's different approach to pedagogy—their different teaching and learning styles (Acker, 1994; Christian-Smith & Kellor, 1999; Lewis, 1993; Luke & Gore, 1992; Weiner, 1994). Teaching performance indicators, such as those commonly culled from student evaluations, do not always account for students' (skeptical and often negative) perceptions of women in positions of intellectual authority (Luke, 1996; Nicholls, 1994). Women's high concentration at lecturer level suggests that they are more likely to teach large-enrollment courses for undergraduates, particularly first- and second-year undergraduates, which puts women's teaching performance at the mercy of students who are often less than fair in their assessment of women academics. Peer review is another mechanism for evaluating teaching that is based on male models of academic success: "peer review...can be problematic for women where women are more junior or do not conform to the male 'publish or perish' career stereotype. Women teaching in 'service' areas or in elective enrichment subjects may also be held in low esteem, both by students and their colleagues" (Nicholls, 1994, p. 6).

The push toward measurement for research has also been viewed as disadvantageous to women. Women academics tend to be concentrated in the humanities and social sciences where the research process is often more time consuming and where output is generally quantifiably less than in the natural and pure sciences. Research performance indicators do not account for women's common, although not exclusive, position as junior or secondary in a research partnership, whether in grant applications or research publications. The lack of senior academic women on university research committees can often lead to skewed ranking of research applications by junior academic women and can also mean a scarcity of senior female mentoring partners. At the national level, women are seriously underrepresented on the Australian Research Council panels and committees. As Wells (1995) puts it: "All women researchers are aware of the frustrations and difficulties of getting a seat on the research funding merry-go-round: that vital first step in establishing a record of research funding and activity which will make it easier to get grants in the future" (p. 15). Research topics pursued by women and the disciplines in which they are concentrated (e.g., education, social work, nursing), do not always readily fit into national (economic) research priorities and do not lend themselves to large-scale competitive funding. This further puts women's research performance indicators at a disadvantage in comparison to research output in the natural sciences, which are heavily populated by males.

Moreover, the not-so-hidden connections between QA and work intensification has had identifiable effects on casual and low-ranked academic staff where women tend to be concentrated. This increases their vulnerability to retrenchment in a tightening "more work for less" funding environment. Women's greater representation in short-term contract and casual positions (as lecturers and research assistants) means that they are less likely to have access to and build research partnerships with senior academics. As temporary and/or casual staff, they are less likely to qualify for large internal or competitive external research grants (F. Allen, 1994a; M. Allen, 1994b). Finally, women's social circumstances—most commonly, their child care and domestic responsibilities—have been shown to influence their postgraduate and doctoral completion rates, as well their overall research output. In other words, research or teaching productivity measures or equity indicators verifying improved targets do not account for the differences in women's situated realities and circumstances (cf., Murphy, 1993; Rollison, 1999). Moreover, standardized measures or outcome indicators are unable, conceptually or politically, to challenge the definitional or cultural status quo. That said, QA's lack of discursive sensitivity to the gray areas of gender differences and its exclusive focus on accountability, monitoring, and evaluation of progress toward equity targets do not diminish its historical importance in mainstreaming equity in policy frameworks and institutional practice.

QUALITY ASSURANCE:
AN OVERVIEW OF PROCESSES

The following provides a brief synopsis of QA processes for monitoring and improving universities' quality of outcomes at work in Australian universities from 1993 to 1995. During this period, universities were asked annually to initiate reviews and audits of their procedures and systems in place to ensure quality outcomes. Each year, the Committee for Quality Assurance in Higher Education (CQAHE) set key issues that universities were required to investigate and report on (e.g., research, teaching and learning, community service, equity and participation, etc.). Each institution prepared a portfolio to demonstrate what kinds of systems and procedures it had set in place and which initiatives it planned toward compliance with the quality agenda. Importantly, universities were asked to show how they evaluate their own assessments of the effects of their procedures and systems—a kind of self-evaluation. CQAHE reviewed the submitted documents and subsequently sent evaluation teams to visit each university for one day. Using data from each university's portfolio, existing nationally based data, and data derived from interviews with selected university staff during the one-day visit, CQAHE teams subsequently made recommendations to the Minister of Education for allocation of specially designated "quality" funds. These recommendations were based on how well each university had demonstrated its capacity to show the effectiveness of its policies and procedures in the target areas, as well the university's own assessment of its procedures and outcomes. The final stage was the annual national ranking of universities and the allocation of substantial funds, which amounted to $76 million in 1994.

The process by which QA initiatives were implemented, monitored, and evaluated was, in the first instance, achieved through self-evaluation and self-representation through narrative construction in the quality portfolio. This discursive representation of an institution's identity—its organizational structure, human resources profile, financial management structure, research and "educational" products and outcomes—in a document of narrative prose suggests a textual version of the Foucauldian confessional (1977). In the spirit of postmodernist management principles, which put a premium on team work, devolution, lateral and negotiated rather than vertical and authoritarian decision making, a massive public service sector like tertiary education is best surveilled and held accountable (to government and the community) by forcing each institution to self-profess its identity and operations through narrative self-construction. In this way, state control appears as less onerously wielded from the center, for it invites commentary and identity statements from each institution before tours of inspection are commenced.

CQAHE visits to each institution acted as validity checks on the discursive construct submitted in the form of the quality portfolio, and the inspection team's perception of how those narrative claims held up to the "empirical reality" each team had access to during their one-day visit to an institution. Visits were structured around group interviews (e.g., with the senior executive, staff, students, etc.) organized by each university according to "generically" named groups that a visiting team identified in advance. In this scenario, the face-to-face evaluation of the first-order self-evaluation (the QA portfolio) elevated governmental analysis and surveillance to a second-order level of discourse—the verbal (re)construction and validation of testimony formalized in the quality portfolio. In fact, much hinges on the "quality" of the verbal performance—the language games—of those persons and groups invited internally by a university to represent the university to the government audit team. That team, in turn, though ostensibly involved in a process of triangulation, constructed what amounted to a narrative to be written over the original (written) narrative about the institution.

What this dual-level institutional and personal(ized) representation suggests is what Lyotard (1984) calls "performativity." In the current climate of open systems and accountability, performance is a kind of ontology, and in the case of quality assurance discourse, performativity is structured at the level of representation (of the institution) in a discourse of quality. That is, if the mode of performativity is conceptualized and legitimated as "quality," then there is no space, no practice, no ontology outside of quality. The very core concept and mechanism of the new managerialism is, in fact, "performance indicators." Hence, the entire process of QA, and an institution's *raison d'etre*—its mission, strategic plan, procedures, and systems—hinges on performance, on visible benchmarks and outcomes of quality product delivery. And it is within this discourse of performance and quality management, as I will shortly argue, that women can benefit from having gender equity conceptualized as a quality issue, as a performance indicator foregrounded, made visible, and formalized procedurally and structurally.

I have noted in the previous chapter that there is no doubt that QA is the driving mechanism of new global managerialism and standardization in the administration of universities, and the human and financial resources circulating within them and the educational products they market (deWit, 1995; Mallea, 1999). What used to be educational exports in the form of aid has become an international export trade, a not insignificant revenue source and growth area for many western economies. Yet on another level, QA is a prime example of what Foucault (1977; in Deleuze, 1986) called mechanisms of governmentality and techniques of the disciplinary society. Within a federally mandated discourse of "total quality management," institutionalized processes and social subjects can be regulated, surveilled, and disciplined through mechanisms of accountability. Yet if this kind of surveillance—a diffused panopticism—looks for and monitors equity performance, then such mechanisms of power reveal its productive potential by bringing marginalized groups into view of the disciplinary, panoptic gaze. Therefore, rather than view such systemwide ordering of knowledge and persons as an exclusively negative and repressive act of state power and control, following Foucault, there is indeed a productive dimension to such power/knowledge regimes. Crucial to this argument is that global systems, such as state or federal educational policy

for schools, can have very different interpretations, applications to practice, and outcomes at the local level, or in the case of QA, at individual
institutional, departmental, or even classroom levels.

Because the QA agenda is discourse, it is polysemous and therefore
can have a range of dimensions to its positivity and negativity, to its positive transformational and negative reproductive potential. In other words,
any grassroots outcomes at the level of institutional interpretation and
implementation cannot be seen in simple binarist terms as having either
all negative or all positive effects. Rather, outcomes are always mixed,
local, and contextualized by historical conditions. Hence, the application
of a governmental strategy such as QA to institutions that historically have
lacked systems of open management and accountability can have positive
and emancipatory effects on systematically disenfranchised groups within
an institution. For instance, the collection of data on female students
enrolled in nontraditional areas of study, on academic promotion and
tenure rates for women, and external reviews of a department's or university's equity plan and targets generates knowledge about women that, in
turn, can be used by women in their own interests.

QUALITY ASSURANCE:
EFFECTS ON ONE SITE

As I noted at the beginning of this book, prior to taking up my current
position in 1996, I worked for about 10 years in a small regional university. I have already detailed some of my experiences there. To reiterate, I
would characterize the culture of the university during the pre-QA era as
parochial, patriarchal, and pastoral. Like many smaller Australian regional
universities, prior to QA initiatives, many departments did not have any
visible mechanisms for budgetary and administrative accountability, nor
systemwide mechanisms for monitoring teaching and learning as well as
research quality and outcomes. Many departments provided only cursory
course outlines for students, and student representation on departmental
and university committees was not the norm. In many departments, grievance procedures and accountability to students were either absent or ad
hoc and informal. Staff development programs offered courses such as
career planning, stress management, retirement and pension planning,
effective use of technology, and so on, which catered primarily to a male
clientele. Staff development courses and resources designed specifically
for women academics or female general staff, or to address the needs of

students with special learning needs or those from non-English-speaking backgrounds (NESB), migrant and indigenous backgrounds, were few.

This kind of informal culture and lack of institutional systems can be attributed partially to rapid growth. Over a four-year period from 1989 through 1992, student enrollments almost doubled, yet the university had one of the highest percentages of equity clientele nationally, including high enrollments among mature aged women and Aboriginal and Torres Strait Islander students (Committee on Quality Assurance in Higher Education, 1995, p. 121). Although informality might have been justifiable with a small student body, the increasing size and diversity of the institution had created an environment where the lack of formal systems, procedures, and processes hindered accountability, open processes, equitable practices and access to facilities and resources, and transparently fair processes of governance.

Many departments failed to include staff in financial and strategic planning, and where such plans existed, internal funding allocation remained at the discretion of department heads without accountability to staff. What pervaded in many departments, then, was an ethic of informality—a kind of policy-free zone. This no-systems culture created and sustained an environment of what former College of Advanced Education staff (by then amalgamated with and teaching in university departments) often proudly referred to as "pastoral care." However worthy such an ethic might have been at some other historical moment, it appeared to many of us who joined the institution as junior staff as an entrenched paternalism that both monitored and surveilled students and excluded junior, casual, and quite often, female staff. The lack of formalized systems legitimated a male professoriate in sovereign control of departmental fiefdoms. In this context, many of us who were junior women working in these departments, had to negotiate personally with (usually) male senior staff regarding requests for travel, research, and career support without formal systems for application and adjudication of requests.

Interestingly enough, that ethos and management style constructed itself on one side of what I described at the beginning of this chapter as a credible and politically defensible binarism: that is, a male professoriate ruling over staff and students in an informal pastoral culture, pitted against "big government" and the faceless formality of bureaucratic systems. This position is aligned with the stock Weberian critique of bureaucratic systems. But, on closer analysis, opposition to alleged intrusions of state on matters of accountability enables the perpetuation of traditional patriarchal systems. In some cases, the sovereign control of departments by a (usually) male individual operating without formalized procedures and systems of accountability led to unaccountable decision making about research funds allocation, the hiring of tutorial help, staff workloads, and promotions. Under the guise of a pastoral and benign regime, many junior academics, women, NESB, and indigenous postgraduate students and staff frequently felt disenfranchised and without recourse to formal grievance systems to contest inequitable treatment.

In some departments, this pastoral informality generated particular forms of pedagogy that trapped students, particularly postgraduate research students, in a web of dependency bonds that are part of a department's hidden curriculum or informal culture. Evidence abounded of professors presenting student research at conferences without permission or acknowledgment and professors putting their names as first authors on student papers. Many students felt isolated and vulnerable in supervisory relationships conducted behind closed doors, where intellectual guidance apparently was nothing more than intellectual browbeating, interrogations, and ersatz psychoanalysis of students' personal lives and "problems." Without formal recourse or appeal procedures, women students in particular often sought guidance and solace from sympathetic women academics. The lack of formal grievance procedures, student representation on departmental and university committees, and a uniform system of subject evaluations in many subjects, meant that students had little recourse for complaint other than to go along with unmonitored and often unreasonable demands (e.g., excessive contact hours and assessments).

The CQAHE 1994 audit of that university found that "there is a perception on the part of some students that they have limited access to decision-making bodies." (Committee on Quality Assurance in Higher Education, 1995, p. 123). By 1995, the university was forced to formalize procedures and systems of accountability, which resulted in the implementation of compulsory evaluations for all subjects and subject outlines that included explicit appeal and grievance procedures. Following publicly released and debated audits and surveys, student representation was mandated for departmental research, teaching, and planning committees and for most faculty and university committees, excluding the executive management, hiring, promotion, and tenure committees. All departments also were required to establish equity committees and/or officers.

Predictably, in the course of three-year QA audits, all of the polarized political positions for and against QA, outlined at the beginning of this chapter, arose. However, the initial response among student unions, post-graduate students, new and beginning lecturers, technical and support staff, most of whom had been systematically disenfranchised from university governance, was positive. A senior officer of the student union commented that "there had been more consultation about university procedures and individual student issues during the two years of QA work than any time before." In one department, following a staff meeting to discuss QA systems, a junior female lecturer commented that the meetings with QA staff had been "the first opportunity we have ever had to talk with the professor or with someone from university administration about how the department should be run. We never knew there should be systems there to deal with research support, workloads, or career support." Another senior woman scientist commented that this was the first time the university administration had ever publicly asked questions of the departmental leadership about equity issues, including the status of women students in laboratories, and women academics in staffing profiles. The advent of QA, then, was seen by many female students and staff working in various positions and locations throughout the university as a way forward. It is worth noting, however, that these same measures were opposed by many of the male professoriate and a few women professors, many of whom sided with the Academic Staff Association's extremely skeptical position that QA was simply a means to remove academic freedom and undermine working conditions. Like all local realignments of power and knowledge relations, the advent of QA at that university was complex and contradictory. Yet it appeared to many at the time to have productive outcomes.

CULTURAL CHANGE

Significantly for all staff, the forced and belated implementation of accountability procedures and transparent management and budgetary structures, as well as the collection of data on university performance and its public presentation for external review, made a substantial difference to the culture of the university and particularly to those groups previously marginalized and silenced. Some of this could be quantified via improved indicators of female staff hiring and promotion or tenure rates (to which I now have no access), but much of the cultural change can only be described in terms of the ambience and tenor around equity issues created through the development and implementation of new systems of accountability, monitoring, and evaluation.

The conceptual key to the cultural shifts evident in many universities by the mid-1990s was the discursive framing of performance outcomes in discourses of excellence and quality, and linking those to an annual public ranking of universities and to funding incentives. And since equity objectives are core principles within QA, equity is conceptually synonymous with excellence and quality, which means "valuing equity for its own sake: but it also entails illuminating the links between equity and productivity" (Wells, 1995, p. 10). What this suggests is that an institution's productivity and outcomes can be enhanced as quality and excellence measures if the full productive diversity of its clientele (students) and workforce (academic and general staff) is used and valued.

At that institution, the interpretation and implementation of QA initiatives were used as an exercise in institutional and cultural self-redefinition around equity issues that were repositioned at the center of debate, policy, and practice. In the last few years, all departments have had to put accountability systems in place for teaching, research, planning, budgeting, management, recruitment, hiring, promotion, and so forth. Workloads or research fund allocations were no longer negotiated behind closed doors with department heads. Financial accountability had forced more open budgeting and budget planning, with staff involvement in funds allocation and financial planning. All departments were required to include student representatives on all committees with a special focus on Aboriginal and Islander students, women, and students with disabilities. For many, this was the first opportunity to get a voice on matters that directly concerned their everyday work lives and academic career opportunities, whether as staff or research student. Many departments were using the "new" terminology of the equity agenda for the first time. In devising systems of accountability, department heads and management were no longer able to avoid the use of categories such as "equity," "disability," "older," "indigenous," or "gender." While this might seem a trivial achievement, for many women students and staff in departments previously administered under old-style nepotistic management regimes, this was a huge step forward at the level of discursive naming and recognition.

At the time of my departure from the institution, substantive changes became evident throughout the university. For example, strategic plans that incorporated equity issues and performance indicators were required by all departments. Mechanisms for checking the quality of teaching forced staff to consider equity issues and stand accountable for initiatives aimed at accommodating the special needs of equity groups. For example, when setting consultation hours, staff needed to consider whether they accommodated the needs of working students, rural students, and women with children. In organizing lecture rooms, staff had to take into account the provision of facilities that would accommodate students with special needs (wheelchair accessibility, audio-visual aids to assist the hearing or visually impaired, etc.). Staff were forced to think about how their lecture content, reading lists, and pedagogy accommodated the diversity of learning styles of, say, indigenous students, overseas students, mature aged students, and women. Many male staff members, in fact, had no idea that women, indigenous, or overseas students could have a very different relation to the logocentrism of western knowledge and epistemology.

Better funding for gender equity programs, NESB, and mature aged student support, counseling, and student services were put in place, much of it supported by the federal funds accrued from the quality audits. A Centre for Women's Studies was established and, although its origins lay in the grassroots activism and lobbying of a group of already networked and highly dedicated university women, the climate of accountability, particularly in areas of equity, helped to support its establishment and maintain it against encroaching cutbacks. I had the privilege of serving as foundation director of the Centre for Women's Studies since 1994. Relatedly, policy initiatives for intellectual property rights for research assistants, postgraduate students, and junior staff were developed, and policy drafting about the knowledge claims and intellectual property rights of indigenous groups began. In a previous era, none of these issues were seen as relevant for public debate.

CONCLUSIONS

Following Foucault, I have argued that QA is a form of governmentality and social discipline that regulates social subjects and practices. Yet the very panoptic mechanisms of "making visible," of the occularcentrism implied by performativity, of standardization and normalization, have also brought previously invisible and marginalized groups to light in ways that make them part of a new standard, and new set of norms. QA is a discourse and a set of practices that institutionalized a panoptic and internalized gaze (e.g., via peer review, student evaluations, grievance procedures, and institutional self-assessment) around a set of principles such as quality, equity, productivity, performativity, accountability, standardization and normalization. However, these principles and the mechanisms through which they are actualized have ironically also been able to break the hegemonic, forced consent of "the people" who, under a masculinist regime of university cultures, were positioned to legitimate—and not infrequently be victimized by—sovereign, individual power and exclusionary systems of informal governance. I wish now to close with some comments about what I see as an opportunity for academic women to work as strategic practitioners in the building of coalitions that would make diversity a first principle of equity, quality, and productivity.

First-wave feminism some 20 years ago argued for and achieved *de jure* equity in many areas of women's lives, although many of those early initiatives served primarily the interests of white Australian, not indigenous or NESB, women. As a consequence of those legislated equity policies, and under a center-left Labor government over the past decade until 1996, a relatively powerful femocracy had emerged that made substantial and visible inroads into many state and federal organizations. Large numbers of femocrats in the public sector have worked productively within bureaucratic institutions to transform *de jure* into *de facto* institutionalized equality. But in the tertiary education sector, no comparable academic femocracy, in terms of critical mass, has been evident to force a national systemic shift from equity in legal principle to equity in monitored practice. And, just at a time when academic women were gaining a toehold in middle and senior university management, that moment ironically coincided with an economic shift in postmodern, global capitalism, which has had some of the harshest workplace restructuring consequences for women. These are indeed new times and contradictory moments for feminists, and for women working, teaching, or studying in universities. Yet, as Yeatman (1994b) reminds us:

> Many feminists over the course of the 1990s will find that they are working within organizations and institutions including the State which are following courses of action with which they have little agreement. Leaving will not be an attractive option for those who would find themselves unemployed. Moreover, there is a sense in which we are all in it together, namely facing economic rationalist-managerialist agendas of the services, universities or public sector agencies within which we work. There is a good deal of sense in working as strategic practitioners

to conserve what has been won and, where possible, to minimize the damage. (p. 191)

In some ways, we are not "all in it together" because, for the most part, indigenous, NESB, and immigrant women are hardly part of the handful of women nationally who occupy senior administrative and management positions in the sector. As Leitch (1999) points out, "we are not all sisters" and, indeed, affirmative action and QA discourses have principally benefited white middle-class women. But working as strategic practitioners and forming provisional political coalitions (Mouffe, 1993) through the formal procedures for equity-as-quality can be pragmatic politics for women in ascending positions of influence to reverse the racial imbalance within the gender imbalance by instantiating links among equity, quality, and productivity.

In the corporate-speak of fast capitalism, team work and lateral and negotiated decision making are now recognized as the cornerstones of innovation and productivity (Badenoch, Brown, & Sebastian, 1999; Ledwith & Colgan, 1996). Quality and excellence, likewise, are said to be achievable by harnessing the maximum diversity of ideas, interpretations, and viewpoints. Consensus building and flattened management structures are in, top-down and hierarchical communication channels and decision making are out. What this means, in principle at least, is that performance excellence and quality of product and service are best achieved when the entire spectrum of diversity among human resources within an organization are harnessed and valued.

I think this way of thinking about quality, equity, and diversity may be especially useful for women in regional newly industrializing countries, some of whom have recently been swept into their nations' quality assurance discourses (e.g., Malaysia's ISO 9000). Everywhere in Southeast Asia, women are a tiny minority in higher-education management. In Malaysia, the state manages racial diversity, and there are many contentious issues surrounding race-based imbalances throughout the educational sector that impact particularly hard on Chinese and Indian academic women. There are ways of attacking the problem from within and on its own terms. Appropriating the language and principles of QA in women's own interests is the first step. Second, if women argue for inclusion of the full spectrum of gender and culturally diverse human resources available in an organization as fundamentals of excellence, quality, equity, and productivity, then the culture of university management can be diversified to include women and marginalized ethnic groups. To argue for diversification and inclusivity on the principle of quality strikes at the core of how universities everywhere envision themselves today: quality world-class institutions, globally competitive, and open to the market as much as to accountability and quality audits. It can be an opportune moment for women to step out of the shadows of academe and be counted.

4

Western Feminism,
Globalization,
and Local Standpoints

The question I want to raise in this chapter is how we might reconcile, theoretically and in terms of research practice, aspects of globalization with
locally situated practices, experiences, and identities. Today it is commonplace to assert that feminism is the product of some 30 years of western
scholarship and that the growing body of feminist theory and research on
the subaltern, third world feminism, women of color, or women in various
diasporic configurations is the product of western-based and/or western-
educated women of color. The development of feminism and its global
diffusion (through principally western publishing houses and journals) has
produced a global feminism that has "naturalized and totalized categories
such as 'third world women' *and* 'first world women'" (C. Kaplan, 1994,
p. 137). Critiques of western feminism's theorization of a universal category of women, and of global forms of women's oppression enacted by an
undifferentiated global patriarchy, have been well documented and do not
need rehearsing here (E. A. Kaplan, 1997; Mohanty, Russo, & Torres,
1991; Narain, 1997). However, counter to this global conceptual sweep,
feminism along with poststructural, postcolonial, and even cultural studies scholarship over the last decade has been instrumental in excavating
the local, in giving voice to silenced and marginalized identities and experiences said to have been written over by the totalizing metanarratives of

western grand theory. As I argued in Chapter 2, globalization theory has tended toward the same kind of grand theorizing but alongside persistent calls by some (e.g., Abu-Lughod, 1997; Dirlik, 1996; Featherstone, 1995; Pieterse, 1995) for local analyses of globalization.

Three related questions I want to raise in this chapter are: How local, perspectival, and contingent is the view from the situated "I"? How does globalism, of orientation or intellectual paradigms, infuse the local and thereby mediate local voices and representations? How culturally authentic and local is any indigenous or postcolonial theorizing? I illustrate the questions I pursue about cosmopolitan intellectuals, local situatedness, and global orientations by reference to my own research in the region and the women in my studies.

At the outset, however, I must acknowledge the tremendous linguistic and conceptual difficulty of writing in a "both/and" discursive style, and not falling prey to reproducing the same binarist local/global separations that characterize feminism and globalization theory. That is to say, efforts to write about the "already stitched together," the melded blend of local/global mélange, pastiche, or montage, are defeated by the protocol of academic (rationalist) writing that forces categorical separation: on the one hand "this," on the other "that." Moreover, the very language of debate about globalization forces particular positions and perspectivism: either looking top-down from the center or looking bottom-up from the so-called peripheries (Abou-El-Haj, 1997; Robertson & Khondker, 1998; Wolff, 1997).

GLOBAL COMMONALITIES

It is fair to say that there are indeed global patterns of women's exploitation and oppression, their marginal economic and social status. The same can be said of class differences that reveal global patterns among middle- and upper-class women who share similar levels of advantage through access to education, employment, and consumer goods. Conversely, working class and rural women are globally disadvantaged by lack of, or only limited access to, educational and employment opportunities, to social, cultural, and economic capital. Social and economic indices, such as those produced by UNESCO or the OECD, divide the world into "developed" first world countries and developing "third world" zones, or into more recent transitional economies of newly postindustrializing countries such as Singapore or Hong Kong. Within such differentiated development bands we see further global patterns of similarities among women's economic status, labor participation and income contributions.

Women globally are more likely than men to be the primary child care provider, and they are more likely to earn less than men. On a global average, girls receive less education than boys. From a sociocultural perspective, we can also say that women globally are at greater risk of rape and domestic abuse than men, and it is women, not men, who are globally the object of rape as a weapon of war. Advertising the world over is more likely to use women as signifiers of home, family, and community. TV sitcoms and soap operas around the world, including locally produced programs, reproduce traditional gender stereotypes of women as homemaker mother, gossips, scheming vixens, wronged by unfaithful men. On the other hand, men are portrayed as breadwinners, absentee or incompetent fathers, action heroes or villains, or unfaithful cheats. Religious ideologies everywhere reserve the right to speak and interpret "the word" of scripture, doxa, and transcendental "truths" for men. The list goes on. But my point is that there *are* global patterns of women's differently situated realities across class, nation-state, and cultural differences. We know of these patterns and similarities because 30 years of feminist analyses from across the disciplines have documented local instances of global patriarchal patterns, structures, and cultural forms, including theory itself, which names and classifies those very structures and forms.

However, most of that scholarship has been undertaken in the local sites from which feminist theory was produced and which, in turn, produced feminists—namely, the west and north. And although feminism has exposed the masculine fictions that parade as universal and androgynous theory, feminism's reworking of the canon remains very much a western narrative. Feminist work produced in the south and east is generally not known to western feminists, although the last decade has seen a surge of northern interest, perhaps voyeurism (Chow, 1993), in the voices of diasporic difference. Of course a lot of this north-south, east-west imbalance has to do with the dominance of book and journal publishing empires that are tied to seeking readerships and market share where profits are to be made: Europe, North America, and European outposts in Australasia. Global feminism travels along the same trade winds as global capitalism.

POSITIONALITY

Arguably, there is no "global citizen" per se but only locally situated, embodied subjects. Since globalization (of consumerism, information, or

McCulture) is always only enacted and experienced in local sites—whether at the local Kentucky Fried Chicken outlet or supermall, on the cellular phone or in front of the keyboard or TV—analysis of people doing global things, by definition, remains localized. Thus, the researcher or theorist too is located in a locale, a situated context, despite engaging in global intellectual work: adhering to internationally recognized paradigmatic frameworks and the universalism of scholarly protocols of inquiry. Constituent subjects of "global" scholarly communities in any discipline are situated in place-specific institutions and communities, nation-state governments and ideologies, real neighborhoods and office spaces, staff rooms and classrooms. One's location on the dense grid of sociodemographic particularities of age, educational and employment histories, gender, age, race and ethnicity, partner relationships, and so on further localize or individualize researchers' epistemological and political standpoints.

How we read theory or the world, interpret and write up data or OECD statistics, how we apprehend difference and the "other," or how and what we teach is ultimately grounded and saturated in a view from somewhere, a "centric" view. It is centric in the sense that it emanates from embodied subjective "consciousness" that, in turn, is made intelligible to the self through historical discourses about gender, race, ethnicity, and so forth. This "I" is in charge of "the positions that have constituted me," and it is the "I" that is the transfer or relay point through which culture and discourses flow that position the "I." "These 'positions' are not merely theoretical products, but fully embedded organizing principles of material practices and institutional arrangements, those matrices of power and discourse that produce me as a viable 'subject'" (Butler, 1995, p. 42). Thus, how we read the self and other or adhere to or reject theory is very much a function of subjectively situated politics, gender identity, history, training, social, and cultural circumstance. "Third world" feminists rejecting western feminist theory, feminists rejecting masculinist theory, or men pontificating on feminism (Derrida, 1987) are cases in point.

In short, "there is no view from nowhere" (Bordo, 1990, p. 140). My intellectual lenses, subjective sense of self, and overlaid identities are the product of history, of a particular life trajectory, of the discursive resources available to me because of where and when I was educated, where I have lived and worked, and how my class and ethnic background dovetailed into place-specific opportunities and impediments, variable access to power, cultural, social, and economic capital. Theories of globalization also emanate from particular subject positions localized in specific histories, intellectual paradigms and communities, and local cultural contexts (Friedman, 1997). The debate about positionality, identity, location, and locale has been long running in feminist circles (Benhabib, Butler, Cornell, & Fraser, 1995; Nicholson, 1990), and as Bordo (1990) put it some 10 years ago: "We always 'see' from the points of view that are invested with social, political and personal interests, inescapably 'centric' in one way or another, even the desire to do justice to heterogeneity" (p. 140). Western globalization theory is similarly "inescapably centric," expressing a particular optic.

Theoretical attention to the perspectivism of location and positionality, however, need not obscure larger objective structures, discourses, and processes that flow through and position subjects within vectors of cultural, economic, religious, political, and social ideologies and organization. Nor should particularism preclude links and appeals to normative, "universal" benchmarks be they moral, ethical, or legal. And this I believe to be a crucial, albeit contentious point for feminism. In other words, without recourse to some forms of normative "standards," there is no ground, no criteria to invoke with which to distinguish between morally and ethically defensible and indefensible positions and practices. Contrary to the long-standing feminist critique of any form of theoretical, legal, or moral normativity as normalizing and oppressive, "feminists do need to make normative judgments and to offer emancipatory alternatives. We are not for 'anything goes'" (Fraser, 1995, p. 71). I have argued elsewhere in relation to debates about feminist pedagogy that, without recourse to normative principles, whether of feminist claims of "the good" for women, claims for meritocratic equity and social justice principles, or moral claims that can judge between oppressive and emancipatory theory and discourses, feminism runs the risk of an antifoundationalist stance without authority, where anything goes, where any claim is as good as another—equal but different (Luke, 1996).

Without normative principles, deferrals to infinite differences preclude critiques of what might constitute injustice, exploitation, or subordination, which leaves us with a "veritable cacophony of voices" (Jones, 1991, pp. 107–108), none of which can be judged against another. We *do* adhere to normative standards, although they are never wholly consensual and uncontested (e.g., International Court of Law, International War Crimes Tribunal, UN Human Rights Charter). Feminists do appeal, however tacitly, to global principles of social justice in claims for gender equity—from demanding the vote, wage parity, and equal educational access to judging feminist theories as "better," more emancipatory or ethical or responsive to women than male-stream theory. I would argue then that, first, there is no escape from normativity despite its contested and provisional status. Second, it is politically indefensible for the feminist project to deny its epistemological connectedness to norms and to deny its responsibility to situate and localize them with the same kinds of contextual, cultural, and historical analytic rigor accorded to differences of identity and locality.

Relatedly, feminists have also cautioned that the feminist and postmodernist turn to specificity, to local knowledge and multiply constituted differences, easily runs the risk of creating a totality of difference, where any claims of commonalities or similarities —the basis and potential for coalition building across differences and affinities—is undermined by an endless deferral to differences. A (conceptual) universe of views from everywhere and every body readily slides into views and voices from nowhere and no body—floating signifiers of difference and diversity whose only political or epistemological referents are their unique location, history, experience, identity, and so forth. Foucault heeded that "everything is dangerous," and postmodernism's skepticism of certainty and universalism certainly mirrors that distrust. It is as dangerous to fix on and trust the local as it is to lock on and trust universals, the objectivism of macrostructural theories, explanations, or social indicators. In some ways, the theoretical and practical issues of globalization have brought the Gordian intellectual knot of reconciling that old structure/agency dilemma into new relief.

The problematic of new times, then, is how to proceed epistemologically and methodologically without falling prey to a valorization of local narratives of difference, or of allowing the conceptual frameworks and empirical data of globalization to grind the local into a mirror reflection of globalization. I shall now turn to a more narrativized account to explain my contingent positioning vis-à-vis research on local instances of globalization in higher education, and to relativize my identity and position as woman and western doing research in cross-cultural contexts. This is about optics, positionality, and situated otherness.

First, in relation to women in higher education, global indicators of gendered labor distribution in the sector reveal that, "With hardly an exception the global picture is one of men outnumbering women at about five to one at middle management level and at about twenty or more to one at senior management level" (Dines, 1993, p. 11). As I outlined in Chapter 2, academic research has provided two decades of evidence confirming that women globally are concentrated at lower positions and therefore earn less, have less access to power and decision making in the institution, and so forth. Such "facts" of the global condition of women in higher education, such a "provisional totalization" (Butler, 1995), highlights a general political and sociological problem that requires that it be genealogized through contextualized culture-specific analysis, mindful that such analysis is itself a narrative embedded in a history, a cultural framework, and a location. We can begin, then, from "global facts." However, the way those facts are read, translated into a research model, and executed at the level of interpretation and engagement with local instances of global phenomena remains ultimately a local experience mediated by situated subjects.

Second, as I noted in the earlier chapters, in light of my present historical location in Australia and in a particular institution and department, I am constituted as agent of and a constituent part of the globalization of higher education in a particular geographical location. That situatedness frames my narrative here. My own history and positionality mean that I bring to my work a particular set of intellectual lenses formed by, among other things, a research and teaching history in feminism, education, cultural studies, postcolonialism, and Foucauldian poststructuralism. My own experiences in three universities (one in Canada, two in Australia), 10 years as undergraduate and graduate student, and 15 years as an academic have shaped my understanding and critique of and research interests in women in higher education in specific ways. My recent work in Southeast Asia has thrown what I thought I understood about globalization, and my previous taken-for-granted knowledge about women in higher education, into new relief, the product of which is this book, this narrative.

My second but most proficient language is English, which prevents linguistic access to research and scholarship on women in higher education in Bahasa Malaysia, Thai, Cantonese or Mandarin. While there is not a major "Asian"-authored scholarly corpus on women in higher education, there are some studies and reports in local languages that are closed to me. Hence, my speaking-writing position here is complicit in reproducing a "globalized," English-language narrative that excludes local knowledge and local texts. I am of a particular generation, which shapes my worldview and my relationships with others: it can build bridges in cross-cultural research with women of the same generation as we compare notes on our adult children, having studied in the 1970s, or "getting older" in academics. My partner is second-generation Chinese American. On occasion, we work together in some offshore programs and related academic business in the region. My identity by association to an Asian male gets remediated in different cultural contexts, but in "Asia" it has most often paved the way for me to gain access to people and information that might otherwise be denied a white western academic woman (Luke, 1994; C. Luke & A. Luke, 1999). On the other hand, my visible identity will always position me as a cultural other in nonwestern contexts, which, in turn, has both enabling and limiting consequences. My particular identikit, then, shapes my optic.

Methodologically, cross-cultural research is always fraught with insider-outsider positioning. What happens when women research women in cross-cultural contexts but in same-professional contexts? First, my own gendered professional experience in higher education provides a shared springboard, so to speak, from which I can raise issues with women related to, for example, raising a family while pursuing academic study, attaining promotion, teaching loads or research, and so forth. And as I have already explained, since universities are broadly similar the world over, despite local cultural variations, I am able to share with women a broad frame of reference about our workplaces, including experiences of academic career ladders and academic culture, such as the long haul of the three-degree requisite, study abroad, undergraduate and postgraduate teaching, research and publishing culture, conference circuits, and so forth. This, then, forms a touchstone of shared knowledge and experience.

Despite such shared experiences, in Southeast Asian contexts, I am still perceived as western and white, I embody and am "the other," and I remain an outsider. This has two consequences. First, I have found some women reluctant to raise issues that might be construed as reflecting negatively on their system, their country or political leadership, or their men: "No, the men, the senior men have always been helpful, more helpful often than women." Indeed, I have encountered a few women who have taken this stance by insisting on a rosy picture of equal workplace opportunity, gender equality, and a total absence of any form of discrimination or patriarchy. A second consequence is the reverse: Many women have told me that they feel free to raise issues with me that they would not share with a local. I have found this repeatedly to be the case with issues related to local politics and race/ethnic relations. And yet, as I will discuss shortly, regardless of who is an other and where, academics are part of a larger global intellectual network and elite. Despite culturally distinct locations and social networks, they engage in routinized global practices of inquiry and scholarship. They share more or less the same class-based privileges and speak the "same language"—linguistically, conceptually within paradigms, and semiotically in terms of class-based distinctions of consumer tastes and style. Difference and sameness thus interpenetrate and coconstitute the cosmopolitan academic, the global-mobile intellectual.

But to return to the issue of standpoint and identity: The sedimented personal and intellectual history any researcher brings to an analytic task, particularly in cultural and intercultural research, can never be discarded in hopes of achieving some untainted pure space from which to apprehend an "other" local, the nuanced spectrum of cultural difference and diversity. In that regard, I believe it behooves western researchers to come clean on the impossibility of *not* seeing through western eyes. The "far east" is only far and east from the vantage point of Europe or America. Overseas is only over there because it is not here, not home. Let me provide just a few unspectacular examples of positionality and situated otherness that are common enough to most "tourist-researchers" and part and parcel of fieldwork in a country not one's own.

Scene 1: I am in a taxi, some 45 minutes outside one of Asia's megacities, on my way to a suburban agricultural university. We are driving on a two-lane road through villages and sugar cane fields, and I have no idea where we are. I am somewhat anxious because I don't know whether the cab driver is literally taking me for a ride, what I would do if this turns into an unpleasant experience (which it has on other occasions), and whether we are in fact on our way to the university. The cabbie is uncommunicative, and I don't speak the language. My cellular phone probably wouldn't do me any good, and since the meter seems no longer to be working, I feel a bit helpless and worried. I do not know the cultural code and feel powerless to take charge of a situation that seems unclear to me— I am female and the tourist.

Scene 2: I have finished late Saturday afternoon interviews at the City University of Hong Kong (CUHK). I make my way out of unfamiliar campus territory and finally find a taxi stand. It is late Saturday afternoon and, oddly enough, there are no taxis in the dock or on the streets. Dusk is approaching, and I am in an unfamiliar area, but finally an empty cab picks me up, and I give directions to the YMCA where I am staying. I know Kowloon well enough to recognize after a few minutes that we are heading in the wrong direction. I try to redirect the driver, but suddenly he no longer speaks English and starts yelling at me in Cantonese. Again, I have no vocabulary to contest what's happening and no alternative other than to get out and find the nearest MTR or bus station, although I am short on coins, have no transit tokens, and staying in the cab suddenly seems like the least stressful alternative. We did take a circuitous route back to the Y, and I was ripped off for almost twice the cab fare I paid going to CUHK, but noting the cabbie's name and number to report the incident hardly seemed worth the hassle. Not a major drama and one that besets tourists anywhere, but one that has never occurred when I travel with my partner, whose visible identity as male and Chinese reframes cultural recognition in Asian contexts as insider.

Scene 3: I am in a two-star hotel in a small town in northeastern Thailand. My university contact calls and offers to take me to a silk-weaving factory out in the country. It is Sunday, and there isn't much else to do except watch CNN and organize my tapes, paperwork, and gifts for the women I interview the next day. We head off in a pickup truck (with no air-conditioning), and 40 minutes later we arrive in the silk-factory village. We are dusty, drenched, and thirsty. First stop: a small roadside snack bar for Coke poured over ice. Because I do not have local immunity against stomach bugs, I quickly fish the ice cubes out of my Coke, and we all chuckle. I am the tourist. Next, we saunter through town to the silk shop and pass countless mangy, flea-ridden dogs and some cats, and my heart goes out to them: I am seeing as a westerner and I know it. We enter the silk factory, which is a low, sprawling, somewhat ramshackle building with an iron corrugated roof that makes the heat unbearable—for me. It is Sunday, but there are about 10 very young girls sitting at looms in dim light, clicking away with hands and feet. Some women sit on the tiled floors running silk threads through their toes and onto spindles. I ask my hosts about the age of the girls. My interpreter knows what I'm thinking and tells me they are between 12 and 16, although some girls look no older than 10. I am told that it is good money for the girls and that this is a very poor part of the country where everyone has to contribute to the family income. I am not that naïve to be astounded by child labor, by what western eyes see as impoverished "third world" conditions, but I think my interpreter, a deputy dean from a Bangkok university, knew what I was thinking and she was right, for I was seeing through western eyes. I made a mental note, and we moved on to look at the looms, the bales of silk, the patterns, and so forth. Returning to the front entrance, we stopped for more Coke—this time without ice—and then I am taken to the sales counter with obvious expectations of a purchase. I buy some silk, although I have drawers of it at home from previous visits. It is the right thing to do. I am the visitor from Australia, and I think of the girls in the back rooms.

I am on the plane to Bangkok later that week, and my deputy dean friend and I talk about macrobiotics and tennis. She is a tennis fiend, and we have been watching excerpts of the U.S. Open on CNN the past week.

We talk about counting calories vs. kilojoules and the Pritiken diet, and she shows me a nutrition book she's recently purchased at Borders bookstore in Singapore—the first Borders outpost in Southeast Asia. We talk about bookstores and stumble on amazon.com and agree that it's a much more up-to-date and comprehensive bibliographical source than most online university libraries, including our own. We have moved to another level of social and knowledge exchange thoroughly marked by our common professional and class status and academic engagements with aspects of globalization.

DISJUNCTURES AND COMMONALITIES: CLASS, COSMOPOLITANISM, AND GLOBALIZATION

In the examples I have just noted about shifting identities and location, cultural insider-outsider ways of seeing, I have tried to illustrate difference in reference to positionality. I now turn to look at how commonalities of class and orientations, engendered in part by aspects of globalization, inhabit difference. Notions of class have been among the most contested terms in social theory for most of this century. It has always been notoriously difficult if not impossible to fix groups within precise socioeconomic or class-consciousness strata. More recent postmodern, "new times" arguments "have raised serious doubts about identifying classes as concrete entities in late modern, high modern, post-modern societies" (Gibson-Graham, 1996; Stivens, 1998, p. 15). I am mindful of the problematic of using middle or professional class as an identifying marker. I agree with Kahn (1995) that there is "no new middle class, only new middle classes" (p. 150) and with Stiven's point that groupings within Asian middle-class strata "are better seen as comprising a number of classes or class factions, rather than as a unified, single class" (p. 15). Such factions in Southeast Asia pivot principally around historically sedimented race-based politics and hegemony. These are variously tied to diasporic residues of colonialist regimes, ethnic Chinese economic elites, a post-boom nouveau riche, and political elites formed out of family dynasties.

Yet across the region, new middle classes are also developing out of large segments of the working class and rural poor, who are emerging as a rising consumerist class just beginning to tap into what might be called lower-middle-class aspirations and lifestyles (Abraham, 1997; Chua,

2000; Kahn, 1998; Stivens, 1998). On the other hand, in Singapore, the government actively promotes an ideology of a single homogenous middle-class society. It "denounces criticism against social inequalities" and accuses those who argue for a more egalitarian distribution of wealth and resources as "indulging in the 'politics of envy'" (Chua & Tan, 1999, p. 154). Instead, the myth of meritocracy is heavily promoted by the government "as the basis for allocation of material rewards so as to individualize success and failure" (p. 154). Public debate about class inequalities is not tolerated and it is the "newly rich middle class [that] sets the standard for the society, giving credence, at the ideological and perceptual levels, that it is a 'middle-class society.'" Class stratification is a capitalist universal despite governments' manipulation of policies and control over public debate about social inequalities. Across the region, whether in Thailand (Ockey, 1999), Indonesia (Heryanto, 1999), Malaysia (Shamsul, 1999), or the Philippines (Pinches, 1999b), the term *middle class* has taken on new, contested, and varied meanings, but everywhere it has been at the center of academic, economic, and governmental elaboration. In industrializing Southeast Asia, changed global capitalist circumstances have unfolded differently in different countries, but everywhere across the region they are said to have generated a new social force, a new middle class, which accounts for the "emergence and popular usage of new class vocabularies" (p. 43). Here, however, I want to use the notion of class in relation to an intellectual class of career academics who are professionally positioned to be relays or transfer nodes in globalizing activities, to express aspects of globalized consciousness, to be economically privileged and thus more likely to engage in middle-class and bourgeois levels of consumption, lifestyle activities, and cultural translations.

Contrary to the modernist notion of an intellectual as a "generalist commentator" or "gentleman ethnographer" and critic of public life, culture, capitalism, or the state (Bauman, 1992), the cosmopolitan intellectual of postmodernity is the disciplinary and interdisciplinary professional specialist, the technical expert, whether in cultural anthropology, education, environmentalism, engineering, or social geography. She is multilingual, globally mobile, a cultural code-switcher and "armed with free-floating credentials and go-between talents" (Wilson, 1998, p. 352). She is advisor to NGOs or UN bodies, does research on WTO-funded AIDS projects or World Bank educational programs, or represents her or his university, country, or region at international governmental or academic congresses where issues of globalization are on the agenda. She works with industry and government on tourism development and environmental impact studies, heritage listings, or wetland habitat conservation.

Much has been said of an emerging global middle class (Cheah & Robbins, 1998; Friedman, 1995; Pinches, 1999a; Robison & Goodman, 1996), "an international elite made of top diplomats, government ministers, aid officials and representatives of international organization such as the UN who play golf, dine, take cocktails with one another, forming a kind of cultural cohort" (Friedman, 1995, pp. 79–80). Friedman goes on to say that these groupings overlap with internationally mobile cultural elites, including culture industry VIPs, publishing and media moguls, and professional experts such as academics. Leaving aside for the moment Friedman's classic masculinist assumptions—golf?—so typical of globalization arguments that repeatedly fail to read gender specificity into their equations (Wolff, 1997), a new global academic elite has indeed emerged in the last few decades. Pnina Werbner (1997) frames a description of this new mobile class of cosmopolitans in a zoological metaphor, noting that they

> are multilingual gourmet tasters who travel among global cultures, savoring cultural differences as they flit with consummate ease between social worlds. Such gorgeous butterflies in the greenhouse of global culture are quite a different species from the transnational bees and ants (immigrants, colonialists, corporate expats) that build new hives and nests in foreign lands. (p. 11)

However, "butterflies" or "bees and ants" always emerge in specific histories that are not everywhere the same (Clammer, 1995). For example, Thailand's history as an indigenous/Chinese/Buddhist hybrid has already shaped its culture as a mélange, a product of hundreds of years of complex cultural change and blending of Khmer, Hmong, Lao, Chinese, and Burmese—a process that predates westernization. In fact, it is this capacity to absorb, hybridize, and appropriate that has enabled Thailand to survive without colonization and to infuse a particular slant to the processes and practices of globalization (Girling, 1996; Phongpaichit & Baker, 1996; Unger, 1998). "Thai intellectuals many of whom come from a radical, leftist background, are playing a crucial role as the mediators of global culture. Indeed, globalization is itself a central trope of Thai intellectual discourse" (Kahn, 1998, p. 8).

In Malaysia, attempts to contain the particularism of indigenous and racial cultural diversity have been underway since independence in 1957 as part of a larger political project of Malay nationalism and Islamic identity. Although the project of retooling national identity remains incomplete (cf., K. Raslan, 1998), it has "become universalistic . . . reified under a globalizing impulse" (Kahn, 1998, p. 9) of a greater world Islamic state, which has particular implications for middle-class women who become the bearers and cultural symbol of Islamic modernity (Stivens, 1998; Yuval-Davis, 1997). Here a globalizing impulse woven into a global religious ideology also predates postmodern, ostensibly western-driven globalization. In Malaysia, as elsewhere in south and east Asian Islamic states, women's role and social status has long been subsumed under global categories like "Islamic womanhood." There are many globalisms, and the cosmopolitan intellectual circulates within many overlapping orbits of globalized narratives and practices.

This new intellectual elite of cultural globalizers has been pulled into global discourses in various capacities ranging from working for or conducting research for NGOs, as advisors for the World Bank or members of national ministerial bodies, and so forth. Several women in my study were working with NGOs in girls' literacy programs in Laos and Cambodia, with the WHO in AIDS education, with prostitution rehab centers in Bangkok, and sex education programs among Thai Karen, Lahu, or Shah hill tribes whose daughters are most vulnerable to Bangkok procurers of "hostesses." Relatedly, in 1993, the Thai Royal Institute commissioned a group of distinguished academics (from history, political science, economics and the social sciences) along with business leaders and journalists to debate and develop a definition of *globalization* that would express Thai understandings and sentiments and its perception of place in a global world (Reynolds, 1998; Robertson & Khondker, 1998). The agreed-on term, expressing a sense of outward oriented and adapting to the world, was accepted by the Office of Royal Literature and included in the Thai Royal Dictionary in 1994. This conceptualization embodies a much stronger lexical sense of place and center that looks out and adapts to the world rather than the more totalizing rollout effect implied by the English term. It also illustrates the politics of positionality and locale in constructing a speaking and reading position from the point of view of nation and geopolitical place—but interpreted by a small elite of postcolonial, thoroughly cosmopolitan cultural spokespersons.

Academic historians, architects, archeologists, geographers, and environmentalists work with UNESCO councils in the identification, authentication, and listing of structures and sites for the World Heritage listing, which brings enhanced prestige to "this place" on the global tourist circuits. Whether in Malaysia or Thailand, academics collaborate with the local tourism industry on environmental, social, and cultural issues in the marketing of their heritage buildings, rainforest parks, temples and spiritual sites, indigenous communities, wetland habitats, or pristine "exotic" beaches. As Reynolds (1998) points out, locally produced tourism campaigns often "unabashedly play on the orientalist clichés about the exotic east" (p. 135). Local intellectual, business, and culture industry elites are active agents in a strategic local positioning, a relativization, vis-à-vis the global through appropriations of western orientalist referents to export the local to a world audience. And that world audience is not exclusively the west, implicitly dictating consumer demands elsewhere, but the affluent middle classes of the region from Hong Kong and Japan to Indonesia and belatedly China. Conversely, academic experts call on global discourses and global public concern to secure and protect local environmentally at-risk sites, indigenous groups, and endangered flora, fauna, and animals. In turn, local objects saved from the ravages of global, principally northern, excess and saved by appeals to global "save our planet" discourses are then marketed globally, whether as indigenous medicines or healing practices or as rare species protected in heritage-listed parks, in turn, promoted through eco- and cultural-tourism packages. These are the push-pull, coconstitutive dynamics of local-global trade-offs and appropriations.

This new middle class of public intellectuals, as I have already noted, are western trained and therefore bring analytic, organizational, or even interactional skills and epistemologies to conceptualizations of and solutions to current local problems. But because they are nonetheless locals empowered to articulate local agency, they "have the power to twist and bend standards set elsewhere" (Reynolds, 1998, p. 130). But there are other layers of insider-outsider politics implicated in local intellectual work and academics' cultural-textual productions and community involvement vis-à-vis less privileged and less educated communities in their own countries that are the objects of academic research. Featherstone (1995) raises this issue in relation to the distanced positioning, the "betwixt and between" identity of the cosmopolitan:

> Cosmopolitan is, in identity terms, betwixt and between without being liminal. It is shifting, participating in many worlds without becoming part of them. It is the position and identity of an intellectual self situated outside of the local arenas among which he or she moves. The practice of cosmopolitanism, common to the self-styled global ethnographer of

culture, is predicated on maintaining distance, often a superiority, to the local. (p. 78)

Postcolonial scholars in Southeast Asia are not exempt from the western intellectual paradigms that have dominated scholarship globally, and questions of local authenticity are recurrent (Clammer, 1995; Rajan, 1997). Western postcolonial scholarship has engaged in a long-standing debate about positionality: Can the subaltern speak? Who can speak for whom? On one hand, "the 'post-colonial' middle classes themselves, journalists, artists, academics, among them many women, are simultaneously creating, living in and contesting their own middle-class and cosmopolitan cultural forms" (Stivens, 1998, 20). But academics who inhabit the urbanized, middle class and the globalized spaces that they theorize, describe, or critique are in fact "the identity spaces of the identifiers themselves" (Friedman, 1997, p. 85), and hence those who define and master this "constantly mixing world" are the intellectual elite, the "cultural theorists" theorizing themselves (p. 73). Stivens is worth citing at length on this point:

> The role of these intelligentsia can become extremely complex in such contexts. Some of them espouse the somewhat second-hand globalized, post-colonial (actually mostly U.S. academy-based) agendas of speaking as and for the subaltern underdogs; their position is made even more complex when they sometimes embrace versions of anti-Western modernity. . . . The elite situation of 'Third world' intellectuals, however can undermine [their] claims to authenticity. They have to distance themselves from their own privileged practices, tied as these are into global scholarly enterprises. (p. 20)

As we shall see in the testimonies presented later in this book, many of the women in my study (only a few of whom would consider themselves, but not formally label themselves, feminists), rejected western feminism, western approaches to breaking glass ceilings or implementing gender equity programs. Their ambivalence about their own local identity and political commitments to local problems and solutions, and their connectedness to global debates, issues, and scholarly enterprises, came up repeatedly in our conversations. My deputy dean friend, whom I mentioned earlier, does research in remote communities on technology transfer, and she spent considerable time describing her fieldwork and explaining the importance of working with the people, investigating local problems. Her research and analytic models, however, were entirely based on American scholarship, and her analytic models (pre- and posttests and statistical quantification of instructional program exposure, skill reproduction, transformation, or loss, etc.) seemed to me somewhat questionable in a rural Thai context.

Two postcolonial feminist literary scholars in my study (one each in Hong Kong and Malaysia) provided astute analyses of current political conditions, crises in national identity issues, and the role of women in society and in nation building. Their conversations were heavily referenced to western postcolonial scholars with whom I am familiar, and this common stock of knowledge provided an intellectual bridge for our discussion. Both do research on local literary works but, again, principally through western intellectual paradigms that frame the very terms of debate about the local. To what extent reading social reality off literary works (always the cultural productions of a literate elite) provides a theoretical or descriptive window to the world is a separate but related question, particularly since the "literary critic" is itself a modernist and western invention (Friedman, 1997). Nonetheless, the women's critiques and explications of the local mirrored what has been raised in the western postcolonial literature and therefore did not seem to generate any new, locally voiced insights. As Stivens (1998) points out regarding the Malaysian intellectual elite: "Claims of some Malaysian intellectuals to be providing (more) authentic knowledge of their own conditions run the risk of overlooking their own location within dominant Western ways of knowing and their own elite position" (p. 90).

Another woman, a dean in management and administration, spent considerable time at the beginning of our interview demonstrating her thoroughly western scholarly credentials, querying me if I was familiar with certain authors, where and with whom she had studied, etc. I was then given a mini lecture on the importance of her work to local entrepreneurship, especially small business enterprises in remote communities where barter and traditional family connections still dominate, and where food stalls or small shops are often the only means for women to earn an income. I could not help but wonder what insights could be gained from applications of business administration theory to women's food stalls, or from statistical analysis of rural women's use of technological knowledge for fixing water pumps or mechanized farming tools.

And yet these same women expressed strong antiwestern sentiments, often in terms such as *westoxification* and *dollarization,* the very issue

Stivens (1998) raises about the complexity of postcolonial academics' double-bind positioning of adhering to western intellectual paradigms and yet embracing "versions of anti-Western modernity." They readily reject what they consider western feminism's exclusive focus on women as a special class in need of special treatment. Yet they are active in organizations and grassroots movements to combat domestic violence and prostitution rackets, to improve girls' and women's literacy, and to provide legal aid and emergency shelters for women. Arguably, this new class of globally oriented yet locally based academics cannot wholly be seen as organic intellectuals, tied to and the voice of "sons and daughters of the soil." Their identities, class position, and academic labor traverse within ambivalent and often contradictory layers of insider-outsider politics in their own local sites.

But these are also the same class of women I meet at conferences in Australia, Europe, and the United States. They are all fluent English speakers, and many are multilingual. They all have a stock of global stories to tell that typify the new cosmopolitanism: whether of the best frequent flyer programs, best airports or cab drivers around the world, or which five-star hotels in Bangkok, Singapore, or Kuala Lumpur offer the best Mother's Day lunches. As is common among women, our children were a common topic. As I noted in Chapter 2, class status and privilege extends to positional goods of educational qualifications, and conversations almost always included talk about their children's overseas credentials from the best universities or private schools. Several women had property in the United States and England and spent part of (northern) summers there to spend time with their children studying abroad. Academics everywhere are usually "high in status but low in income" (Clammer, 1995, p. 27), and women's income alone would not account for their class privileges. The conduit for women's access to material affluence, positional and symbolic goods, was through husbands who held positions ranging from high court judges and senior military personnel to CEOs in the corporate sector or their own companies.

Indeed, a significant number of the approximately 60 women I interviewed in four countries lived in levels of affluence that far exceeded the sorts of class-based signifiers I associate with my own western middle-class milieu. This became apparent mostly in situations where the women invited me into their homes. Many of these residences, whether single-dwelling houses in Kuala Lumpur or condominiums in Hong Kong and Singapore, seemed palatial in contrast to my own typically Australian little "hut" back home. These homes were staffed by servants, filled with expensive and opulent furnishings, and had garages packed with top-drawer European cars. In fact, I recall one evening on the way to dinner at a posh country club with one of the women and her family. I was sitting in the back seat of a Mercedes 600—my one and only experience inside this hypersignifier of wealth and status—and wincing at the thought of "How am I going to write this up?"

Westernized, globalized, and middle class but at the same time differentiated, local, and often antiwestern. That antiwestern, antimodernization stance is best illustrated in Malaysia's Islamic revivalism and its pro-Muslim social policies. As Stivens (1998) has argued so well in her case study of "modern" Malay women, middle-class women's embrace of the Malay version of *hijab* must be read as indicative of a new Islamic globalism as well as Malaysia's (or rather the ruling party's) political-cultural stance in opposition to western-style modernization and, indeed, in opposition to an economistic version of globalization.

The legal enshrinement of Islam (such as Islamic banking or state-legislated Muslim family law) and a national Islamic revivalism are a powerful symbolism of antiwesternization and homegrown modernization that attempt to counter images of a Malaysia and Malays made "backward" by successive colonial regimes. Malaysia's Islamicization drive is an anti-colonial, antipostcolonial and anti-western-style globalization stance but dovetailed into a global cultural-religious system (Mohamad, 1994). That antiwestern inflection of Islamic revivalism has only recently (most notably associated with Khomeini's Iranian Islamic revolution) reconstructed a new imaginary specifically "tailored for the present global context" (Beyer, 1998, p. 90; Howell, 1998). Within the most recent fine-tuning of the Malaysian government's Vision 2020, the making of *Melayu Baru* (new Malay) is a key ideological strategy, and it positions women as the most visible cultural bearers of that symbolism.

Women's socialized compliant behaviors within patriarchal family structures and their universal role "of symbolizing their nation or ethnic collectivity" situates them in "crucial roles in hegemonic ethnic projects" (Yuval-Davis, 1993; 1997, p. 195). As in the west, in times of legitimation crises and cultural change, women's bodies readily become passive objects of representation and social discipline. In that regard, Malay middle-class women represent, indeed embody, that confluence, that intermediary relay point, where they are active agents of various cultural messages and translations. Under *hijab*, Rolexes flash and cellular phones go off in Italian designer purses.

I do not suggest that all academics or all academic women fit the image of the cosmopolitan intellectual elite that globalization theorists such as Friedman (1995, 1997), Cheah (1998), Hannerz (1992, 1997) and others have described as key agents in globalization processes. But certainly among my own social-academic network in Southeast Asia and the women in my study, many fit the characterization of a cosmopolitan and global intellectual elite that I have described so far.

WOMEN ON INFORMATION TECHNOLOGY
AND MEDIASCAPES

I have so far not discussed how women or the academic enterprise factors into the electronic flows of the global infoscape, but I will briefly address it here. The global circulation of cultural representations and social subjects is the mostly widely popularized aspect of globalization. Commonly excluded from such popularizations as well as critical inquiry is the productive potential of electronic connectivity that enables new relationships and communities. This, I believe, has been particularly beneficial for women. Yet local differences in cultural protocol and state regulation mediate electronic global exchanges as well as media content and access. I take these issues up in reference to the women in my study.

The electronic socioscape of the IT superhighway has some barreling down the center lane and others waiting on the on-ramps. Vast populations without electricity or phone lines are disconnected from the global multilogues that the cosmopolitan elite takes for granted and for whom connectivity is the key to global networking. Unquestionably, "rapidly increasing levels of technical sophistication in southeast Asia, culture and society in the region are already being shaped in significant ways by the linking of (some of) its citizens both to each other and to the outside world by the Internet" (Kahn, 1998, p. 10). And it is mostly the middle-class professional elite and intellectuals who are technologically literate and the shapers of cultural and national identity in global contexts (Castells, 1996; Mees, 1998; Robison & Goodman, 1996).

Most of the preliminary groundwork for my study was conducted on e-mail and Web sites. Every woman's business card included an e-mail address, and a few had personal URLs—the latest identity markers and symbolic cultural capital. Discussions about transcripts and drafts of my papers for each case study were conducted via e-mail. Many women put me on local women's network mailing lists. Their engagement with a global electronic community is no different than among women in the west, although there are some cultural differences in terms of intersubjective protocol and political differences in terms of freedom of speech. I will turn to this issue shortly. But, contrary to the popular view of women being IT illiterate or at least reticent users, these women are globally mobile fiber-optic travelers. Yet what local resistance, appropriations, and contradictions flow out of this global electronic switchboard, this so-called open and democratic mediascape? A few examples will suffice.

Singapore has long constructed itself as a global city, a financial and IT hub that is currently pushing a renewed national identity theme focused on harnessing diversity through unity encompassed in visions of a unified, highly IT literate, networked society (Birch, 1999). The government's document of its IT future vision, "IT 2000—A Vision of an Intelligent Island," is an information, economic, and cultural management strategy. Plans to hotlink and wire every home, school, office, and factory by 2005 mean open slather to the world "out there" and the potential for Singaporeans to gain access to morally questionable and politically dubious material. Legislation "to safeguard public morals, political stability and religious harmony" was enacted in 1996 and prohibits "material that jeopardizes security or defense, or undermines confidence in the administration of justice; misleads and alarms the public; tends to hold the government in hatred or contempt, or incites disaffection against it" (Vervoorn, 1998, p. 235). The risk of cultural and moral contamination is real enough because electronic access to limitless information, western values, and social relations (queer MUDs?) has the potential to "undermine the sorts of political, social, cultural and economic stabilities which were actively used to attract the investment capital of the multinational and transnational corporations in the first place" (Birch, 1999, p. 32). So government control of the print media, monitoring of electronic communications, and censorship of "unsavory" Web sites, judged as potential threats to national security (cf., Brown, 2000) and the cultural well-being of the nation, hopes to sustain a cheery and protected citizenry untainted by westoxification.

E-mails in and out of Singapore often lurk for days in cyberspace waiting for "authentication." E-mail, as we know, is ultimately not private at all, and in dialogue with Singaporean colleagues, we all speak a cautious politeness, we don't gossip, talk politics, or drop names. That sense of caution, indeed paranoia, and pressure for proper public political correctness extends to the publication and conference presentation of academic work. Malaysia and Singapore "have governments that are quite sensitive to criticism, and academics can face problems if they are too critical of government policy; potentially volatile ethnic and religious questions must be treated with extreme care by the academic community" (Altbach, 1989, p. 25). My friends tell of chapters pulled by local publishers out of anthologies, judged as too critical, too borderline politically. My own heavily self-censored paper on women in higher education in Singapore went through repeated edits with colleagues there who helped me water it down to the point where it would not arouse undue attention. Similarly, I sufficiently sanitized my paper on the Malaysian study before sending drafts via e-mail to the women in the study. Publishing "critical" work outside Singapore or Malaysia is no guarantee of safe passage back into either country as tourist or academic.

There is nothing particularly remarkable or unique about state censorship and control of media, because it is common fare around the world in promoting national ideologies and maintaining national security and political and cultural control. However, despite the recurring antiglobalization, antiwestern innuendo that infused parts of conversations I had with women, they all resented media and Internet censorship and were avid western media fans while voicing the obligatory criticism of advertising, Hollywood-style violence, and teen pop culture.

In Malaysia, on the day that the driver of dismissed and criminally charged Deputy Prime Minister Anwar Ibrahim gave damning court testimony about police coercion into giving false statements (about having been sodomized by Anwar), I got the news midafternoon from CNN and BBC in my hotel room. That evening the women who picked me up for dinner immediately asked me what had transpired on the cable news because there had been no print or free-to-air TV coverage, and apparently by late afternoon, the plug had been pulled on CNN and BBC household subscribers. A few months earlier, during the Commonwealth Games and Queen Elizabeth's visit, "reformasi" street protests broke out (in response to Anwar's removal from office and charges of corruption and sodomy), and immediately all satellite TV coverage was halted, which itself became a CNN, BBC, and Australian news item.

The women, none of them political radicals as far as I could make out, referred to this incident with some dismay. Earlier during interviews, they expressed strong antiwestern sensibilities, particularly in light of then recent International Monetary Fund (IMF) directives. But they felt strongly about their right of access to global information sources from which they could choose and make up their own minds about issues and events. It also became apparent that they were among the small elite who could afford satellite service, which is not standard issue on the rooftops throughout Malaysia. Women in Penang and Kuala Lumpur were getting their news off the Web and, as educated urban women, they wanted information and access to global—that is, western—media fare and expressed resentment at being treated like a nation of duped children. They reject globalization and westoxification in broad ideological clichés yet want to be tuned into global media fare. They argue for an indigenous feminism, for local resistance to western cultural imperialism and IMF packages, but "off the record" they take an antilocal stance against government censorship, suppression of political opposition, and turning riot police against its own people.

A similar conflation of local proglobalization and antilocal sentiment is evident in Thai students' preference for English, which also illustrates Robertson's "relativization" argument and Water's point about "positive preference for western and capitalist possibilities." Much has been said of the cultural and knowledge imperialism wrought by McMicrosoft. The information processes, organization, and iconography of a global product such as Microsoft Windows and Word have standardized all our information and knowledge processing practices. Yet in Thailand, where keyboards and software text commands are in Sanskrit, academic staff and many of my students complain that that doesn't help them to hone their English skills. One of the IT assignments I give graduate students in our on-site programs is to develop a web page with curriculum resources and analysis of those resources. In the spirit of culturally relevant pedagogy and curriculum, I encourage them to use local Thai resources that I can mark with translators. However, students don't like this idea and insist on using English—local antilocal responses within global contexts, a local relativization vis-à-vis the global.

Admittedly, the historical, cultural, and political diversity across Southeast Asia, or even across the four countries I focus on in this volume, cannot be fully detailed and explicated in one chapter. Mindful that there is much more to the push-pull and discontinuities of local-global intersections and dynamics, I have attempted to provide a snapshot of how I understand the links and connections between globalizing trends and processes and the politics of local standpoints and centric vision. The fusion of local and global, as I have tried to show, is always already scripted (to use a logocentric metaphor) in the academic's intellectual, social, and cultural *modus operandi*. This is particularly the case with senior academics who, because of their seniority and academic and institutional status, tend to be more globally connected and mobile and are more likely to comprise the cosmopolitan intellectual elite of their nation. Most of the women in this study represent such an elite.

By virtue of the global nature of the academic profession, we are all in this together, so to speak: from quality assurance and corporatist discourses and practices that are restructuring our academic labor, to engaging in global debates about globalization itself. Yet we come to the global roundtable with our local baggage, which is never exclusively local, culturally pure, or neatly bounded and untainted by the global. Local and global orientations coexist among academics who contest local traditionalism or myopia as much as they might contest global intrusions, who may claim to speak for a culture and nation as a whole and yet speak (and theorize) primarily of and for themselves. This text, admittedly, is not exempt from speaking of and for itself.

Globalization is as much about difference and ambivalence as it is about sameness and similarities at the level of local uptakes, appropriations, identities, and engagements with global processes, structures, and ideologies. As Kahn (1998) states:

> our earlier understandings of global cultural flows which envisaged a culturally homogenous world as its evolutionary endpoint (the classical understanding of 'cosmopolitanism') or a world culture produced almost entirely through western cultural hegemony needs to be substantially revised as we recognize that globalization is as likely to generate difference, uniqueness and cultural specificity as it is to produce a genuinely universal or homogenous world culture. (p. 9)

The local standpoint of the cosmopolitan academic is ultimately never wholly local, although it is localized. But the global citizen, the cosmopolitan whose orientation and life-world may be substantially global, is nonetheless a local subject and locally situated—each infused with the other.

II

Women, Education, and Equity: South/East

5

Women in Academics:
Views From the South/East

This chapter provides a context and overview of the research presented in the next four chapters and examines sociocultural and political issues related to women and education in Southeast Asia. I investigate locally authored research and UNESCO and census bureau statistics on women and education to provide a backdrop against which to discuss women's underrepresentation in higher-education management. Where data is available, I present brief country profiles of women's participation and outcomes in higher education and tie these to local political contexts, cultural politics, and state regulations that converge to construct variable educational opportunities for women. Throughout I draw illustrative links to the women in my studies to contextualize the cultural politics underpinning discourses of "Asian values," "Asian femininity," and "Asian family values." My discussion of local, indigenous research remains framed in the local globalism issues I have raised so far, but in this chapter, I take a closer look at the politics of difference and standpoints raised by so-called "third world" feminists. I look at epistemological issues about local theorizing that have been raised by local feminist scholars, some of whom argue for adaptation and translation of western theory and others who argue for "indigenization." I begin and close with reflections on my fieldwork in the region to contextualize local contingencies, the messy and chaotic nature of research in which this study and the women's dialogues were situated.

I began in Chapter 1 with mapping the historical trajectory of western feminist research on women in academics. In this chapter, I present views from the south and east. However, to foreshadow, my attempts to locate research on women in Southeast Asian higher education were generally futile. Gender issues or gender equity in educational contexts is not a high priority in the educational literature in any of the four countries. Higher education in Southeast Asia is not addressed in the western or "Asian" organizational and management literature. Research in the politics, history, economics, or sociology of education draws heavily on development theories and arguments, but here too, women and women in higher education, whether as students or staff, are largely excluded from analysis and debate. Education ministries, census bureaus, and state statistics divisions rarely provide data on women in education, whether at the level of teachers in schools or women in academics. In short, I have searched far and wide beyond the standard texts on education and "Asia" to find women. Women *are* in the development literature, but there the persistent focus is on girls' schooling, women's literacy, and to a lesser extent, women's tertiary education participation. Women's invisibility as an analytic category thus mirrors one more aspect of local globalism: a global invisibility in local academic and research discourses.

SETTING UP THE STUDY

The case studies I report in subsequent chapters were conducted in 1997 and 1998. I began in Thailand, where I had already spent considerable time with senior management personnel, academics, and students observing and learning about institutional protocol and national and local issues related to schooling and higher education. On numerous previous visits, I had already been observing and making mental notes on women's role, status, and the gender politics in academic contexts and engaging women in discussions about the kinds of glass-ceiling issues that had always interested me. Site visits are "total immersion" experiences. After a 9-to-5 teaching day, evenings are almost always taken up with formal and informal dinners and related social amusements such as karaoke. Weekends usually consist of packing the "foreigners" into minivans and heading off to do the local sights. Along with hosting staff representatives, a few students invariably accompany us as interpreters and to practice their English with us. In other words, these are full-on academic and social encounters and relationship building blocks with steep learning curves. I was feeling relatively comfortable in Thailand, despite my lack of Thai language skills, and so Thailand seemed an obvious first choice for me to get started on a larger regional study on women in higher education.

I already had an established network of friends and colleagues in Singapore and Hong Kong and felt confident that I could negotiate these three sites with relative ease. Culturally and socially, my choices were based on the need for me to have a sense of security and relative control in countries where I would be traveling on my own and in charge of fieldwork logistics without the help of research assistants. My site choices were also limited by financial constraints. I had received a modest university grant in 1997, which was just enough for one return overseas airfare and about 10 days of accommodation, meals, and related costs. To remain fiscally prudent within my meager budget, I decided to add the Thai and Singapore fieldwork to one of my teaching seminars in Thailand and to schedule Hong Kong as one separate trip later in the year. Hong Kong accommodations are among the most expensive in the region, and 7 days of interviews consumed as much accommodation costs as airfares. Since my department covers all travel, meals, and accommodation associated with off-shore teaching programs, I was able to save my grant funds by remaining in Thailand for another two weeks after my teaching commitments there. I added the Thai and, later, the Singapore fieldwork onto this "prepaid" research trip. Singapore is only an hour by air south of Bangkok. I managed to stretch my modest research budget to cover accommodation and incidentals in Singapore, accommodation and domestic travel to various universities in Thailand, and a separate, very expensive, trip to Hong Kong later in the year. In other words, counting pennies on a small budget certainly shaped the scope and sequence of my study.

In 1998, I received another small departmental grant of AU$4,000, and at the end of that year, I conducted the Malaysia study. Malaysia is usually cheaper than Singapore and Hong Kong, but at the time of my trip, the Australian dollar had deteriorated to an all-time low, and the Malaysian *ringgit* had just been pegged to the U.S. dollar, which meant that my initial grant had suddenly lost a fair amount of spending power. In Thailand a year earlier, the situation was reversed, as the Thai *baht* was just starting its downward spiral at the time of my fieldwork. The scope and trajectory of research can be as much about personal choices as it can be about unforeseen external contingencies.

The case studies are organized chronologically to reflect both the sequence of political events in the countries visited and the chronology of my research journey. My Thai study was conducted just months before the currency meltdown, when an atmosphere of crisis was already in the air. I visited Hong Kong eight weeks after the historic July 1, 1997, handover of the colony to China, when a sense of optimism and anxiety was evident everywhere. My visit to Malaysia in November 1998 occurred during the prolonged political crisis surrounding the dismissal of Deputy Prime Minister Anwar Ibrahim and his imprisonment on corruption and sexual misconduct charges. This same period also saw the first major civil "reformasi" protests since independence, staged in the civic center and on university campuses, in response to the Anwar affair. My visit coincided with these protests and occurred only weeks after the APEC summit, during which U.S. Vice President Al Gore's comments about the "brave people of Malaysia" engaging in prodemocracy reformasi demands raised the ire not only of host Prime Minister Mahatir but other leaders in the region, who are very sensitive about external meddling into internal affairs. In short, it was a tense period, and everyone from cab drivers to academics were very much thinking and talking politics, although academics' comments were usually in "off the record" conversations. Besides anxieties about my own security and mobility, the politically charged atmosphere also enabled me to raise political issues that would be seen as acceptable questions from an outsider. Research is always imbued with personal histories and choices, and for me, the selection of fieldwork sites had to do with financial resources, with where I felt I could negotiate the situation and feel relatively safe and comfortable, coupled with where I had established core networks from which I could fan out and snowball my sample.

When I started this study, therefore, I relied on my colleagues in the region to help network me into further contacts, to be on the lookout for local research on women in academics, and to provide any links or sources that could be useful for my study. Our international students also helped with contacts, advice, and information. When I began, I knew very little about the educational histories, current contexts, and issues in higher education in these four countries. I had a general but limited knowledge about colonial histories and some "on the ground" knowledge and experience from having taught in Thailand, having given seminars and presentations over the years in the region, and learning mostly from the academic colleagues, administrators, and students I encountered. Local newspapers, TV, and English-language books bought locally also added some insights into current political and social issues. Armed with this eclectic stock of knowledge, experience, anecdotal and popular media information, I set about researching Southeast Asia in earnest and from several disciplinary areas, all new to me: revisionist and narrative history, locally authored postcolonial and cultural studies, comparative and international education research, development studies, political science and economic research, NGO reports and data.

(RE)SEARCHING WOMEN

Research on women and higher education was easy enough—there's plenty of it, all of it western authored and focused on western higher education, and most of it I had already collected over the years for previous research. But locating research on women in higher education in Southeast Asia was very much a needle in a haystack search. The categories "gender" and "women" are often not even entries in book indices. Mainstream development research focuses on education and occasionally segregates for gender on educational outcomes but, as with economic, comparative, or international educational research, the focus is consistently on educational participation at primary, secondary, and tertiary levels. Theoretically this work is based in human capital theory and its relationship to economic development and socioeconomic mobility, the politics of nation building and maintenance of state legitimacy. Women appear in these accounts conceptualized primarily as a reserve labor force and, in accounts of the postwar period, as a quantitatively increasing cohort at all levels of education. In this literature, nobody seems to be noticing or querying the historical or contemporary politics of gendered control and authority over the educational enterprise: from the management and administration of knowledge, students, assessments and credentialing, or policy, whether in ministries or departments of education, in schools or higher education. Other than an occasional observation that primary teachers are mainly women, that girls' education and women's tertiary participation has increased in the postwar period, in this literature there is no substantive view and no comment on women's role in educational decision-making, administration or management.

The literature on women and management has contributed significantly to western research on women and glass ceilings, although the focus tends to be less on the public sector such as universities, and more on the private, corporate sector. Organizational theory guides this research, which has provided insights into the patriarchal workings of formal and informal organizational cultures. With few exceptions, however, analyses of workplace cultures have not been transposed to investigations of organizational and gendered cultures in management or different industry and service sectors in cross-cultural contexts (Adler & Izraeli, 1994). Women's educational participation, outcomes, and subsequent professional opportunities figure significantly in this literature, but again, women's role in higher education (as managers or teachers and mentors of future generations of women managers) is generally neglected. However, this research supports findings from educational research on women in higher education. Both claim that women's increased investments into education coupled with enhanced professional opportunities through various kinds of equity legislation in many countries, has *not* translated into "significant breakthroughs into executive ranks . . . women in every country remain only a tiny fraction of those in senior positions" (Adler & Izraeli, 1994, p. 7).

The literature on women and development also tends to focus on compulsory and postcompulsory educational participation and outcomes (Mak, 1996). Southeast Asian women are often the object of inquiry in western-authored research on women and development but as immigrants to the United Kingdom, the United States, or Canada (Marchand & Parpart, 1995). Highly regarded, internationally refereed, and locally published English-language journals such as Hong Kong's *Education Journal*, Singapore's *Asia Pacific Journal of Education* and *Soujourn— Journal of Social Issues in Southeast Asia*, or South Korea's *Asian Journal of Women's Studies* also failed to provide any research or reference links to higher education or women in higher education.

As I noted in Chapter 4, my research is limited to English-language publications. But as I discovered in short order, regionally located sociologists, economists, educationists, postcolonial scholars, and cultural theorists are publishing in English, on European and American presses, in overseas and local English-language journals. Moreover, on checking with all the women in this study who are in education faculties, the resounding response has been that "women in higher education" is not a research area or priority. In fact, a few women commented that this was a peculiar research topic and seemed surprised that a university would be funding such a project. Others said that it was high time somebody was investigating this topic, that "maybe now we can know more about what is happening with us and other women and why," and were keen to know what I was finding out in other countries. In any case, efforts to find locally authored research didn't lead me very far. A few women did find a few local reports and some conference presentation papers, and some had saved newspaper clippings on issues related to women and education that they gave me at the interviews.

In Hong Kong, for instance, I received newspaper and news magazine clippings on items profiling senior women in the public service sector. In Singapore, women had saved me several weekend newspaper editions that focused on International Women's Day and featured accounts of high-profile women and government progress on women's issues. Several women in the Singapore sample were members of the Association of Women for Action and Research (AWARE), which proved an invaluable source for numerous publications, although none specifically dealt with women in higher education as students or as staff. Some of the Malaysian women also brought a few local publications to the interviews and provided addresses and sources to pursue, one of which was the Women's Affairs Division. This government-funded unit publishes working papers and monographs on women's issues in English and Bahasa Malaysia, but the publications focused principally on women in the workforce (excluding women in education), women and development, fertility rates, changes in household composition, and so on.

Searches of university Web sites failed to locate any annual university reports in which I thought I might be able to find data on gender distribution in academic staffing and classification levels. Web sites for ministries of education all have links to universities or higher education, but here again, data was inconsistent on academic staffing in terms of total numbers, position classifications, and gender distribution. Departments of statistics do not all provide educational data, and those that do generally do not differentiate for gender, levels of enrollment, or graduate rates. UNESCO's Statistical Yearbook provides country data on percentage of female participation in third-level educational participation but does not disaggregate for public and private institutions, diploma and degree courses. Only Hong Kong's University Grants Committee, the funding body for public universities, provided data on sex distribution in academic staffing. In short, the search for a body of academic research on women in higher-education management, a position and view from the south and east, has been an arduous journey of picking up bits and pieces here and there across a vast range of data sources and disciplinary and analytic orientations. Occasionally, I would stumble onto a line or paragraph in a journal article or monograph mentioning women's role or status as academics in higher education, and this was always a big find worthy of multiple Post-it notes and yellow highlighter marks.

"Women in Higher Education Management," a UNESCO-commissioned report published in 1993, remains the one anthology dedicated specifically to analyses of women in higher-education management in 12 countries. Although by now somewhat dated, it provides locally authored country case studies that include several Southeast Asian countries, and as such, it has formed a useful backdrop to this study. I was able to interview one of the contributors to this volume, and her involvement was a useful introduction to other women. Editor Elizabeth Dines' position on the authors' contributions is that despite the cultural, ethnic, and religious diversity among the countries represented in the volume, recurring themes within that diversity reveal universal dimensions beyond cultural difference. Dines identifies two themes that match the glass-ceiling explanations many women in my study provided. First are pipeline theory effects, which suggest that lack of girls' access to schooling translates into reduced tertiary participation and outcomes for women which, in turn, produces a trickle rather than a flow of qualified women suitable for senior appointments. Second are the institutional barriers or glass ceilings that confront women once they ascend the career mobility ladder. Given that this is a UNESCO report, the links between education and development remain at the core of arguments for improved gender balance at all levels of schooling and tertiary education including women's access to senior decision-making positions. Indeed, any discussions on women "and" or "in" education are consistently linked to local development histories and politics, whether authored by local or western scholars.

WOMEN, EDUCATION, AND DEVELOPMENT

"The unifying theme of education as a tool for development" (Mak, 1996, p. *x*) is common among all international or "global" feminist studies of women in management (e.g., Adler & Izraeli, 1994) and women and education (e.g., Conway & Bourque, 1993). Reform to improve girls' and women's access to education is a long-standing and global issue, particularly in the postwar period. Educational access and participation and government commitments to reform differ country by country in relation to religious, ethnic, and class differences, urban and rural differences, legacies of colonial regimes and postcolonial development, and the various educational models implemented by postindependence governments. Yet

Hong Kong and Singapore are among Asia's wealthiest and most western-ized countries with near gender parity of primary, secondary, and tertiary participation. The adult literacy rate in Hong Kong is 88% for men and 96% for women. In Singapore, the rate is 86% for men and 95% for women, and in Malaysia the rate is 78% for men and 89% for women (UNESCO, 1998). In Malaysia, more girls than boys complete secondary education (equivalent, as in Singapore, to the British GCE "O" level), although in 1990 this combined female/male cohort represented only 19% of the 17- to 18-year-old age group (Sidin, 1996). Women are underrepre-sented in vocational education but comprise about 45% of university undergraduate enrollments. Arguably, the pipeline theory of "trickle" effects from schooling to university does not hold as single-factor expla-nation for women's underrepresentation in senior higher-education man-agement in these three countries.

As elsewhere in the region, Thai women "have participated strongly in educational enrolment," but the "teak ceiling" nonetheless remains:

> Few women make it to the leading ranks of business. Posts which have any association with political power are strongly biased towards males. The militaristic male tradition of the court was handed down to the mod-ern bureaucracy. Few women ascend the heights of politics or adminis-tration. Few even occupy roles associated with political power—such as public intellectuals or political journalists. In 1995, women accounted for 24 of 391 MPs, 8 of 270 senators and 5% of village and district coun-cillors. Most women work. A few manage. Almost none govern. (Phong-paichit & Baker, 1996, pp. 113–114)

Thailand's adult literacy rate is 91% for men and 96% for women, but compulsory schooling ends in ninth grade. In 1994, 90% of the relevant age cohort completed sixth grade, a vast improvement from 1969 when only one-third of students continued past fourth grade (Unger, 1998). Thai-land has the lowest secondary school participation rates among ASEAN nations, and only about 6% of 18- to 24-year-olds get past state examina-tions to attend university. The most recent data issued by the Ministry of University Affairs (1998) lists staff distribution at position classification levels and student entry and exit rates across the private and public univer-sity sectors, but none are disaggregated by sex. Again, gender breakdown of educational participation or staffing is hard to come by, but certainly in Thailand, as elsewhere in the region, the huge expansion of education in the last three decades is "viewed as a strong force for Thailand's industrial expansion and economic well-being" (Chutintaranond & Cooparat, 1995, p. 56), and is seen as a key indicator of the burgeoning Thai middle class (Girling, 1996), which itself is now producing the boom in educational demand. Current moves to extend compulsory schooling from nine to twelve years have been temporarily thwarted by the economic crisis, but educational and political arguments for educational expansion continue and are premised on human capital investment and development theories.

Women's literacy rates are consistently higher than men's, women's first-degree enrollments match male rates, and in some countries women parallel and sometimes exceed men's participation rates in professional degree programs historically the preserve of men. In Malaysia, for instance, women outnumber men in dentistry and law and comprise almost 50% in medicine, basic and applied sciences, economics and public administration, business, and accounting (Sidin, 1996, pp. 132–33). In Singapore, women's university enrollments increased dramatically from 44.2% in 1980–81 to 55.3% in 1983–84 following revised admission requirements that awarded higher weightings to language achievements that favored women (Lee, Campbell, & Chia, 1999). The Singapore Department of Statistics provides no gender differentiation for student enrollments at any levels of education, educational attainment, higher-degree graduate rates, or teaching staff across the sector. However, the National University of Singapore, the oldest and most prestigious of only two in the city-state, provides some gender-disaggregated data on student completion rates. In the 1996–97 academic year, women comprised 55% of first-degree graduates and 49% of higher-degree and postgraduate diploma graduates. Academic staff statistics account for classification distribution across institutions, promotion rates, permanent and visiting staff qualifications, and nationalities but provide no gender distribution data. In 1997, 11.5% of women in the workforce were tertiary educated (Lee et al., 1999).

The administrative and funding body for public universities in Hong Kong, the University Grants Committee, provides limited gender distribution statistics for staff and students. In 1997–98, out of a total of 17,000 academic staff, 25% were at senior–lecturer level and above, of which 14% were women (Hong Kong University Graduate Committee, 1999). Coincidentally, that rate of 14% matches 1998 Australian figures for women at senior-lecturer level and above. Women comprised 49% of all full-time students in government-funded public universities, 49% of all part-time students (most of whom are older studying at the Open University of Hong Kong), and 31% enrolled in technical colleges. Female participation rates at all levels of higher education have increased from 39% in 1991–92 to 53% in 1998–99. A total of 18.6% of Hong Kong's 17- to 20-year-old cohort is enrolled in first-year first-degree programs (1998–99). Despite the limited statistical accounts of women's educational participation and outcomes rates in Thailand, Malaysia, Singapore, and Hong Kong, the figures nonetheless suggest that lack of education cannot be seen as the primary cause of women's underrepresentation in senior management, whether in private or public higher-education institutions, or public sector employment.

GENDER EQUITY: WOMEN'S INTERVENTIONS AND STATE RESPONSES

Another common argument claims that western colonial regimes did not encourage girls' education (Vervoorn, 1998), nor did "western modernization as imported into Asian societies . . . carry within it any concept of gender equality" (Mazumdar, 1993, p. 17). That may be the case. However such arguments ignore the political influence of numerous women's groups, associations, and councils that had been active at various times throughout this century in Singapore, Malaysia, Hong Kong, Vietnam, Cambodia, and China. In Indonesia, individual women were publicly active and have been credited for "improving their fellow women's status through education" as early as the late 1800s (Setiadarma, 1993, p. 105). Many of these groups emerged out of what used to be church, YWCA, or university-linked "ladies' clubs," or charity groups consisting of educated middle-class women, many of whom were overseas educated, the daughters of progressive parents who themselves supported and modeled the importance of a woman's education. The women's groups of the 1950s were networked within global, worldwide women's councils and confederations that enabled women to attend international conferences, go on lecture tours, exchange information and devise action plans and policy strategies. Throughout colonized Southeast Asia in the early part of the century, and in Singapore particularly, British neglect of the civic welfare of the colony led to the formation of many voluntary civic organizations that provided basic vernacular schooling and "some welfare, legal and minor infrastructural services" (Chua, in Hewison & Rodan,

1996). Historically, then, the formation of women's groups at the onset of 1950s industrialization and modernization was based in an already well-developed ethos of community social service organizations.

Equal access to education for girls and improvements in women's cultural, social, and economic status were core principles upon which women lobbied for the elimination of a range of "customary" laws and cultural practices that were seen to deprive women of their rights. As in the west, the objective of these early "women's liberation" groups was to emancipate women which required the massive tasks of changing cultural attitudes and lobbying for legislative change (e.g., polygamy, traffic in women as secondary wives, and child marriages). Underpinning these reforms was a more fundamental need to further and broaden girls' education and to change the cultural mindset that devalued the importance of girls' education. Although "Confucian" societies have traditionally placed a high premium on education, cultural attitudes have historically favored the education of boys (Edwards & Roces, 2000; Low, 1997). The struggle for women, then as now, remains with changing deeply embedded cultural attitudes and value systems that are historically resilient enough to flourish in spite of successive policy or legal interventions, public rhetoric, or institutional or government positions. The legal changes effected in these countries to enhance girls' and women's rights and opportunities were due in large part to women and women's groups of the day that, as Chew (1994) notes, "have contributed significantly to social and political movements, [but] they have been neglected in historical accounts and often their contribution has been excluded altogether" (p. 1).

"Western development models imported into Asia" may not have banner-headlined an explicit concept of gender equity, but in the postwar flurry to modernize and industrialize, economic growth, whether in Malaysia, Thailand, or Singapore, was closely linked with educational expansion as fundamental to human capital development. And educational provision in the pursuit of economic growth and nation building was an investment in the citizenry and future workers, regardless of gender. Education for girls was necessary to train up a docile and reasonably literate labor force to work the machines in the manufacturing, textile, and later, electronics industries. The goals of rapid economic development also required the training of a female consumer class courted by advertising and new media such as radio in the 1940s and TV in the 1950s. This is not to say that governments went out of their way to ensure gender equity at all levels of education. Indeed, as late as 1993, Hong Kong produced a government report titled "Equal Opportunities for Women and Men," arguing among other things that higher-education outputs remain gender skewed, that women lag in labor-force participation and earn less than men for comparable work (Lui & Suen, 1993; Sweeting, 1995).

Relatedly, in the late 1980s, the Singapore government attempted to reverse the consequences of "too much" education for graduate women who were delaying marriage or not marrying at all and having fewer or no children. The consequences of these "unruly women" were seen as national security issues, as birth rates dropped and the long-term population survival of the nation was called into question. Educated women were at fault for this population "disaster," so women had to pay the material and symbolic price of returning to the "normal" Asian family to tend kitchen and kin. The earlier "Two is Enough" population control policy is now reversed as former financial incentives, tax rebates, and housing and other privileges are now used as withholding, punitive measures against married women who have no or few children. Instead, a third and fourth child means extra cash and benefits (Hill & Lian, 1995; Lee et al., 1999).

In Asia, women's education, social status, and role in public life have always been complicated and difficult to reconcile within often sharply opposing cultural-religious systems and modernist development and market ideologies. In her analysis of gender issues and educational development in Asia, Mazumdar (1993) argues, "Most Asian political elites, after encountering Western imperialism, have accepted the ideal of gender equality, but the principle has been hard to square with the traditional value systems and social organization" (p.16). Different postcolonial regimes have indeed attempted to combine western gender equity ideologies, particularly in regards to marriage laws, employment and educational policies, with "Asian" or "Confucian" or "Muslim" ideologies based on patriarch-headed family hierarchies, filial piety and obedience, the maintenance of an intergenerational family unit, a strong work ethic and an ethos of self-reliance, and so forth. Insistence on the virtues of alleged "Asian values," combined with the goals of rapid economic growth, allows governments to promote and sustain Asian traditions and values with "western free-market notions such as competitive individualism and meritocratic equality" and to selectively craft a "composite of 'Asian' traditional and 'western' middle class elements [that] resonate with the core values of the family within the Confucian social system" (Hill & Lian, 1995, p. 155).

This ideological blend not only allows governments to support equity (of pay, employment, or educational opportunities) in principle and in law but also enables the sidestepping of commitments to social welfare provision typical of the liberal western welfare state (Chua, 1991), although traditional welfarism is fast eroding in the west as well. The family, not the state, is the locus of social and financial support and security in times of individual or family crisis. Women are thus double-bound and easily recuperated into the normative construct of the "Asian family" fold. As the intergenerational glue of childbearers and childrearers, carers of kin and aged parents, women bear a disproportionate burden of family and cultural maintenance and continuity, regardless of how well-educated they are. Women are responsible for the transmission of cultural values and the educational success of their children, for the emotional support and care of husbands and family elders, and for developing their own abilities and potential as a family asset. And yet, the best educational qualifications and professional credentials, and the legal enshrinement of meritocratic equity, are no safeguard for women against state-sanctioned cultural and religious ideologies that continue to control the social status, role, and containment of women, despite allowing them access to the material and symbolic goods signifying the "modern" Thai, Singaporean, Hong Kong or Malaysian woman. Nirmala PuruShotam (1998) likens the normative construct of the Asian family to political and ideological *hijab*, an insidious boundary of male-defined cultural constraints supported by civil codes and sanctions that let women roam, consume, get an education, and hold a job but always tethered "to do the family first." Women are ideologically shrouded and "cannot see and so reread the frames by which they do their lives" (p. 161).

Structurally, the state can legalize and perform a rhetorical commitment to gender equity. However, subtending public proequity sentiments and government rhetoric, far more deeply entrenched cultural attitudes toward women maintain powerful gendered hierarchies in public and private life that both men and hegemonized women enact and collude with. And this is certainly the case in the west where, despite decades of very public debate and feminist consciousness-raising about equity issues, a broad array of institutionalized and legalized proequity interventions coupled with support programs for women, accountability measures, and so forth have only marginally turned the tide in favor of women in high-status leadership positions across the professions, in politics, and in the corporate and civil service sector. In Southeast Asia, the picture is even more complex. The political traumas of decolonization, nationalist movements and postindependence nation building, the rise and iron grip of political elites, all coupled with the drive toward modernization, industrialization, and economic growth, create historical environments in which women's education and their emergence in the public sphere has been caught between conflicting pressures. "On the one hand, nationalist leaders campaigned to promote the education of women, but, on the other, the patriarchal values of existing elites undermined any real commitments to changing gender or expanding women's opportunities" (Mazumdar, 1993, p. 21). Interestingly enough, the leaders of those political elites, including many nationalist leaders and heads of postindependence governments, were themselves western educated (e.g., Indonesia's Sukarno and Suharto were Dutch educated, and Singapore's first prime minister now Senior Minister Lee Kuan Yew, were British educated).

CULTURAL POLITICS,
CULTURAL DIFFERENCES

"Asian" cultural values and attitudes, rooted in contemporary reworkings of Buddhist, Confucian, or Muslim religious codes, cast a pall everywhere in the region over women's political struggles for equity reforms, their professional aspirations and opportunities, their autonomy and self-determination *on their own terms*. The women who speak in the chapters that follow all had much the same thing to say about "the cultural mindset"; "Asian", "oriental", "Chinese", "Muslim", or "Confucian" values; and cultural politics that enforce what some consider a romanticized, traditional "oriental" construct of femininity. Yet others, mostly Muslim Malay women, defended women's traditional roles and responsibilities as their "natural" place, as "the true nature of women," as a refuge from the excesses of western and modernist visions of feminist women. Yet they also argued for the need for greater workplace flexibility to enable women to pursue both professional aspirations and duties to family and home.

The women in this study are urban, upper middle class, highly educated and professionally successful. They, as well as all the authors I cite and textually reproduce here, are all successful products of the very education systems that some critique and that others hold up as a model of meritocratic equity, of women's ability to succeed within that system. Without exception, they all felt that the educational system in their countries had not held them back. What is holding them back now at more senior levels are sexist and racist ideologies, legally enshrined in some countries but in all countries deeply embedded in the cultural imaginary. However, many women also held educational curriculum and pedagogy (as well as parents) responsible for diminishing girls' and women's aspirations, of inculcating early and thus reproducing gender ideologies of male superiority and sec-ond-class status for girls and women. And yet in Thailand and Malaysia, women also felt strongly that education in rural or indigenous communities ought to be tailored to reflect traditional cultural values, customs, and norms, although they acknowledged that this can easily keep girls tied to traditional family structures and gender roles with only limited opportuni-ties for upward and outward mobility. As I already noted in Chapter 2, "insistence on local 'purity' may well serve as excuses for a reactionary revival of older forms of oppression as women in particular have been quick to point out" (Dirlik, 1996, p. 37). Indeed, many women I spoke to expressed mixed messages and ambivalent attitudes toward gender equity, women's role, cultural traditionalism, and modernism.

One thing is certain, "the use of educational systems as a mechanism for achieving gender equality has clearly not been pursued by Asian gov-ernments with much energy or enthusiasm" (Vervoorn, 1998, p. 266). Moreover, comprehensive or "realistic analysis of gender roles was never undertaken in Asia" (Mazumdar, 1993, p. 16) which is evident in the rela-tive paucity of locally authored research and the lack of "gender" as a demographic category in the databases and reports for censuses, universi-ties, or ministries of education. Where feminist or women's groups and associations have some visible presence, such as in Singapore and Malaysia, gender analysis and political lobbying for legal reform or social programs in support of women (e.g., domestic violence) are more evident and publicized, albeit within the tolerance parameters of governments.

What unifies "feminist" perspectives from the south and east is the recognition that economic development in these regions has been founded on the backs of women at least as much as on men, but universally on the exploitation of lower-educated, lower-waged working women and their unwaged domestic service. As women are catching up in workforce par-ticipation and educational achievement, their wages remain below men's, and they are largely invisible in senior civic and governmental affairs, cor-porate boardrooms and executive management. "Asian" cultural values, in many places legally enshrined, keep women tied in bonds of social and economic dependency to husbands and families. Capitalism and patri-archy have always been a deadly combination for women. But in South-east Asia, the discourse of "Asian values" mesh with complex political, colonial, and postcolonial histories; different development trajectories; the resurgence of religious and cultural "core values"; various historical roles and influences of Sultanate royalties; constitutional monarchies; and military powers and governments—all coalescing in ways that put a very different ideological spin on Asian patriarchy and capitalism. And it is within these dense grids that constructs of femininity and of women's "reality" and status, opportunities and constraints are experienced, legislated, contested and reproduced, and enacted by the state and in the courts, by women and men, in the classroom and the boardroom, in the factory and the kitchen.

Many of the women's experiences and analyses of career impediments match those documented in the western literature: balancing the double-day, guilt over professional aspirations and commitments that shortchange family and children, feelings of having to work twice as hard for half the reward, and so forth. Yet cultural differences are evident in regards to the politics of gender relations across a range of institutional encounters that women in the west do not experience. Cultural attitudes remain skeptical of women who socialize professionally with male colleagues. Women told me about turning down research opportunities because they would involve too much time with male colleagues in their offices or in laboratories. Women spoke of fears of "being seen" with men, which would "lead to "whispers," "gossip," people thinking "that something hanky-panky is going on." Single women well into their 50s said they would not attend after-hours university functions on their own let alone bring a male friend or partner, they would not "go to lunch with my deans too often," or would avoid being seen on or off campus in the company of men. Some women said that it was easier to interact publicly with European males, but not "our own kind." Cultural rules of feminine propriety curtail women's social-professional conduct and rule them out of networking opportunities where important information and institutional allies and deals are formed. Married women spoke of husbands who disapproved of and prohibited women working after hours, which often meant being allowed "out" only for graduation ceremonies where the presence of deans is mandatory.

Filial responsibility puts pressures on men and women within the "Asian" family. Unmarried women, unlike their married brothers or sisters, are technically freed from child care and husband-household duties, but they are expected to look after aging parents. Filial obligations exert different costs from sons and daughters: Women provide the day-to-day emotional and routine care of elderly parents, whereas men, particularly first sons, are responsible for financial support. All the single women I interviewed in Singapore and Hong Kong had at least one parent living with them, and all had live-in or part-time domestic help. The women appreciated having a live-in companion, a good and lifelong friend who also happened to be their parent, but these arrangements also came with time-consuming responsibilities. In the words of one Singapore dean, "just because I don't have a husband and children doesn't mean I have no family. I have aged parents, and that's responsibility. And because your siblings are married, they think because you are not, you look after them. You become the family babysitter." Women spoke of having to organize care arrangements for parents, which they claimed were at least as time consuming, expensive, and complex than those organized by married siblings for their children, particularly when academic work frequently means travel overseas. Remaining single in a family-oriented society carries a price. Cultural ideologies and social policies shape women's choices and lifestyle options, particularly where housing policies militate against women's independence and autonomy.

I noted earlier that in some countries, governments had made some gestures throughout the 1960s and 1970s toward gender equity in regards to marriage law reform, including antipolygamy legislation and the legal abolition of underage and arranged marriages. But law, social policy, and civic regulations maintain gender-based social engineering that disadvantages women. In Singapore, women are disqualified from unemployment benefits and medical benefits for their children—benefits only available to men (Chan, 2000). Housing policy excludes single women with children from government subsidized housing. As noted, the government provides extensive financial benefits for women who have more than two children. In higher education, only men can obtain sabbatical leave funds for spouses and children who accompany them overseas. A 33% enrollment ceiling for women entering medical school has been in place since 1979 and remains one of the most contested issues between government and proequity reform lobbies. Citizenship laws have long disadvantaged women. Citizenship rights have always been granted (after a two-year residency) to foreign female nationals married to Singaporean men; however, this right was not extended to Singaporean women married to foreigners until January 1999 (Lee et al., 1999). Based on assumptions that women follow husbands, this legal provision curtails women's career decisions and, not least, constrains women's mobility in a highly mobile and global academic environment. Citizenship and residency laws in Malaysia are similarly gender-biased and are the focus of ongoing lobbying by feminist lawyers and women's groups. Economic rationales of "brain drain" sustain reform arguments: "If the present law persists, we may see the departure of many highly educated and skilled women from the country for the simple reason that their husbands cannot stay. This will prove costly to our country's economy" (Ariffin, 1994, p. 131).

Legal inequalities that disadvantage women persist in Malaysia, where polygamy was finally outlawed in 1982 for non-Muslims under the federal Family Law. Muslim law (*syariah*), administered by states, allows Muslim men to have up to four wives, whereas a Muslim woman can marry only one man. Divorce initiated by husbands requires only a declaration of repudiation (*talaq*) of the wife, although reconciliation provisions and various religious committee hearings are now required. Women who initiate divorce must present a litany of proof of breach of promise, abandonment, infidelity, unequal treatment among wives, or consorting with women of ill repute; financial compensation to husbands is another option for women of independent means. Divorced men are granted custody of their legitimate children, while women become custodians of their husbands' illegitimate children (Ariffin, 1994). As noted earlier, women outnumber men in law degree programs. One law professor explained the surge of women's enrollment claiming that most *bumiputera* (indigenous) women study law for their own protection, not for career purposes. Because Muslim women are subject to Islamic customary (*adat*) as well as civil law, what better way to protect their status, children, and assets than to have a good working knowledge of the legal system. Others hinted at the trepidation many young Muslim women today feel at the prospect of marriage: It is the *de rigeur* "career" choice for a Muslim woman but also one that does not guarantee her economic security, rights over her children, or a place as the sole or permanent wife.

Cultural ideologies hierarchize gender as much as they hierarchize race, and this, of course, is not a particularly Southeast Asian phenomenon. In Thailand, Hong Kong, and Singapore there are no legal or constitutional provisions barring ethnic groups from holding government office or civil service jobs or gaining access to education. In Malaysia racial discrimination is embedded in legal-juridico discourses and social policies such as those governing civil service sector employment and higher education. Race-based policies confer a host of privileges on *bumiputera* Malays and erect "ethnic concrete ceilings" for non-Malays (as students and staff) and, thus, for non-Malay academic women.

Other significant and distinctly "Asian" cultural values that can work against women are the politics of "face" and an ethos of connections or patronage. Some of the women claimed that the cultural protocol of face combined with a social debt economy of patronage shapes social relations and identity crafting in everyday professional encounters and exerts a particular toll on women's already subordinate social status. Contesting one's senior in public forums such as committees or councils is considered inappropriate institutional conduct because it is seen to "diminish your superior's positions, his status." In the west, as I noted earlier, speaking up, arguing against issues on principle, a point of law or policy, or in support of social justice issues are the very core skills women are encouraged to perform to get recognized, to demonstrate leadership, and so on. In Asian contexts, the rule of face prohibits contestations from subordinates, which extends to expectations of compliance within systems of institutional patronage whereby duty to senior personnel "who groomed you" tends to limit autonomous action and decision making. In other words, "your tongue is tied for a good part of your career and basically you toe the line" (Chinese Malaysian). The crafting of "enabling relationships" requires compliance and subservience to those who groomed the subordinate, and skillful cultivation of connections: "it's like you must be able to get certain people to like you to be able to get, say, a scholarship or a signature to go and do your sabbatical."

In the words of one Singaporean dean: "If you are there at all and got these positions, it was some male who recommended or promoted you, so there is this sense of obligation and loyalty." There is always a payback, a debt, an obligation, and eternal gratitude to those who supported one's institutional advancement or promotion. Failure to pay due respect to the system of obligations and hierarchies of subservience extends to loss of face for both senior and junior players in such relationships. For women, who are more likely to be "sponsored" by senior males, rules of face within patriarchal hierarchies can be particularly debilitating to their attempts to get ahead. Institutional gender and sexual politics cast suspicion on male-female collegial relationships, and cultural expectations of docile, loyal, and subservient femininity stipulate that "women are not supposed to come on too strongly, so you hold back, not wanting to offend your superiors." Women's professional skills and intellectual contributions, their career aspirations and managerial or administrative skills, and their potential have to be managed within a context where discourses of equal opportunity are publicly mapped against the ideological rhetoric of meritocratic opportunity but mediated by and exercised from within cultural value systems that reflect particular Asian forms of patriarchy whether at the level of the state, the law, or the academy.

In an analysis of Malaysian feminism, Maznah Mohamad (1994) likens women's "maneuvers" through this minefield of equal opportunity, systemic male privilege, and discrimination against woman as a form of "gaming." She writes that out of this "interplay of access and exclusion," women are led to believe that "there is nothing to stop a woman from achieving what she wants, provided she is clever enough to tread carefully and not upset the 'unchangeable' norms of a gendered society" (p. 135). In the face of social and cultural barriers, women "have to be resourceful to know how to 'negotiate', 'maneuver', 'bargain', 'manipulate,' or 'manage' the situation for one's benefit. The above gaming strategies operate within the rules of the male privileging system" (p. 135). In other words, patriarchy writes the rules and enacts them with ease, for they are the mirror image of their authors. Women's lifetime project is to learn and play by the rules, and because the rules are not of their own making, they either "reread the frames by which they do their lives" (PuruShotam, 1998, p. 161) or else sneak around the rules, maneuver and manipulate the game to find a gap, a small space within which to assert an already culturally mediated and contested "I."

LOCAL THEORY

Feminist views from the south and east are not uniform, not in agreement, and constitute only a minority voice on issues related to women in higher-education management. Given the more urgent health, employment, and educational issues facing rural and working class girls and women, the limited research focus on academic women is not surprising. If anything, an academic preoccupation with gender equity issues in a relatively well-paid and high-status profession such as university teaching can easily be seen as a bourgeois preoccupation among a professional elite at the expense of attention to discrimination and exploitation of women in far less privileged positions.

At the risk of generalizing, in my interpretation, feminist views from the south and east are divided between those who accept western theoretical models as adaptable and useful lenses for examining local systems of patriarchy, gender discourses, and systemic inequalities, and those who reject western feminist thought and argue, instead, for "indigenization" of theory and analytic templates. For the most part, feminists who have applied western theories to analyses of their own local sites have modified and recontextualized theories of, for instance, the state, power, modernization, or capitalism to culture-specific *in situ* analyses of how women become historically inserted in those east-west confluences of capitalism and Confucianism, or modernization and Islamicization. Whether such theoretical and analytic reworkings are indicative of a local standpoint, an "indigenous" exposition of itself, remains open for debate. There are at least three issues pivoting around the question, "What constitutes indigenous?" (Mohamad & Wong, 1994).

First, feminists who reject all forms of western theory as inherently unable to speak to, for, or from the point of view of nonwestern local sites assume a culturally untainted, pure space from which to speak and theorize. This position commonly valorizes indigenous voices as concrete, as "true windows to the real," contrasted with western theory as abstraction, myth, and fiction. It is not my place to contest such positions. However, from an admittedly western point of view, I would argue that theory itself is a western artifact and, as such, there is no guarantee that the "indigenous community," however defined, will theorize itself in the terms by which theory is generally understood—that is to say, theory as abstract epistemology, as macroanalytic and generalizable category building (even for microunits such as the individual, a behavior, or a process), as hypothesis building and testing, validity and verification checks, deductive and inductive (as in grounded theory) reasoning, and so forth. I have already argued earlier, and will raise the point again shortly, that there is still a need for big picture theorizing, for generalizable and normative principles from which to evaluate, adjudicate and make claims for a better, more equitable world.

Second, there is a tendency among postcolonial scholars (and, of course, others as well) to accuse capitalism and its historical offshoots of imperialism, colonialism, and the economic development models that followed of introducing social and economic inequalities to the rest of the world. Few would disagree. However, this position fails to acknowledge that gender (and race) hierarchies and inequalities predate capitalism and that gender, in fact, is *the* primordial and most universal division of labor.

Third, if by *indigenization* antiwestern feminists are referring to themselves, that is the postcolonial feminist scholar, then, as I have already argued, theory building and analysis is always already mediated by the class and educational privileges that locate the intellectual or theorist in urban, cosmopolitan, and globally networked orbits and ways of seeing. If, however, *indigenous* refers to traditional communities untouched by modernization, the excesses of westernization, the telephone or TV, then this begs the question raised above about presumptions of local authenticity and indigenous propensities to "do theory." Sensitive to the complexity of these issues, Mohamad and Wong (1994) note that "the impulse to unearth indigenous elements and paradigms is timely" but that caution needs to be exercised

> if this move is not to result in a more reactionary, and more enhanced patriarchal perspective. For instance what constitutes "indigenous"? Does the "indigenous" mitigate the evolutionary discourse thus promising a better alternative for women? Is there a danger of a return to parochialism to the detriment of a new and forward-looking universalism? (pp *xi-xii*)

I already raised issues of locality and polyvocality, universalisms and normativity in Chapter 4, but I reiterate here what I consider a still important political commitment and inescapable epistemological standpoint for any feminist project: the need to challenge and continually reform and refine larger universal (moral, ethical, theoretical, or legal) "standards", benchmarks, or criteria, and to posit provisional and normative ideals toward which to strive, and against which to judge discrimination and inequalities. Harding puts it in simple terms: "there have to be standards for distinguishing between how I want the world to be and how, in empirical fact, it is" (cited in Scheurich, 1997, p. 35).

East or west, north or south—indeed, important markers for a politics of location, and identification and contextualization of standpoint. Geographical location notwithstanding, issues of who can speak, where, how, and for whom remain globally intractable epistemological and not least political issues. The politics of voice, identity, and speaking position are always situated and thus embedded in any attempts to disentangle what local standpoints might mean—constrained as such attempts are in the language of theory and the academic discourse of western inquiry in which I speak here, and which frames the so-called "third world" scholarly work that I engage in and cite here.

IN THE FIELD

I now return to where I started in this chapter and will close with a narrative account of the local contingencies of this research process. My aim here is to provide a contextual backdrop, a snapshot of the haphazard, chaotic, socially "messy" nature of research that does not claim a separation between the researcher as social subject "I" and some abstract entity masquerading as impartial researcher seeking objective truths, facts, reality

(Scheurich, 1997). In explicating methodological choices and procedures, I make no claims to clinical precision, decontextualized social analysis, or uncontaminated data collection. Instead, I want to provide a living context in which I and this research, and the women's dialogues that follow, were situated.

I have already explained the various financial and logistical limitations of scope of this study and my decision early to frame this as a set of case studies. Case study research consists of fine-grained qualitative data collection from a relatively small sample within a local context. Its aim is to paint an in-depth picture of a local site (e.g., classroom, courtroom, factory, or community), of local individual or group experiences (e.g., family, workers, women, teachers, or students) and peoples' interpretations of social events, processes, or structures within a local context. In group case studies, the researcher looks for unique characteristics as well as common patterns across cases. Case study research makes no claims to being generalizable, although it does aim to identify and theorize patterned events, processes, or structures that can be transferred across similar although distinct social and culturally situated contexts.

As noted earlier, I initially identified women in each site through my own academic and social network, and through identification on university Web sites, which subsequently led to snowball sampling. Many women made a point of contacting other women on my behalf, and many connections and recommendations opened up while I was on site. Indeed, in Hong Kong and Malaysia, women were very forthcoming with offers to arrange interviews on the spot. Although I was always well stocked with extra audiotapes, questionnaires, and confidentiality and consent forms, I was not always able to fit in fresh contacts in the course of a day when prearranged interviews in different universities had already been scheduled and confirmed. Walking back from lunch with a colleague to the Hong Kong Polytechnic one day, we ran into one of the deans who volunteered on the spot to see me later that day. I was already committed to an interview that afternoon across town at the Baptist University. To solve this logistical problem, I offered to call her later that day at the end of my last interview, but when I called at 6:00 p.m., it was too late. I was leaving the next day. When someone volunteers or offers help, it is impolite to turn them down, and I felt guilty about committing a cultural *faux pas*. These missed opportunities quickly become part and parcel of feeling out of control. Despite studying maps to approximate travel times between universities, allocating extra time to find my way around campus and to arrive early, research logistics invariably take on a life of their own. Often research of this kind is less about having control of a situation and more about staying afloat in a rapid current of events, and all the while retaining a sense of humor and optimism.

I initiated contact with all the women through postal and e-mail correspondence, which included a four-page research brief of my project, participation requirements, and a questionnaire. The questionnaire sought standard demographic data and asked questions about women's career aspirations and experiences, which subsequently served as interview entry points. The questionnaire was devised in consultation with local women in each site to ensure cultural and linguistic appropriateness, although all questions remained conceptually the same.

In each country, I initially sought women in senior management positions of dean or above. It quickly became apparent that I was not going to find any female vice chancellors or deputy vice chancellors and therefore moved my definition of *senior* downward to center directors, deputy deans, and heads of schools or departments. In each site, I also made arrangements to speak with women in nonmanagerial positions at classification ranks from lecturer to associate professor. Sometimes I had opportunities to speak with them in groups, at other times they were one-on-one sessions. Most of these sessions were spontaneous get-togethers over coffee or lunch where audiotaping was inappropriate but I did get the opportunity in Singapore to gather a relatively large group of women over dinner at one of the women's residences where part of the evening's conversation was audiotaped. These more informal conversations attempted to gauge women's views on glass ceilings, their career aspirations, and their interpretations of opportunities or impediments among women in nonmanagement posts. Many of their comments confirmed statements made by the more senior women and also shed some light on how women perceive other women's management and leadership styles.

At the close of each interview, I provided copies of my university's gender equity annual report, current programs for women offered by the Equity Office, and a sample of recent papers I had published on women in higher education in Hong Kong, Singapore, and Thailand. Since Thailand was my first case study, I had no previous published papers on the topic to leave with the women there. I offered my papers so that the women would get a sense of my writing and of the sociological and feminist approach I take on the issue of women in higher education, and so that they would feel comfortable with the ways I had represented and interpreted other women's experiences. Everyone was advised that they were free to withdraw their transcripts if they had any reservations about how I was writing up the research. All interview transcripts were returned for checking, editing, and validation. None of the women in Thailand, Singapore, or Hong Kong asked to make changes to their transcripts. From several Malaysian women, however, I received repeated e-mails querying me when their transcripts would arrive and when they would receive a draft paper, and several edited their transcripts to improve grammatical clarity and to delete statements they thought could be misread and considered "racially insensitive." I also explained to all the women that I would make an effort to publish the ensuing paper in a regional (English-language) journal and to present findings at local conferences to return the data to the site and community of women from where it was derived. This is a crucial ethical and political strategy in feminist research that is particularly important in contexts where the researcher is not a cultural local (Haraway, 1988; Scheurich, 1997). I presented the last case study of Malaysia at a joint conference between the Singapore and Malaysia Educational Research Associations held in Malacca in late 1999.

Transcripts were generally returned within three to four months. None of the women withdrew her transcript. Once I had prepared a draft of a paper for publication, it was sent to all participants for comment. Again, only a few Malaysian women responded, all with supportive comments about "fair interpretation" and representation of their contributions. Following this final validation, I subsequently submitted each case study paper to regional journals for publication. Once each paper was published, I sent all women a copy of the published paper. I am still in regular touch with several women in each country.

During the course of this study, I was also involved in a three-year study of interracial families in Australia (C. Luke & Carrington, 2000; C. Luke & A. Luke, 1998, 1999). That research was conducted by a three-member team consisting of my partner, a full-time research assistant/project manager, and myself. That project was well funded, and we traveled to six capital cities in the course of three years as well as visiting families in a few rural and provincial towns. Interviews with approximately 80 interracial families where one partner was of Indo-Asian descent enabled me to gather a range of related information and insights from women and men who themselves, or their parents, had emigrated to Australia from Malaysia, Indonesia, Japan, the Philippines, Singapore, China, India, and South Korea. Many of the women were professionals in their home countries and, although our research focus was on the politics of race and racializing practices, they provided valuable retrospective insights into women's issues and their own professional experiences back home.

That project, however, also spoiled me in the sense that a three-member team provides a lot more latitude for data gathering and engagements with subjects than does running a project solo. One person engaged in conversation always leaves two to make notes, to observe and record artifacts around the home or people's behavioral and gestural repertoires, to prepare for a follow-up question, to review the interview schedule and check what we had missed or where to redirect a probe. After interviews, we were able to debrief and exchange impressions and initial interpretations. A research assistant takes care of all technical and travel logistics, provides synopses of questionnaire responses, organizes preinterview briefing papers on families, and so forth. I had none of these support mechanisms on my own study—I was "multitasking" on my own.

Paying full attention in a one-on-one conversation while also writing a few notes, making mental notes of what issues to probe further while staying on schedule within the conceptual organization of my questions, glancing at questionnaires to follow up on responses, keeping an eye on the time and the tape recorder, and so on, can be very stressful, and cognitively consuming experiences that often create lost opportunities. Basic logistics such as struggling with tape recorders that go into resistance mode, despite new batteries and double-checked leads and connections, while trying to focus on and keep a conversation on track are common experiences of interviewing. One doesn't want to appear rushed, yet there is only the one hour in which to cover a range of issues. Most of the women were seeing me between meetings or classes, and there wasn't always the latitude to run over time. Although I attempted to schedule interviews at the same universities on the same day, that didn't always work out, and I often found myself panicking to find a cab to get to the next interview which, in places like Bangkok or even Kuala Lumpur could often be several hours away.

Other unforeseen problems crept up along the way. In Thailand I conducted two interviews while the university lawn mowers were wrecking noise havoc outside the ground floor offices of the women I was seeing. The tapes were almost inaudible. Hong Kong University at the time of my visit was basically a construction site no matter which building I was visiting. Jackhammers, cement machines and a host of related construction noises drowned out conversations and obliterated big sections on audiotapes. I learned early on about the intrusion of noisy air conditioners, and despite purchasing state-of-the-art microphones and always running a second tape recorder, many tapes were very difficult to transcribe due to incessant noise.

In Malaysia, several women were keen to visit me at my hotel to save me the costs and hassle of long cab rides to their universities. I met three groups, in fact, on one Saturday during lunch and afternoon high tea. We agreed to meet and talk over food rather than in a sterile hotel conference room. So we met in the hotel restaurant, which was booked solid all day and jam packed with families, wailing kids, the noise of hundreds of conversations, the splash of water fountains, an incessant piano, and so forth. I ran two tape recorders and had one lapel mike that the women passed among themselves. In group interviews, it is, of course, impossible to regulate conversations so that only one person talks at a time. That one Saturday I ended up with seven hours of taping, most of which was extremely difficult to transcribe because of the background noise. Some women arrived late, which meant we ran over time as the next woman arrived two hours later. Tapes quickly got marked and packed in and out of premarked envelopes, fresh tapes and new batteries were inserted, a quick sound check was done, and off we went. In such contexts, there is often no time to prepare adequately for the next interview, to write up notes at the conclusion of each interview, to review the next interviewee's questionnaire responses or refamiliarize with the women's research area or institutional details. There were many days like this one, emotionally dense and cognitively exhausting.

I have been dropped off by cab drivers at university main entrances or central administration buildings, and then walked what often seemed like miles in stifling heat and humidity to find the right building, all the while hauling my bag of papers, university brochures, maps, recording equipment, a bottle of water, etc.—eventually arriving drenched and exhausted. I have had harrowing high-speed taxi rides—with no seatbelts—in Bangkok and Kuala Lumpur, rushing from one interview to the next, changing tapes in the backseat, getting out the next lot of paperwork and university maps, and always double-checking that I left nothing behind. And, of course, on occasions I did lose things in cabs.

Few research handbooks, feminist or otherwise, pay much attention to the lived experience of qualitative research, other than to focus on the logistics of data gathering, coding, analysis, write-up phase, and so on. Feminist research and methodology books give advice on feminist ethics of self-disclosure and self-representation to break down traditional boundaries between researcher and researched. We generally exclude the nitty-gritty of the mundane aspects of research. The few experiences I have sketched here are a consequence of the situatedness of research. Most would not have been an issue had these studies been conducted on home turf.

Lastly, a comment about women researching women, which is a very different experience from researching men or mixed-sex groups. In general, I would say that women on the whole are more socially engaging, conversationally inclusive, and polite than men. Their conversations are less bureaucratic, they generally do not pose as "knowers" in the way men often do, and they rarely lecture when providing answers. Women introduced me to their administrative staff and other women in their offices, whereas men rarely consider such a gesture. As a woman and an academic, I took great interest in the way women remake their institutional office spaces, which is quite different from men's organization of their work spaces. Not all the women's offices signified feminine spaces, but many did. In Thailand, for instance, there wasn't one office I visited without orchids, porcelain or carved figurines, and silk cloth over couches and under plant saucers. Patios and balconies were full of plants, and women often took me on minitours of their little gardens. In Singapore and Hong Kong, women's offices appeared more western, businesslike, but here too some women had adorned their spaces with their children's artworks, family pictures, and other personal mementos.

I have found that going to lunch with male academics is usually organized so that the visitor from overseas can meet other "important" and high-ranking academics. With women it is just the opposite. Repeatedly, when women had the time for lunch or afternoon tea, they had already arranged or would call their friends down the hall or across campus to organize a group lunch. They wanted to share a meal or snack with friends, not with influential Big Name academics. Again, when the time was available, we would drive to local shopping malls or a restaurant off campus to talk, laugh, relax, and eat. In fact we all talked a lot about food. With women it all seems a lot less pretentious. In contrast, I have spent hours over the years with men in suits in faculty club lounges performing institutional scripts for "doing lunch with the boys."

As a woman researching women, there was always room for talking about women's issues outside the parameters of my research questions. I suspect similar gender specific discourse patterns occur among men talking sports scores, cars, or fishing. On the whole, women seem more forthcoming than men in talking about personal issues, from stories about family and children, about missing their adult children now overseas, about life after divorce or widowhood. I have found most women's discursive style much more inclusive: They invite the researcher into a conversation rather than providing minimalist answers or lengthy theoretical expositions. The women asked questions about my own life, about why I was doing this research, what I had found elsewhere, where I was from, did I have children, and so forth. Despite all the cultural differences, there are many common bonds between women that *can* build bridges, even in the short instant of the one-hour interview, from which issues can be jointly explored. We may well have different cultural codes, reality and plausibility structures, and ways of seeing, but those differences and the codes in which they are inscribed are what constitute "the real." The real is always a *code of representation* (Trinh, 1989, p. 84), and it is as close as we can get to speaking ourselves, and speaking to each other.

Thailand

Population	61.3 million
Language	Thai
1998 UN Gender Empowerment Index ranking (out of 174)	59
Female combined primary-, secondary-, and tertiary-level gross enrollment ratio (1995)*	55.5%
Number of tertiary-level students (male and female) per 100,000 inhabitants (1996)	2,096
Public universities	21
Private universities	34
Gross enrollments (male and female, all levels), all universities (1998)	1,021,011
Total full-time academic staff (male and female), all universities (1998)	27,159
Public expenditure on education as percentage of GNP (1996)	4.1%

*Expressed as a percentage of the population age group corresponding to the national regulations for these levels of education.

Sources: Thailand Ministry of University Affairs (1999), UNESCO Human Development Index (1998), UNESCO Statistical Yearbook (1998).

CONTEXT

Thailand was my first study in this series, and although it took the longest to complete, it is also the shortest textually. I found few English-language resources and publications on women in higher education, or gender and education. All the women I interviewed spoke English but with various levels of proficiency. My assistant dean friend from Bangkok accompanied me to every interview in the capacity of interpreter. Although there were many instances of women clearly struggling with English, the politics of "face" meant that none of the women asked for interpretive help, and my friend politely refrained from any interventions. However, after interviews, she augmented information and explained things that apparently went right past me. Parts of transcripts were difficult to transcribe, and some sections were lost because neither my Singaporean transcriber nor I could make clear sense of what was being said. As I mentioned earlier, some data was literally mowed down by the noise of university lawnmowers. The Thai data, then, is somewhat limited in depth and scope.

In the first week of interviews, I was still fine-tuning my questions, probing techniques, and sequencing my hardware and paperwork logistics. That week it also became apparent that my focus on male academic culture was too narrow. Repeatedly, women alluded to other women "keeping us down" and implicated them in glass-ceiling politics. I also learned that deans like to talk about their own programs and university initiatives. Not wishing to cut women off, and aware of the need to build a repertoire and some sense of trust in the short span of an interview, I spent too much time early on engaging in conversations about enrollment numbers, programs, and so forth. In Thailand particularly, and later also in Malaysia, deans and department heads were keen to find out about costs and enrollment criteria for postgraduate study at my university. Always the ambassador for my own institution, I was happy to oblige with the information, but it did use up valuable time. Time management, then, was an early lesson. Later I started packing my university's brochures and enrollment forms for international students, and I also mentioned at the beginning of each interview that I was keen to hear about their programs and the university more generally at the close of the interview. Thailand, then, was an early lesson in logistics and preparation, and in reshaping some of my questions. My colleague and I traveled extensively throughout the country, and we had sufficient time everywhere to go sightseeing and to visit her friends. This social backdrop provided a very different context compared to my subsequent research in Singapore, Hong Kong, and Malaysia.

As with my other studies, I identified women through social networks, which led to subsequent snowball sampling several months prior to interviews. Each participant received a research brief outlining the parameters of the study and a questionnaire that sought basic sociodemographic information. Consent and confidentiality forms were explained and cosigned at the interview. I scheduled interviews with 12 women, of which two in rural universities were unavailable on the scheduled days because of unforeseen commitments in Bangkok. The remaining women were located in three public universities (Kasetsart in Bangkok, and Khon Kaen and Mahasarakham in two northeastern provinces), two Rajabhat Institutes in Nakonpathom and Ayutthaya, and King Mongkut's Institute of Technology, all about a two-hour drive from Bangkok. Rajabhat Institutes are similar to what used to be polytechnic institutes in the United Kingdom, Singapore, and Hong Kong, or colleges of advanced education in Australia. Since the mid-1990s, Rajabhats have been upgraded to offer postgraduate degrees.

The women held positions as deans, deputy deans, and assistant deans, department heads, research center directors, and presidents of Rajabhat Institutes. They were located in faculties of science, industrial education and technology, agro-industry, education, arts and humanities, and social sciences. The women's ages ranged from 43 to 55. Three women were unmarried (single, divorced, or widowed), and all the married women except one had children. One married woman listed "economist" as her partner's occupation, and the others listed "government official" or "military official." With the exception of Rajabhat presidents, all the women listed "associate professor" as their position classification. Nine of the ten women had doctoral qualifications, of which eight were American Ph.D.'s and one was a Japanese degree. Their average length of service in higher education was 26.8 years, with the longest service record being 37 years and the shortest 20 years.

Most of the women had begun their academic careers as instructors or lecturers between the mid-1960s and early 1970s, a time when few women held mid-level or senior positions in the Thai tertiary sector (except teaching colleges). Moreover, given low female participation rates in lower to upper secondary and tertiary education during the 1960s, the decade when these women passed through schooling and their first academic degrees, suggests that these women are indeed trailblazers—the first generation of women at the vanguard of education expansion and the shift throughout the 1980s toward "the feminisation of tertiary education in general and the predominance of women in all but vocational schools" (Knodel, 1997, p. 68).

"Doing academic business" in Hong Kong and Singapore is a business-like affair, not that dissimilar from western academic protocol. In Thailand, by contrast, academic business is a more social and ceremonial affair, providing occasions to entertain a visitor, to serve food and tea and exchange gifts. In Hong Kong and Singapore, most interviews were conducted across the dean's or director's desk; offices were generally sparse, and decoration limited to framed credentials. In Thailand, I was seated on couches, served drinks and food before we exchanged gifts and began our "official" interview. All the women introduced me to their support staff, and all insisted on lunch after mid-morning interviews. Some of the women's offices revealed much about the gendered constructions of institutional space.

In the course of my own academic life, I have spent a lot of time over the years in people's offices, always attuned to how men and women organize and construct their spaces differently, how they create and use the space that is a public workplace and yet a private niche within the pre-set architecture of university buildings. In Thailand, the women's offices were filled with flowers and potted plants. Some women took me on short walks through their patios or gardens outside the building. We talked about plants, orchid raising, and water-lily culture. I know I would not have had similar conversations with men. Pictures, carvings, and figurines spread across walls and furniture; doilies and pillows adorned the couches and easy chairs. One dean's office was decorated with pink silk curtains matching the upholstery fabric and a similarly pastel-colored carpet, which led to a lengthy conversation about Thai silk dyes. These spaces were decidedly "feminine," framing a cultural space organized and inhabited by women. All clerical, reception, and personal assistant staff were women. The only males I encountered in the women's immediate sphere were their drivers.

I began our conversations by explaining that in the west, the concept of the glass ceiling has been used to explain the invisible cultural and structural barriers that exist in institutions and keep women locked in low- and mid-level positions. I explained that the overt and invisible rule of patriarchy is generally considered to create a masculine workplace culture that may grant women mid-level administrative, paper-shuffling posts but keeps women out of positions of real authority, power, and budgetary control. I then asked each woman to reflect on what she viewed as the main structural, cultural, and social impediments to women's career advancement in the academy in terms of their own experiences and their knowledge of other academic women colleagues. I asked the women if they thought men and women had different concepts of career, whether gender differences existed in management and leadership styles, and how such differences might impact on women's career mobility. I also asked them to reflect on whether marriage and child care impeded career advancement, and how Thai cultural values mediate women's single or married status as a senior academic manager. I concluded the interviews by asking each woman about her career aspirations and future professional plans.

GENDERED MANAGEMENT STYLES

The initial response among all the women to my question about the position of women in Thai higher education today was one of meritocratic idealism. Most women felt that young women today can achieve anything in Thailand "if they work hard, have the qualification to be the leader, they can get there." Most of the women agreed on these points:

- "In Thailand, there's no limitation or constraint. If any woman would like to go for administration, she could go ahead."
- "We [women] have a chance. It is up to you, if you can improve yourself and you can develop yourself."
- "Generally for women in Thailand, we don't have any barriers. If we would like to go ahead in our work or anything, we can do it."
- "I think we can go up to any high position. In Thailand, I think we are still lucky, we don't have very obvious sex discrimination."

However, on closer probing, it became apparent that behind the rhetoric of meritocratic opportunity, historical and cultural factors remain strong determinants of women's professional career opportunities. Out of 21 universities, Thailand has "only one lady president", and only 6 out of 36 Rajabhat Institutes are headed by female presidents. One dean summed it up succinctly: "The top is always a man." One woman—the first female director of a major research and development center in a Bangkok university science faculty, the first female president of a highly prestigious scientific association, and the only woman in my sample who considered the possibility of seeking further career advancement—made this comment: "In most of the universities, women do not yet go to the very top rank; probably it's a bit of a custom or tradition of the people. They think that in the high-ranking positions, male is better than female." Another woman had this to say: "I think that maybe it's cultural—because in Thai custom, usually it's older men who should take high positions." And another stated, "Some don't separate between men and women but many do. They say 'Oh, it's a lady, ah, we don't want her, she's emotional, talkative. Women are not good for executive positions.' I have observed this in appointment committees when they discuss candidates."

A deputy dean distinguished between academic equality and professional equality:

> In terms of academics, in Thailand we don't have any barriers, and we don't lack equality. But when they [women] grow professionally and get to a status in the higher administrative positions, to some extent, yes, there is inequality. If we have to do a big job in a higher position, we have to dedicate ourselves totally to the job. And because of our role in Thailand, men don't have families to take care of, but we do, so men can just go ahead in what they are interested in. But for women, even though we have domestic or child care help or whatever, we still need to be with our children and we need to take good care of our husbands. That's just one part of cultural barriers or traditional barriers. Academic barriers no, but professional barriers in higher positions, yes.

What is also keeping women from reaching the upper echelons is women themselves:

- "I think we work harder [than men]. Maybe it seems we are busy all the time. Our subordinates, young women, they think 'I cannot do that, I don't want to work that hard.'"
- "I think what's keeping them [women from advancing] is that they think of the past, of traditional values. They think that women should be more at home, with children. We have only one woman [university] president. Women have to work harder to get to that position, and many don't want to."
- "When young women students see how much we work, no time to relax, maybe they think, 'No, I don't want it.'"

Most of the women were first-time female appointments to their positions. How did they fit into an exclusively male culture? Again, most claimed that gender had not been a problem, but on closer questioning about potential differences in women's and men's management and leadership styles, the perceived differences in expectations and performance became apparent:

- "You have to prove that as a woman, she can be very good in her mind and her work. She has to be very open-minded. Don't do everything by detail, but you have to think big. Big picture."
- "Women tend to be more careful working with the people. They focus on collaboration, partnership, consultation with people."
- "I think women have some advantage in the administrative region because if the top management is a lady, is a female, we can use that softness to bring in or soften down some critical situation."
- "The quality for me is my potential to work. I can make good relationships, join every group, bring people together to work as a team. I help people and am sincere to everyone. I have [social] justice. I can administer better than some men."

Two women said they come to work early every day, around 6 a.m. and "I walk around and just say hi to the people, you know, the gardener and cleaners. People seem happy about that." Another woman relates, "I have to wake up at 4 o'clock and go jogging in the morning about 5 o'clock. When I'm jogging, I see a lot of temples, buildings, gardens. It makes me feel good, and after that I talk with my staff, before work starts." Women "show sympathy to the people" and they are "gentle." Thai women see themselves as having a tremendous capacity for work, and for recognizing and looking for "the little things," the details:

- "Women can do more than men and they get all the details. I think that is the benefit of women's quality."
- "I mean they work more than men. Women work hard at work and work hard for men: We have to take care of the family, take care of students. Two or three jobs at the same time. Men have the wife. Women don't have the wife."
- "I have a very strong intention to do this job. As women, because we do so much at home, with family, children, our own research and studies, helping parents, we have strong attitudes to working and we work very hard. Even in traditional times, women knew how to work."

On the other hand, one woman had this to say about men: "You cannot see that from the guy. Maybe the man is thinking, 'This is just a little thing,' but a little thing is very important. [Men] ignore the little things." One woman insisted on the need to change men and male culture:

> Sometimes we feel like we are supposed to adjust them, to get them across to us. For example, our president is a man. When he has some kind of special activity, some important event, he doesn't know how to present himself to the public. But we try to tell him. They miss a lot. They say, "Oh, that's a little thing," but little things can be big in the future.

Several women felt passionate about the need for women to be able to operate like men in order to be heard, treated with respect, and accorded institutional legitimacy. A director explains:

> I found that it is necessary for women in administrative positions to be able to be just like a man when you are among men. Because at the top level, they are mostly men, very few women. For example, you must be able to drink with them their drinks. After work, it's always a banquet or party, and you have to be there, you must be able to join them. You must be able to join in the group without talking about women's things like shopping.

Unlike some women who claimed women's strength lies in their gentleness and softness, this woman insisted on the importance of "aggressiveness" (I believe her use of the term *aggressiveness* was meant more along the lines of assertiveness) as crucial to maintaining her credibility and status in a high ranking position:

> If you look into the background of successful women in high-ranking positions, you would see, I think, aggressiveness is a must. Self-confidence, promoting yourself, being visible, arguing for issues. You must be able to dare to say things in any situation because, in Thai culture, we were taught to be shy, quiet, you know, you must behave like a traditional female.

How women present themselves in public is clearly fraught with contradictions and conflicting values about women's expected decorum: balancing expectations of traditional femininity with assertiveness and "drinking with the boys"; managing in strategic "big picture" terms and yet attending to the detail of "the little things." However, one woman who claimed to have successfully integrated into the old boys' club, had experienced some backlash. She says:

> I get along with the men more than the women. I don't know why. I need to get experience from the men, so I talk more with the men. For me it is better than women. Men can tell a joke and I laugh, and I say, "Why don't you tell this to the other women?" and they say, "I don't dare; I don't dare."

Apparently, some of her staff "told me that I need to look more of a lady. They say, 'When you talk, you talk like a man . . . it doesn't look so good for a lady.' When I wear jeans, someone told me it's impolite because 'you are the president now, you should dress like a lady.'" But, in her words, what is important is that "I do the work, I am on time, I know when to dress formal like this for official occasions." One assistant dean who considered women's ability to think in "big picture" terms crucial to their success also claimed that women "have to learn to work like men, to be able to get acceptance from the men," which does not imply that "to work as a man does not mean that I'm like a man."

The perception that women need to fit in with male culture and to learn to work like a man departs significantly from the western literature on women in management. That research (e.g., Davies, Lubelska, & Quinn, 1994; Eggins, 1997; Itzin, 1994; Morley & Walsh, 1996; Oerton, 1996) has argued strongly for the institutionalization of women's networks, mentoring programs, and gender equity policies in the workplace as formal political interventions to move women up through various glass ceilings and thereby to change the masculinist culture of organizations. Performing masculinity to get along and ahead in primarily male organizational enclaves is not a political or theoretical option in the western literature. However, I got the sense from the Thai women that they were infiltrating male culture by assuming masculine practices selectively in strategic and informal ways, quite different from the formal policy interventions common in the west.

There was general consensus among the women that one significant gender difference in management style derives from Thai women's great strength of determination and commitment to stand by their decisions:

When Thai women decide something, after they decide, they don't change. Before she decides right or wrong, before she gets to a decision, she will use a lot of information, searching to try to get the reasons for the decision. She will gather information before she gets to the decision, but once she has the decision, she never changes. She sticks with it. Very determined.

Women are also seen to use power differently. As one woman said, "women use power more than men." For example:

A woman who wants to get someone to do what she wants, she will do anything to make it happen. It's different for men. Like my boss, he is a man, and he wants this guy to do something and he won't do it, so he [my boss] tries somebody else, he just switches. But women don't.

According to another woman, "men they don't think so much before they make a decision. I have to think a lot and then try to see what to do and then I make my decision." Only one woman thought that women were worse decision makers than men, noting, "I think the most distinct point between male and female is the decision making. Women mostly cannot make very good decisions. They are more shifting, more indecisive. And this is one point men always say about women."

Although all the women began by telling me about women's equal opportunities and the "lack of barriers," when pressed further, all had something to say about gendered cultural expectations and attitudes, about women's different approaches and orientations, and how such differences might help or hinder women. When asked about their early career decisions, interpretations of gendered patterns also emerged. Some women referred to husbands and sons to illustrate how men and women construct different career orientations.

CAREER PATHS

Looking back over her 30-year career in the higher-education sector, one dean of an industrial education faculty summed up the situation of women and academic careers best: "Men have the wife. Women don't have the wife." All the women started out as lecturers or instructors, most of them in teachers' colleges during the 1970s. When they started their first teaching posts, none had given much thought about career planning, and none had ambitions to attain senior administrative or executive management positions. For most women, career advancement just happened":

- "I had only the idea to go into my research. I never had any idea of coming to an administrative position."
- "No, it just happened. I never thought, 'I am going to be the dean.' I myself don't want to be dean because I don't like paperwork."
- "I just started and it was the intake of the Bachelor of Science and my major is in science and I was asked if I could help with the intake. I didn't think much of continuing for my further degree until a few years later. So it happened, no plans."
- "Well, to me, I just let things happen. I know I never had any career path or any ambition. Even though I got into the Ph.D. program, I never had ambition at that time. It's by accident, when something comes up, okay, I have a chance so I go. But I don't have any determination to be in administration. I just let things happen."
- "When I first started, I had no expectations. But it is my personality that I try to do everything the best. One day my boss said, 'I need one of you to be the head of the project but it is difficult, you will work hard.' Two said no so I said 'Okay, I can do it.' And I succeeded. After that, my boss asks anything of me, and I say yes, yes. So that's how I started."

Men, on the other hand, have more clear-cut career goals and ambitions because, in one woman's view, "men don't have families to take care of but we do, so men can just go ahead and do what they are interested in."

- "Yes, the men know they want to move up when they are young. Like my sons. They know what to do."
- "Men are focused with their career plans. I can tell from my husband."

With only one exception, none of the women had further career ambitions. As presidents, deans, deputy and assistant deans, these women put in 12- to 14-hour days, teaching undergraduate and postgraduate courses, working late most nights to catch up on paperwork, attending banquets or other official events, running evening seminars, and all worked on Saturdays. In Australia, work intensification is the current buzzword, and certainly we all easily put in more than 60 hours a week working evenings and weekends marking papers, writing, catching up on e-mail, etc. However, even middle-management positions do not require the huge loads of undergraduate and postgraduate teaching, including Saturday mornings, that are common in Southeast Asia. In fact, some of the Thai students I supervise are department heads and assistant deans and experience tremendous difficulty doing their Ph.D. research and writing theses in addition to their workloads.

As is the case with their counterparts elsewhere, Thai academic women engage in the "mom work" and "smile work" (Tierney & Bensimon, 1996) of nurturing students and departmental "housekeeping." It is women, not men, who scurry around to make sure everyone has food on their plates during academic social events, who fuss with tablecloths, pour tea, rush off to run errands for senior males, or stay late to help cleaning staff tidy up. As several women in the Malaysian study observed, the gendered division of domestic labor is mirrored in the division of academic labor.

All the married women's children were adults, some living away from home while studying in overseas universities. Several women in provincial universities whose children were studying in Bangkok claimed they take every institutional opportunity to go to Bangkok: "I go to as many meetings there as I can. I miss her and so I go all the time." All the women lamented that they missed spending time with husbands, children, parents, and in-laws, and they all regretted not being able to continue reading, writing, and researching. One dean had been asked to seek a vice presidency and had refused: "The people came to ask me to be the vice president, but I don't want to be the vice president. I don't want it [deanship] any more. Just one more year is enough for me. I want to go back to teach, to go back to spend my time writing."

I asked one deputy dean if she would consider applying for the deanship for which her colleagues were strongly supporting her. Her response was, "I don't think so. I would like to retire about five years earlier. I'm in my second term already. Too long, long enough. Almost seven years now. I would like to travel more, follow my husband, and do something I would like to do for my personal interest." Another woman also looked forward to early retirement: "What I have planned is to retire early and to do something that I like. I have a lot of people under me and have to manage them, and do a lot of things for them, not for myself. And I'm getting tired, and I want early retirement and do something for myself." A 58-year-old dean, in the sixth year of an eight-year term said: "Another two years, that is the time, I am happy, I retire. I have no plan but I think I will maybe write a book. I will do some research or write a book." Another dean whose staff had encouraged her to pursue the vice presidency was also looking forward to stepping down from the deanship, but not before she had completed her agenda of "transformation" and "academic change" to which she had already committed many years:

> I don't want it any more [deanship]. I have another three years from now to be the dean. It's two jobs. I teach four courses and I have my research projects. So that's why it's too much for me. I enjoy writing. My teaching, I love it. I want to go back to teach, to go back to spend my time writing. But I cannot finish yet. I still have some things to do, like a building, like new curriculum, academic change, a new department that I set up by myself. I have a proposal for a building. All that should settle a bit more and then when everything is done, it's okay, let somebody else take care of it.

The only woman who still saw her career on the ascent was the first woman director of a high-status, high-profile research and development center in a science faculty. At age 50, she was widowed with one adult child:

> I am the first lady director of this institute, and you know, it is quite difficult to come up to this position. It's an elected position, elected by all the heads of departments of the university. So this position is quite difficult to be taken by a female, and many people said that I have broken through. It used to be difficult for women to rise to this position because this is one of the key organisations in the university.

All previous directors of this center had gone on to become the vice president or president of this university. In her view, her appointment to this position suggested a clear career path in terms of the history of previous directorships of the institute. Without seeming too brazenly ambitious, she put her career aspirations in these terms: "So when I was chosen for this position, I have already foreseen into the future. I know already where I should go, which direction I should take. It's like, you know, you're already jogging and then you just run."

Like the other women in this study, this woman's career aspirations and concepts of successful achievement were linked to her dedication of effecting institutional change, having influence, making a difference. As a research scientist, she saw the importance of having a powerful and high-profile position as the best way to generate and disseminate knowledge, develop large-scale research projects, and attract major funding to support those projects:

If you are doing research by yourself, you only have limited power, and you can extend your own ideas only to a small group of people. But if you come to a major research administration role, you can extend your ideas into very wide group of people and that is good. That is what I see as challenging. I put all my effort in the formulation of big research projects.

As a single divorced woman with no child care responsibilities, she was not under pressure to balance work and family but could devote most of her time and energies to work "without [feeling] guilty." In her view, "What I would like to say is, for a woman to go up to the administrative level, there are many factors, and family is the key factor. If the family does not understand the problem, it is very difficult. Guilt. Stress." All the women agreed that women's domestic and family responsibilities were key impediments to career aspirations and advancement, that single women are somewhat advantaged in that regard, and that without family support and understanding, "it is very difficult". But single women experience other cultural pressures.

SINGLE WOMEN/
MARRIED WOMEN

Single women in the Singapore and Hong Kong groups mentioned that just because a woman is single does not mean she does not have family responsibility. In fact, all the single women I interviewed in those two sites were living with one of their parents and claimed to be immersed in a substantial share of extended family care and responsibilities. For the single Thai women in this study, the picture was similar in terms of the gender stereotypes they perceived people held of them, and workplace expectations of and attitudes toward single women. I asked all the women if they thought that having children, rather than just being married, was a significant factor mediating women's career opportunities. One married woman without children said:

Yeah, everybody looks at me and they think, "You have no kids, you can come to work more." That is what I heard them say when they appointed me. I asked the dean why they appointed me to that position and he said, "Oh you don't have kids, you have the time. Even your husband can take care of himself."

One woman attributed her early career success to the fact that she only had one child "after I got my master's," and was married to a "very talented" and "supportive husband": "I was lucky because my husband, he understands very well, so he always gives me the opportunity. So I was lucky. He was a professional administrator and I learned from him how to manage, how to administer a big organization." Another woman also attributed part of her early career success to the fact that she didn't have to balance family with study and/or work: "I already finished my degrees when I got married. I got married last." And another woman said, "No conflict because I have no children. I also have my [domestic] helper at home so I can be at work early in the morning." In the Hong Kong study later that year, women in their 40s would repeatedly raise the issue of having deferred marriage or having children until Ph.D.'s were completed or tenured positions were secured. Career planning for women clearly ties in with family planning, an issue not faced by men with the same kinds of professional consequences.

One single 48-year-old president spent considerable time discussing her life as a single woman in her current position and institution:

> For me, as a single woman, I can do things by myself. I am strong. I can go everywhere alone. But I think some ladies don't like me. Not everyone likes a single woman. So I think that if you don't get married you can do this job. But ladies who get married, it is harder, more than for single women. But if you are single, you have a chance to do more.

This is the same woman, a very athletic person who jogs and wears jeans around campus on days off, whose staff encouraged her to "dress more like a lady." Her residence, the president's quarters, is on campus property, which means that her private life is in public view. She has been called the " the jogging director—they call me that." My impression was that she had undergone some rather traumatic experiences for which she was not prepared. Without reading too much into her comments, I got the distinct impression that she had a difficult time being accepted and combating various Thai stereotypes about older single women. She said that "someone told me that 'you are like a boy more than a girl,' but I don't it take seriously." I suspected that she might be seen as a threat by other women because she chose to socialize with the men in order to network, to get insights into "what they do" and "what they think": "For me, because I am a new person, when we have meetings or lecture time, I will join with

the men, to ask things. I talk with the men more than the women, to learn
what they do, what they think. The women don't like it."

One of her first executive decisions was to appoint a female vice president, to which her staff responded with skepticism:

> Some of the staff don't accept her. But I tell them, "I think that she can
> do the job. She has intelligence." But I know that most of the staff here
> don't accept it, and when they have a chance to talk to me, they say,
> "Why, why did you get her to take this position?" For me, I know that
> some of the staff don't accept me because I am a lady. If a man is in an
> executive position like this one, no one wonders. But if you are a lady,
> and a single lady, then they think different.

In some ways, she has had to construct her relationships with colleagues
and staff, in ways that a married woman in the same position may not have
found necessary, to overcome the assumptions and perceived concerns
about her single status. For instance, she told me, "After I became president, at first no one invited me, you know, maybe because I am single or
of a higher level. But why? So I said, "'Hey, why don't you invite me?
Why do you do this?' So later they changed. Now they tell me, 'Party
tonight.'" I got the sense that she was actively reconstructing the role of
president, which, from my own experience in the Rajabhat Institute sector,
is a highly venerated and high-status position, circumscribed by cultural
practices of strict hierarchy, deference, and social distance among
"unequals." Members of the senior executive eat in separate dining rooms,
and many have their own support entourage of waiters, cooks, gardeners,
and drivers. This president, however, felt isolated in this system and tried
to break the formalities, the old rules of status difference and decorum:

> If I see anyone, I can't shout, "Hey, where are you going? Have you
> eaten already or not?" I am alone, you know. Everywhere, everyday. So
> as president, I have to take lunch alone because they have the president's
> restaurant and they buy it for you. I say that I don't need that. I need to
> go to the same cafeteria as before I am president. I don't need a driver, so
> I walk to the cafeteria. I walk to the restaurant. I want to join with staff.
> But, it is difficult and now it is changing.

Reflecting on the experiences of her women colleagues, one dean had this
to say:

For Thai women, especially if you are single, it can be very difficult in terms of getting together with the men. Like if they have a meeting somewhere in the night time, if you are single it is very difficult in terms of going to celebrate something. Thai women cannot go. It is difficult to ask a male friend to go as a partner and difficult to go alone as a single woman. In a couple, it's easier.

Another women commented:

One of my friends, she's dean and she's single, and every time when they have some kind of meeting, or celebrate, or entertain people from abroad, in the night time, she cannot go. She says, "Oh I cannot go, they are coming back so late," and it's difficult for her to drive by herself back home. She feels uncomfortable with that.

Clearly, being a single and older woman in senior administration is an isolating experience. Cultural rules of propriety curtail lifestyle choices (e.g., appearance, dress) and set limits on single women's social conduct (e.g., going out alone at night or asking a male friend as escort to social events). Consorting with male colleagues in professional contexts can alienate single women from other women colleagues, which, in turn, can isolate single women further. Although being a single, older woman in the west is not without social stigma, I would argue that their social behaviors and professional relationships are less constrained and publicly scrutinized.

The social status associated with marriage may give Thai women more social legitimacy in the eyes of some, and perhaps more professional and geographic mobility. But all the women agreed that having children was the biggest impediment to the freedoms and autonomy required to respond to professional demands and pursue career aspirations. These are some typical responses:

- "Some of my friends, when they get married and have children, they have to think, 'Okay, I have to get back home to cook, to take care of kids, the house.'"
- "Frustration. Sometimes when you have to do something in the office and then 6 o'clock comes, and you have to go back home, even though something important needs to be done at work."
- "When the kids are sick, you have to stay home, have to bathe, have to cook. Men, no. Thai men are not changing much."

All the married women claimed to have exceptional husbands, all supportive of the women's choices, and all willing to pitch in with housework and child care. As one woman remarked, "Like my husband, he cooks by himself, for the kids, you know, he takes good care of the house and laundry by himself." All the women's husbands were professional men, and when I asked whether they thought such enlightened husbands were a product of educational advantage and class privilege, most agreed that the "reconstructed" Thai male was indeed a product of educated parents:

> parents who understand, so there won't be any difference between son and daughter; they give them full and equal opportunity. When they are husbands, they think different about what their wives want to do. But in the sense of class, because the lower-income people have to struggle for their lives, they normally feel that being a woman, you don't have to learn too much. You just look for a good husband, and then you would be supported. They will take care of you, and you will be happy. Particularly in the lower-income group, people think like this. And that is [lack of] education.

Another assistant dean made a similar observation about the link between lack of education and diminished opportunities:

> In Thailand, we still have a lot of people who don't even have a high school certificate. So we have a lot of women who work in factories or do the jobs that they shouldn't do after grade 6. And boys often leave school earlier to work on the land or to get fast money in Bangkok. So then there is no change. For low-income people it is a struggle . . . no education, no change in attitude, in opportunities.

Married or single, all the women in this study had overcome overt and invisible entrenched cultural perceptions about women's capacity to succeed in traditionally male defined and occupied positions. Several of the women were in the second half of an eight-year term as dean and were looking forward to retirement. Having given so much for others, they were looking forward to having time to themselves, whether to travel with husbands, research, or write. Some women had postponed having children until their postgraduate studies were well underway or completed. In the late 1960s and even 1970s, such choices would have been a radical departure from traditional expectations of Thai women, even among the middle class (Girling, 1996).

Eight of the ten women were the first in their families to attend universities, and eventually these women would go overseas to study for doctoral degrees. On their return to Thailand, they started their first jobs in entry-level positions as teaching assistants, instructors, or lecturers. Eventually, those with proficient second or third language skills worked their way through the system, principally in traditional women's administrative posts such as assistant dean or deputy dean of student affairs, academic affairs, or international affairs.

Clearly, these had been long careers in which opportunities "just happened" and no clear career paths or promotion structures were evident. Election to senior posts, as several women pointed out, was a relatively recent innovation, replacing processes of internal appointments that lacked open competition, and systems of accountability. Two women talked at length about how they had been the first candidates appointed by election in a process in which all university department heads or institute presidents had voted. This process had given added significance to their appointments and, in my interpretation, to their personal sense of professional achievement.

"I DON'T SEE ANY GLASS . . . "

Although all the women initially claimed that no gender bias exists in Thai society, many gendered differences of cultural perceptions and institutional treatment became evident in the course of our conversations. At the end of each interview, I asked whether institutionalized gender equity programs would benefit young women coming up through the ranks. I explained the kinds of equity programs prevalent in western universities, many of which the women were familiar with through their time in American universities as doctoral students and/or on sabbatical leave. Uniformly, the women rejected such ideas, often hinting that such initiatives would "divide the sexes":

- "We don't do anything like this. I think that is a very western thing."
- "Women would not go if there are committees based on sex difference or about equality, because we have been brought up in a society where we don't take sex differences as a factor differentiating people."
- "No, because everyone thinks there is no difference; women have it equal, so why have committees, why have quotas? I know your gender equality. But it does not mean you get promoted. Here it would divide the sexes."

- "I think people would not like it. Because a woman is on a committee, like an appointment or promotion committee, that doesn't mean she makes it equal for other women."

All the women except one had studied in the United States and were therefore familiar with the concept of glass ceiling in relation to women's career opportunities. However, the common response was

- "The glass ceiling, no, I don't feel that I have experienced that."
- "I believe that ours [glass ceiling] is not so concrete as in Australia. I studied in Australia...and I can see that the glass ceiling is thicker."
- "I am working here for 20 years and I don't see any glass that men can block me. I don't see it."

It was my impression that this small group of women, all in their late 40s to mid-50s, were the products of a particular generation to have come of age at a time in Thailand's history when women did not hold high-status positions of power and influence in the workplace (Smock, 1981). Indeed, in the late 1960s when most of these women were in their 20s, only one third of all students continued past four years of schooling (Limanonda, 2000; Unger, 1998). Until the 1970s, the university sector (primarily Chulalongkorn and Thammasat Universities) was dedicated to training bureaucrats and administrators to staff government and the civil service, which was principally the work of men (supported by lower-level female typists and clerks) (Phongpaichit & Baker, 1996). In other words, the generation of women in this study went through tertiary education when relatively few women did. For instance, the 1990 census found that among women then between ages 40 and 49, which accounts for the women in this cohort, only 4% held a tertiary qualification compared with nearly 13% of 20- to 24-year-old women (Thailand National Statistical Office, n.d., in Phongpaichit & Baker, 1996). These women were an elite minority in their day and having achieved the positions they now hold, it is understandable that they don't "see an glass ceiling."

CONCLUDING REMARKS

The women in this study had broken with traditional expectations for Thai women of their generation (Siengthai, 1994), and each had overcome cultural attitudes toward achieving women who had been taught "to be shy, quiet . . . like a traditional female." Several women postponed having children until they completed at least one degree, almost all went abroad to study for at least one postgraduate degree, and all had experienced various forms of exclusion and resistance, skepticism and mistrust of their abilities *as women* from colleagues and seniors. Some of the women considered it important to socialize with male colleagues to break into the inner circles, to find out "what they do" and "what they think," even if that meant disapproval from female colleagues. Others found it necessary to operate "just like a man when you are among men."

In their own ways, these women were renegotiating their positions through various attempts to change colleagues' and subordinates' perceptions of their role and status, and by bringing their specific vision of institutional change and women's abilities as senior managers into the mainstream. In light of Thailand's low educational participation rates well into the 1970s and a university system geared toward credentialing a male bureaucratic elite, women now in their late 40s and 50s can be seen as pioneers or trailblazers who, in the context of their generational histories, can claim not to "see any glass that men can block me." Although these women had not planned their careers or held leadership aspirations, for them meritocratic principles of hard work, commitment, and ability had worked in their favor.

7

Singapore

Population	Chinese (76%), Malay (15%), Indian (7%)	3.47 million
Languages	English, Mandarin, Tamil	
1998 UN Gender Empowerment Index ranking (out of 174)		28
Female combined primary-, secondary-, and tertiary-level gross enrollment ratio (1995)*		57.5%
Number of tertiary-level students (male and female) per 100 000 inhabitants (1996)		2,722
Public universities		2
Institutes of education, technical education, and polytechnics		18
Gross enrollments (male and female, all levels), all higher education (1998)		114,974
Total full-time academic staff (male and female), all higher education (1998)		7,714
Public expenditure on education as percentage of GNP (1996)		3.0%

*Expressed as a percentage of the population age group corresponding to the national regulations for these levels of education.

Sources: Statistics Singapore (1998), UNESCO Human Development Index (1998), UNESCO Statistical Yearbook (1998).

CONTEXT

I conducted this study the week after I completed the interviews in Thailand (Chapter 6). This chapter begins with profiles of the women in this study and then outlines aspects of state legislation of family values and housing policy to set a framework within which to situate the women's comments and my analysis. Next, I consider how cultural values and practices mediate Singaporean gender politics in the context of higher education. This is followed by an explication of the women's career aspirations, their perceptions of gender differences in management and leadership styles, and their views on the value of institutionalized gender equity programs.

I identified the women in this study through my own personal network and with the help of two women who are personal friends, both senior lecturers in Singapore. As with my other studies, the sampling proceeded through snowballing techniques, and each participant received a research brief and a questionnaire prior to my visit. Confidentiality and consent forms were cosigned at the start of each interview, and at the close of interviews I left each woman copies of my university's gender equity materials.

Ten women were originally scheduled for interviews, but one withdrew during the week due to illness. The women held positions as deans, vice deans, subdeans, and heads of departments, divisions, and units. They were spread across faculties of science, arts and humanities, and social sciences at the National University of Singapore, Nanyang Technological University, and Ngee Ann Polytechnic. Several of the women were also long-time members of AWARE (National Association for Women for Action and Research), currently the most politically influential women's lobby group and prolific publisher of feminist scholarship through its journal, *Awareness*. A few of the women were past and current members of the association's senior executive group. Most of these women have highly visible profiles in Singapore, and several received laudatory mention in "A Who's Who of Women in Singapore" published in *The Business Times* on International Women's Day 1997. Eight of the nine women were ethnic Chinese of various (second- and third-generation) national descents, including Hong Kong and mainland China. Most, however, were *Peranakan* or Straits-born Chinese (i.e., born in Singapore and/or the Malay Peninsula, particularly in Melaka or Penang, all located on the Straits of Malacca). Their ages ranged from 32 to 56 years. Five women were single, and of the nine women all except one held Ph.D.'s from the United Kingdom, Canada, or Australia.

I also met with four women who held positions as lecturers or senior lecturers. We met over dinner at one of the women's residences and discussed the same issues I had raised with the other women. All the women in this group considered themselves feminists, although it is not a term they use to describe themselves in Singapore. This group provided insights into the viewpoint of middle-rank staff, giving me their interpretations of the leadership and management styles of some of the senior women I had interviewed with whom they had current and past working relationships. In many ways, this group of women provided a more politicized narrative than that of the other nine senior women. Singapore is a small place with a small academic community, so academic career mobility is confined to a handful of institutions where "everybody knows everything about everyone" within and across institutions and disciplinary fields. Unlike the Thai women I had interviewed a week earlier, I found the nine Singaporean senior academic women comments constrained and self-censored. Indeed, many of their comments were prefaced by "off the record."

POLITICAL CONTEXT: FAMILY VALUES

The politics of gender in Singapore must be situated in larger sociopolitical and cultural contexts to analyze and explain the position of women in senior management in the public and private sectors. I will outline here only a few salient issues that shape Singaporean women's career opportunities. Given Singapore's unique multicultural, colonial and postcolonial history and the subsequent powerful involvement in the nation's economic development and social organization by the People's Action Party, the ruling political party in power since 1959, the social control and engineering effects of some three decades have left their mark on people's ideologies and interpretive vocabulary, resulting in a "depoliticisation of the citizenry with practically non-existent interest groups" (Soin, 1996, p. 192). However, the focus group and "off the record" comments were anything but depoliticized. Instead, they revealed sophisticated and highly politicized analyses of the gender and cultural politics in Singapore. But in formal taped interviews, the women skirted or stayed silent on many issues. They were cautious, restrained, and reticent to be openly critical of existing conditions for women, or to articulate issues with reference to concrete examples, events, or persons. In fact, several women themselves acknowledged Singapore's depoliticized polity and public culture, and instead of speaking candidly about issues, they gave me articles, newspaper clippings, books, and other materials they had saved for me. As one woman noted on a yellow Post-it note attached to materials she gave me, "Singapore women today are a shadow of their former selves."

Over the years, I have spent a fair amount of time in Singapore and am reasonably well versed with local issues and recent developments in both higher education and women's issues. I knew that no gender equity policies exist in the government, corporate, and public sectors. I have also followed debates over the third-child campaign and government efforts to curb women's delay of marriage, which is seen to have a worrisome effect on an already declining birth rate. The women were insistent that I understand the dilemma facing Singaporean women today. Regardless of women's professional aspirations and allegedly gender-neutral educational and employment opportunities, the need to reverse the declining birth rate, to retain a strong intergenerational family unit, and to retain professionally qualified women in the workforce, means that women must balance childbearing, childrearing, and domestic family responsibilities with professional career aspirations. As I was repeatedly told, "people are our primary and most valuable resource," and women must play their part in fulfilling the responsibility of population building and maintenance. In Koh's (1996) view:

> Being by nature or culture nurturers, many women accept this [traditional] role. However, at the same time, the interests of capital and nation require the woman's contribution too. Yet if she takes advantage of the six-month no-pay leave so thoughtfully provided for mothers only, to look after a newly born child or young children, she will lose her advantage and promotional prospects. (pp. 25–26)

Added to a long list of government disincentives designed to promote procreation and the nuclear family are ministerial pronouncements and legal constitutional definitions that seriously disadvantage women, regardless of whether they conform to or divert from the traditional path set out for them by government policy. The recent reversal of the 1961 Woman's Charter's definition of *head of household* from a gender neutral definition to one that now legalizes men as "principal breadwinner" and "head of household" (Koh, 1996; Perera, 1996; Soin, 1996), legitimates existing and generates new disadvantages for women. These include barring women who are homemakers and nonwaged from contributing to the Central Provident Fund (a retirement pension fund), and disqualifying women from unemployment benefits and medical benefits for children (awarded only to working fathers). In higher education, male academics on sabbatical leave receive return airfares for wives and children under 18, but as one woman explained, "Women academics don't get it for the spouses and children. There is the inequality, so in effect there is no equal pay, because this is payment in kind, isn't it? They changed *spouse* to *wife* so that effectively the woman [academic] can't have a wife.

Unchanged since 1979, a 33% quota on women's enrollment in medical schools is premised on a national objective of maximum utilization of the educational dollar (Lee, Campbell, & Chia, 1999). Women doctors, the government argues, "tend to work only part-time for a few years because of childcare responsibilities" (Soin, 1996, p. 201). Clearly, the state's construction of women's secondary legal status has serious ramifications for their educational, employment, and economic opportunities and aspirations. Echoing Yuval-Davis' (1993) observation that women tend to be the symbolic and embodied bearers of ethnic and nationalist ideologies because of their socialized compliance and secondary social status, Soin (1996) notes that

> In Singapore there has been a trend of using the women and the family as instruments of social change and this has characterized government policy since the '60s. The Government has used its executive and legislative powers over women and the family to attain general and specific national objectives without analysis of gender consequences. Women's empowerment has hardly been a consideration for policy-makers. (p. 194)

To arrest the declining birth rate, the government instituted a third-child campaign (with highly lucrative financial and housing rewards) in the late 1980s, which women have taken up with enthusiasm: "A lot of people are having three children now and it's across the board, it's not just university graduates but is also the nonuniversity graduates. As long as they feel they can afford it, they will have a third child. The social engineering is very successful."

To encourage married professional women to both work and have children, the government provides tax incentives of 15%, 20%, and 25% of her earned income for the second, third, and fourth child, respectively. In addition, "a further tax rebate of S$20,000 for the second, third, and fourth child" is available "to promote childbearing." Child care, recently altered to include before- and after-school care, is "good but limited," servicing only about 10% of preschool children (Soin, 1996, p. 199). Child care is limited because parents, grandparents, and relatives are expected to look after children while their parents are at work, which is supposed to help promote the emotional and social links between the intergenerational family. Moreover, child care is widely relegated to live-in maids, especially among upper-middle-class and high-income families. Six of the nine women had live-in maids, some of whom had worked for them for up to 20 years. As one women said, "Here they say that behind every successful man is a woman and behind every successful woman is a team of servants."

FAMILY VALUES AND HOUSING

Housing policies may seem an unlikely and remote issue related to women in higher education. However, in Singapore, housing is no simple matter; rather it is a political issue (estates that vote for the incumbent party invariably receive massive financial infusions into facilities upgrading) as well as a "politics of space" issue through which cultural ideologies of gender and the family are woven (Rose, 1993; Spain, 1992). Numerous legislated housing schemes provide financial support for home ownership for married couples, encourage married couples to live close to their families, encourage two- or three-generation families to live together, and give housing priorities to families on the birth of a third child. Singles under 35 without parental coregistration do not qualify for state-subsidized housing schemes, although a Joint Balloting Scheme allows singles under 32 to copurchase a flat with their parents as long as it is within the same estate as the parental residence. According to one woman, this "was a very good policy because it required you to have an intact, nuclear family, two generations, daughter or son, and mother. I had my parents with me, so that helped me to get my housing." All the single women in this study lived with at least one of their parents.

Clearly, such incentives are the cornerstone of a social policy founded on a particular vision of family that has powerful implications for the choices women can make and, relatedly, on their career aspirations and opportunities. The legal structures built into just one aspect of Singapore life—housing—construct a specific range of options and life experiences for people that is derived from and constitutive of specific cultural gender values and roles embedded in a particular "Asian" vision of the normative family (PuruShotam, 1998). Such a politically motivated ideology, although promoted by the government as the preservation of core cultural and religious values (Hill & Lian, 1995), effectively eliminates lifestyle choices that fall outside that normative vision. As the women in this study testified, remaining single in a family-oriented society carries a price. A single 32-year-old woman commented:

> Just because I don't have a husband and children doesn't mean I have no family, and it doesn't mean you don't have responsibilities. In fact I'm told "you have no family" by women. I have aged parents, and that's responsibility. And because your siblings are married, they think because you are not, you look after them. Right, you become the family baby-sitter.

Cohabitation with parents, however, does have advantages. Two single women saw live-in parents and live-in help as built-in social support systems:

- "Look at what she [live-in mother] does for me when I go home. She cooks for me and . . . she enjoys being the manager of the house. Yeah, I've never had it so good."
- "It's so good . . . my mother lives with me and she's 82. Now she's sick and all that, but I have a maid who lives in full time. She has 24-hour care in that sense. I can come home late and it's okay; I don't have to worry."

Another 54-year-old single woman had this to say about being single and female in professional contexts:

> If you are divorced and single . . . it is still extremely difficult for another woman or man to accept, for example, your moral conduct. If you are single, you go out with another single man, even then that is being talked about . . . a lot of small talk, it will be a mark against you. In the west, people tend to accept that you can have a social life without affecting the public image, but not in Singapore. For very senior appointments, they will start to worry whether you will disgrace the director, the company, the institution, or the country if they offer you a very visible position . . . whether or not you are going to be what they consider as a very free

woman. And then, that is not acceptable in the oriental context. There will be whispers.

In Singapore, glass-ceiling politics are subtly structured into the social organization through policy and financial incentives that reward marriage and childbearing. Social policies shape lifestyle options and, by extension, career opportunities for women in ways that leave little room for alternate pathways around expectations of marriage, motherhood, child and kin care, and expectations of workplace participation in the meritocratic state. In one dean's opinion:

> There is the rhetoric that says women are equal . . . then at some point, you meet a glass ceiling; you get married, have your children and all the other domestic work and child care and so on. So we are going back because of the rhetoric of the children and family coming first. So I get very annoyed seeing my male colleagues racing ahead because they have got this woman, and I would joke and say I wished I had a secretary and a wife.

In addition to the pressures exerted on women by economic and demographic imperatives for population maintenance and nation building, women are embedded in another layer of cultural politics that has been suitably tailored by the state to balance and sustain Asian traditions and values with western free-market notions such as competitive individualism and meritocratic equality. Next I look at women's role within the construct of "Asian values" in the context of filial responsibility, one of Singapore's five legislated Core Family Values.

"ASIAN VALUES" AND CULTURAL HEGEMONY

Singapore is a multicultural and multiracial society, populated by three distinct cultural groups: Chinese (76%), Malay (15%), and Indian (6.5%). A labor shortage brings in large numbers of guest workers from Malaysia, Indonesia, Sri Lanka, India and Bangladesh, and the Philippines who collectively comprise 20% of the workforce. Senior- and middle-management posts in the private and public sectors are held primarily by Chinese. As noted earlier, eight of the nine women in this study were ethnic Chinese. The position and experiences of women in higher education, therefore, must be considered in light of the ideological narratives, cultural values, and social practices of this location-specific diaspora of Chinese culture and Confucian value system (Cheng & Katz, 1998; Kuo, 1987). I asked the women how Chinese cultural values and tradition, transformed and reinvented within a paradigmatic showcase of western capitalism, might influence women's experiences, opportunities, and interpretations. Once we got through the obligatory rhetoric about individual motivation, skills, and aspirations within what most women unproblematically accepted as a race- and gender-blind meritocracy—"Women can do almost anything in Singapore . . . if they demonstrate that they have the capability, the intelligence and the expert knowledge"—several women explained how traditional cultural values mediate Singaporean gender politics:

- "The Confucian bind, it's used against you and it colors both men and more insidiously women's attitudes. So like talking vehemently is seen to be very unwomanly. You are not being the typical Asian woman."
- "I think there is some element which says, yes, if you are to be a filial daughter, you give in, even if it's at an inconvenience to yourself, and that creeps into my relationship with my parents and the workplace."
- "It exists in all three cultures; there's still this thing about having a son is a wonderful thing. People say 'Oh, a boy, how wonderful, how lucky you are' and so on."
- "Indian men can be very patriarchal. Malay men can be very, very demanding. But actually, in Islamic religion, men and women are equal. But the men interpret it differently."

The gendering of orientalism (Lewis, 1993) is embedded in what several women noted as the value of filial piety and responsibility, the self-sacrificing stereotype of Asian femininity, and the identity politics of "face." As one woman put it:

Women are the self-sacrificing ones, holding the family together, and these women in Asian society are held out as heroines. So that is giving up the self for the good of society, and you hope that your children will become good citizens of tomorrow. But the price is your own self-fulfillment and your own happiness, and you seek it vicariously in your children. And woe behold, because if your children don't turn out well . . .

Filial piety applies to both women and men in terms of respect and life-long responsibility for family elders. Yet the actual and emotional caring work for the elderly, although the formal and financial responsibility of the first son, is considered the work of daughters and daughters-in-law:

> I live with her [mother] because it's a very convenient arrangement, and she would say "My son has never even thought of providing me with a house or a home, but you have done that and I am so glad that I have a daughter who could feel that way." So it's cultural—it's daughters who would do that for their mothers.

Among the five legislated key family values of Singapore, filial responsibility, only recently changed from filial piety, is ranked third after love, care and concern, and mutual respect, followed by commitment and communication (Ministry of Community Development, 1995). *Singapore's Family Values* (Ministry of Community Development, 1996) is a skillfully balanced "composite of 'Asian' traditional and 'Western' middle class elements [that] resonate with the core values of the family within the Confucian social system"—but sufficiently "deethnicised" to "make it acceptable to a multi-ethnic population" (Hill & Lian, 1995, p. 155).

However, in real terms, filial responsibility in Singapore exerts a different cost for men and women: Men may provide the financial means, but it is women who provide the routine day-to-day social and emotional care and support for aging parents and kin. In that regard, this core moral value reinforces the need for women to have the time, or make the time if they are in full-time employment, to nurture and care for both old and young.

> The reigning patriarchal notion today in Singapore is that the so-called Asian "traditional relationship" of male superiority as head of family and female subordination is the factor which holds families together, prevents the divorce rate from climbing and children being neglected. The woman's role is clear: she must be a martyr to hold the family together; if not, she is the scapegoat for its falling apart. (Koh, 1996, p. 30)

In the domestic sphere, women's success is measured by her ability to raise "successful" children; to marry "well" and make marriage a success; to manage servants, finances, and infrastructural support for all family members; and to craft herself as a valuable asset to the family. In the workplace, women's career success is dependent on the careful crafting of traditional Asian femininity in self-representation and public image and negotiating male/female power relationships. As one woman explained:

> She dresses beautifully, femininely, her hair is very feminine, she's always beautifully made up, wears high heels, and she is a manager, absolutely feminine like any tai-tai (society woman), very gently focused, and she is not threatening because she maintains this femininity. Many women here believe that, 'Oh, we will be the women behind the men,' you know. They [men] always pay us this compliment, that behind every successful man is a woman, so long as the woman stays behind, right, and out of sight. Two steps behind or the hand that rocks the cradle rules the world. *They pay us in compliment what they deny us in power.* [emphasis added]

POLITICS OF FACE
AND PATRONAGE BONDS

"We will be the women behind the men!" Social hierarchies everywhere position women as secondary and "behind the men." But in Singapore, cultural expectations of feminine propriety and the politics of face immobilize women's voices and initiative in quite extraordinary ways. The assertive woman who tables new ideas, challenges a senior male or female, or argues a point in public, such as at a committee forum, can easily cause her seniors and herself to lose face: "If you bring up a good idea in the meeting . . . it can be seen to be oppositional, because the head sees it as 'she is making trouble again, bringing up this view' and then you are seen negatively." Hence, common practice is to introduce new ideas or challenge old ones in private with relevant players before issues get tabled in public committee or meeting sessions. "When you do it behind [closed doors] or after [meetings], you have only your own view and the head's view and it is not fair because all the other people are not in the picture and you get favored treatment or it's a way of insinuating yourself" or "currying favour." What this means is that nothing much happens at committee level, for it is there that the status quo is reproduced, ideas are not debated or contested: "Our boss . . . meets with the smaller group and already preempts the discussion, so we go in there [meeting], and there's not going to be any confrontation," This practice denies women opportunities to develop and demonstrate presentational and argumentation skills, and to articulate and take public credit for innovative ideas:

> I find that women do most of the hard work and men take the credit. You do all the hard work for the men and then he's using all your hard work, legwork, he presents it and looks good. He makes it his and he looks good. They take credit for it and then you are out of the picture.

But denying women opportunities to demonstrate initiative in public is also a way of eliminating competition or threats to one's position of security:

> You don't allow anyone to rise up because what you do is that you encourage them to speak to you quietly, and then you take the ideas and say it at a meeting and present it as yours, so you gain in authority and the other person doesn't gain credit. Women are encouraged to do that because here women are shyer, not so forthcoming, and if you were a clever man, you get this woman for a drink, invite her as part of a group, sit down and talk to her and just get all her ideas.

For women in senior positions, threats to self-confidence, control, or security of position can mean that they resist open, transparent, and collaborative managerial strategies. From the focus group, this comment:

> It could be that women tend to be a little more insecure and not willing to take risks, so they adopt this talking *at* people to safeguard themselves from the unexpected, because if they open it to all, they have to feel completely comfortable and trusting. They might feel it is safer to control the parameters of the conversation, preempting so that they won't go into waters that they have not fought in.

Cultural rules of propriety and decorum expect that women raise ideas as part of team collaborations, or else in private, usually with senior males, who then tend to take those ideas as their own in public forums where any contestation from a subordinate, especially if it is a woman, is virtually impossible given the rule of face:

- "In the west at meetings, people are far more frank . . . they can better separate personal from professional. Here in a meeting, you wouldn't want to argue too much with your boss because you would be seen as undermining his credibility or in a way making him lose face. The tendency is to try and understate, or to hide."

- "The thing about Singapore is that you put society or the group above the self. So the tendency is that it is seen as a virtue to contribute as a team and work towards the institution. But the credit goes to the head of the institution or department, and then it remains for how generous he is in sharing the credit he receives."

The politics of face and informal systems of patronage are deeply embedded in a hierarchical social structure and "grounded in a selective refiguration of Confucianism to promote the interests of the state" (Heng & Devan, 1992, p. 351). In one woman's view, "it comes right from top down, from government right down." Thus, the state has managed to combine traditional cultural value systems with postindustrial capitalist values of individualism and personal aspirations, and claims that it has resulted in phenomenal economic growth "accompanied by good social development."

> Singapore operates on a patriarchal basis, with male supremacy as the accepted norm. The political and social culture is male-dominated and influenced by a hierarchical Confucian ideology. The economic role of women is crucial to the country but patriarchal attitudes play this down and women are thus burdened with responsibilities of work and home. This mismatch between economic reality and the traditional expectations of men and society affects the aspirations of women, their quality of life, and the choices available to them to maximize their potential. (Soin, 1996, p. 206)

The basis of women's promotional prospects, therefore, is less likely to be visible performance and more likely to be invisible contributions to one's senior, which with few exceptions tends to be a male. If women can balance loyalty and invisible "behind closed doors" help to senior males with initiative and hard work within "an Asian sense of what it means to be womanly," then "they can rise." But here, too, a double standard exists, as two women explain:

- "We are caught between two things: one, society tends to be authoritarian and hierarchical . . . and male, and the other is that women are supposed not to come across very strongly. So you hold back, you know, for not wanting to offend your superiors. And then you feel that both he and you are caught within this cultural and sociopolitical context. So it is doubly hard to operate. And secondly, also, you tend to feel that if you are there at all and got these positions, it was some male who recommended you or promoted you . . . so there is a sense of obligation and loyalty."

- "I've seen it over and over again with women who are so loyal . . . in secretaries, in my own colleagues. They are so loyal to these male heads, they will do anything for them simply because he is so nice to them and so on. But they don't get promoted because they are never in a position to threaten the men in power. There's something Asian behind it as well. It's Asian and an Asian sense of what it means to be womanly or to be female . . . woman as being self-sacrificing."

The difficulty with informal patronage, is that the politics of loyalty and obligation tend to immobilize initiative and action for change, once the person "groomed" is in a leadership position:

- "The one who grooms the other and then moves down to another position, expects loyalty from the one who has been groomed, and if that loyalty is not forthcoming, it's like you have not been worthy of the patronage and guiding."
- "It causes a lot of problems for those in the department because you have to be loyal to the one who has gone or stepped down and to the one who has just been appointed."
- "It can cause a real problem because someone who is newly appointed is not expected to flex her muscles and go her own way from the start. She is supposed to do what she has been groomed to do and carry out almost like proxy for someone who has left the seat and who wants to keep control of it."

There are two issues at stake here: ability and opportunity. Ability, the careful balancing of achievements, managerial and administrative skills within a cultural value system that has specific expectations for women's conduct, is set against the rhetoric of meritocratic opportunity, which at its core is a system of personal sponsorship through (primarily) male patronage. Opportunity, therefore, can be haphazard, accidental, linked to personal and influential contacts and carefully cultivated relationships, and being in the right place at the right time. Visible goalposts for academic promotion such as extensive research and publications, external grant and service record, are the same in Singapore as in the west. However, the goalposts for promotion to senior management are much more covert, tied as they are to the more nebulous politics of patronage and social hierarchies, of "superior" and "subservient." Women need to self-promote on a much more personal, social, and emotional level of managing colleagues, seniors, their own image, and public perceptions of their image and behaviors:

> You are ever conscious of hurting other people's feelings, conscious of being thought of negatively; you want to be thought of highly, and if those are the terms, then you have to know when to pull back. And if you are loyal and supportive of the males, particularly the male superior, if he plays his cards well, he's very nice to you.

Finally, the women recounted incidents that had a decidedly familiar ring and seem to transcend cultural specificity: Men and women downgrading and invalidating women's status, presence, achievements, and abilities. These strategies of actual and symbolic subversion are evident in countless western studies on women in management, and some mirrored my own experiences:

- "[My friend] she was a surgeon, and she's saying like she was ready to cut and the prof comes in and says 'How are you doing honey?' and it immediately undermines her—her complete image."
- "[My former boss] he refused to address me as 'Doctor.' Even on a recent invitation for a formal occasion . . . he would only address me without any prefix, he just put down my first and last name. He refused to introduce me."
- "We were interviewing this candidate, and she is pregnant, and this woman [on the selection panel] says, 'This is a problem because you are pregnant, you know, we will have to take that into account.' I really think that's kind of jarring, coming from a woman."

CAREER ASPIRATIONS

I asked all the women about their initial career plans on entering postgraduate studies and starting their first jobs. As with the Thai women, few claimed to have had career aspirations beyond becoming teachers in schools or lecturers in tertiary institutions. Only one woman, now teaching management, claimed she had wanted to be a lawyer but got "sidetracked into teaching." For all the women, moving into middle- and senior management posts "just happened" in a haphazard way: "No I didn't aspire to it at all." The opportunities were there, the sponsorship or patronage by mentors had been enabling, and many of the women had demonstrated administrative capabilities at more junior levels. One woman's initial career aim was to go into academics to "do good academic work, to write my books, my articles, and I wanted to make a statement, to make sure that a Southeast Asian perspective was put on the agenda." Now, she can't wait for her term to conclude:

> I fully intend to see this as a short-term thing . . . I am due for sabbatical, and I fully intend to go back to academic work. If I were a superwoman, I would do both, but I can't, and I would have to make a choice. At the end of the day, I want to be an academic, doing academic work, and that's what I want to go back to.

One department head was adamant that "I don't want this job and I am stepping down . . . .. I don't want it because my life is more than my academic life. I don't want paperwork. I hate paperwork." Another department head who is nearing retirement planned to "step down as head and then I can concentrate, spend more time doing the kind of things I like, like writing. Now, no time. I am nearing retirement and frankly I am not that ambitious." Another woman in her early 50s was also "satisfied to step down. I don't want to go any higher, I don't want to go any further."

With the exception of one woman, who had been appointed as department head only months prior to our interview, all the other women claimed to have no further career aspirations for more senior posts. All claimed that the work was too consuming, leaving them little time for teaching and/or research, or a private life. Several of the women were well into their late 40s and early to mid-50s and were looking forward to retirement (compulsory retirement age had recently changed from 55 to 60 for women). A department head said she looked forward to devoting all her time to fundraising for regional development projects for girls in Thailand, Cambodia, and Laos. These women had worked hard over many years to get credentialed, published, and promoted up the ranks through sponsorship or patronage politics while balancing a range of complex family responsibilities. Yet in the end, none had ambitions to push on to more senior ranks.

Some considered that the demands, expectations, and politics imping-ing on women holding senior positions would impact negatively by exam-ple on younger women's career aspirations. As one woman put it:

> They think what more do I get if I move one step higher? What for? I don't want to have more wrinkles and more white hair. I want to enjoy my life, you know, and having that extra added responsibility and recog-nition, to most women, it really doesn't matter so much. So it easily turns to that invisible self-defeating type of mentality.

On the other hand, lack of aspirations "could be the women themselves" because "we are our own enemies in that sense that we don't want to go that high. If you are a mother, a wife, you still have responsibility to your family, and if you get too involved in public life, your life's not your own." Women also underestimate their abilities: "Some of them do not want it. They think they are not able to do it, although they are most able." Other women are seen to "take the easy way out":

- "I find a lot of women say that my husband is bringing home the bread, you know, why do I want the hassle. I love my children and I have an eas-ier way out, I don't want to run that extra mile, or put in that extra effort."
- "Women want to have afternoon tea with the girlfriends, gossip, go for hairdressers, you know, watch fashion shows, to them that is living. They say 'I don't have the hassle in the office, the stress and competi-tiveness.'"

Following discussions about career paths and aspirations, I asked about differences between male and female concepts of career success. On this issue, all the women agreed. For men, I was told, success is a well-paying position that provides career path opportunities, confers power and high status, and it usually doesn't matter where the job is. Women, on the other hand, see success as "seeing a project through," "implementing the idea or project" all the way, "making sure all the detail is taken care of." Western women have a more "open sense of career than men" because they make more relational choices: Their decisions are "life choices and not just career choices" (Marshall, 1994, p. 318). Singaporean women aren't that different. They are reluctant to relocate to jobs outside Singapore because of concerns over their children's education, and because they would find it difficult living away from (parental) family: "Now I complain, but I would really miss them." But then, issues of whether women should relocate because of employment opportunities, expecting husbands to give up jobs and follow them, are the exception, not the rule.

Success, then, clearly means different things for men and women, although most claimed that "you can't stereotype . . . all women are this and all men are that." Women were generally considered to be more focused on detail (concerns about staff, gathering and organizing information, applying or implementing procedures), on the immediacy of project tasks and deadlines, and on procedures and successful completion. In women's view, men are more focused toward open-ended, big picture issues, on "helicopter views" or open-ended career paths. As one woman said, men can afford to be more concerned with long-term goals, larger objectives, and more interested in "big picture issues because they have the women to help them do the detailed work."

WOMEN'S MANAGEMENT
AND LEADERSHIP STYLES

Responses were mixed to my question about differences between women's and men's management and leadership styles. Some claimed women are better managers because "they have more information, take greater interest in the small things, staff issues," and that women "negotiate more," "discuss more and are less decisive in the sense of a coming to a quick decision." Women are seen as having a more inclusive and consensual leadership style, drawing on staff resources, needs and aspirations, and staff input in the development of policies and procedures.

- "I find among my male colleagues that they tend to be more authoritarian and the women more consultative. The men are very domineering. They feel that they are in charge, and they are very reluctant to let women come in and take part."
- "Women are less egoistic. They give off their ideas far more generously. Men I think are far more calculating because they have been so geared up to be competitive."
- "I suppose we have this feminine touch, more caring, more sensitive to our subordinates' feelings. Men normally don't bother so much about these things. Women are more people-centered in their approach, but I also have this female boss who is . . . you know what I mean?"

Women's preoccupation with detail, however, can work against them:

> We need to get everything sort of perfect. Men seem to be much more
> laid back. After having talked about the big picture, they sit back and
> have a good laugh over a beer or whatever while women are still work-
> ing in the office until wee hours in the morning to make sure all the i's
> are dotted and the t's are crossed. Male subordinates to female leaders,
> managers, they feel very frustrated because the role is reversed and they
> are the ones who have to carry through all the details for the woman
> boss. That's where the notion of the finicky woman boss comes in
> because she insists that everything is all right . . . but my colleagues
> would rather be out having a beer with friends.

On the other hand, some women noted that when women in senior positions do not conform to stereotypical expectations of feminine leadership
or management styles and, instead, perform a traditional male model, that
too can work against them: "She was very proper. She didn't do the usual
thing of being housekeeper, and she wasn't popular that way. People say
she lacks the human touch or that she's not very friendly. She was very,
very proper. Never ever go behind anyone's back." Contrary to these perspectives, women's consultative and collaborative style was seen by one
woman as the management model of the future:

> The style that women use now—it's the style of the future. That more
> consensus approach, collaborative management, teamwork, and consid-
> ering the feelings of your employees, their needs and their interests. Men
> have always operated on the patriarchal, hierarchical style of manage-
> ment which I think is becoming obsolete in this day and age. That's
> where women have the edge on the future. I think that hierarchical,
> patriarchal style is going away.

Several women commented that, although women were generally seen as
better managers and leaders, they are much more difficult to work for
because they tend to be much harder on other women:

- "I find it easier to work with men who are my age or older than women
  who are my age or older. Women give me harder time than men."
- "Everyone that I have encountered so far prefers working with a male
  boss. They feel they are less—shall I say, small minded."

SUPPORTING WOMEN

A week earlier, the Thai women had alluded to tensions and lack of support among academic women. In Singapore, I was surprised at the women's repeated references to tensions, rivalry, and lack of support among women: "Women here do not support other women" and they "tend to gossip." "The small talks, unnecessary criticism, the nonsupport offered by the females toward each other, it is so devastating that it is very, very sad." Women were brutally candid in their estimation of other women:

- "It's women-women, in fact, it's more ugly when it's women-women."
- "If a woman is at the top, you don't find things any better. They are worse."
- "The older women are like the men, you know. Old women are like old men."
- "Simply because women are in power does not mean they will be automatically supportive of other women. I find they are not that supportive."

Several of the married and all of the single women told me that they refuse to engage in "chit-chat" with their female colleagues because "of the gossip" that often transforms innocuous comments into backbiting and potentially subversive rumor-mongering:

> I don't mix socially partly because it may give rise to talk. I'd feel quite conscious if I have lunch too often with my male deans. I just avoid it. I can't be very jolly and go "let's have lunch" too often. There's certain things that socially women can't do, proprieties they call them, and I feel that has held me back . . . because this is an Asian society. I think you are more liberal and freer in the west in terms of male/female relationships; it's not true here.

The problem with and consequences of gossip are particularly dangerous in a small academic community such as Singapore with only a handful of women in high-ranking and publicly visible positions. Three partnered women commented:

- "There's a lot of gossiping that goes around, which is very sad. I think women should rally together. Sometimes I find it's very lonely because I steer away from all these and I try to cut myself off. I never stand at any-body's desk or stand at the corridor . . . I don't sit in the canteen or the staff restaurants. I don't listen to any gossip and cut myself off from all these."

- "In my personal and private life, for example, working with a lot of women, I don't like to engage in gossip. It's not that I don't see women, we do, but I try to avoid any kind of gossiping, otherwise I find that emo-tionally it wears you down."

- "Once you reach the so-called top in an organization, you have to just turn yourself off from a lot of gossip and a lot of unnecessary human entanglement. I feel at times, it is very cold up there, you will have to distance yourself in that regard."

The "chilly climate" at the top coupled with women's perceptions that they need to "cut myself off," "turn yourself off," "distance yourself" is remark-able testimony to self-directed isolation and is antithetical to western femi-nist strategies that promote networking and coalition building among women. For single women, there is additional isolation as the pressure of propriety in maintaining an untainted public image is a powerful influence in shaping their professional and personal relations and public lives:

- "Oh, I never would dare to bring anybody. I would never dare to bring anyone as an escort or just somebody to go to a function with me; the whole town will talk."

- "If you are a single or divorced woman, and that's my public image, it is extremely difficult for another woman or man to accept. In the west, you can keep a boyfriend, you can go out and socialize, there may still be whispers, but in the west people tend to accept that you can have a social life without affecting the public image, but not in Singapore. If you are single, you go out with another single man, that is being talked about; immediately there will be a lot of small talk."

Drawing back from other women for fear of wrongful gossip is not the way to build strong women's networks. However, given the prevalence of informal patronage for career advancement, there is often "suspicion among women as well as men in this oriental society" of how positions are "meritocratically" achieved or granted on the basis of obligation, loy-alty, or connection. This creates divisions among women:

- "They think that something hanky-panky is going on, [that] you have been given that position as a token woman [or] because your husband is so and so. But if you made it on your own and suddenly are placed in this glamorous position, then there is suspicion. My appointment here, again there is talk, probably she knows so and so. And this happens to women in our position, and it can be very devastating, and so as we are striving for career independence, there isn't this support or respect given to you by other women."

- "If I were seen with another single or male person, then immediately there will be whispers . . . there's always this perception that if you manage to get ahead, you know here, you must have had a godfather."

One study titled *Successful Women in Singapore* (Low, 1993) noted that "the ability to withstand loneliness at the top is also important" for women to succeed in senior positions. I asked the women whether they feel professionally and socially isolated in contexts where many of them are the only woman, or among only a handful of women, in executive positions in their institutions. I asked them whom they turn to for advice and support when they are faced with problems. None claimed to turn to other women in similar positions either within their own or other institutions because it might signal their inability to cope and deal with issues and things might be taken the "wrong way." One women stated, "I have always found help outside the institution because one of the things I found that within the institution there is rivalry between women." Most said they turn to husbands or personal friends to talk things through.

GENDER EQUITY INITIATIVES

Usually this part of our conversation turned to discussion of whether the women thought institutionalized equity audits, gender equity policies, and/or gender equity units would be beneficial to university women, and whether formal and/or informal women's networks or programs existed in their institution. Several of the women suggested that such initiatives might be important in the west but would be rejected by both male and female academics in Singapore. Most of the women had studied either in the United Kingdom, the United States, Canada, or Australia in the last decade and were familiar with affirmative action and equal opportunity legislation in the west, but none saw any need for such programs in Singapore institutions. Mentoring, I was told, is something that women do anyway, although I was told later by the women in the focus group that they knew of no women in their institution who were either mentors or mentees.

As noted, mentoring in Singapore is more about informal sponsorship and patronage, or "grooming," rather than a formalized system of induction and mentoring. Recognition, respect, and being thought of highly comes from "channeling responsibility" to the right people, which "will bring limelight." A revealing comment about women's reliance on informal patronage and the "reflected power and visibility" derived from association with influential senior staff comes from a recent study on 35 women in public sector management:

> These women had good supervisors who not only became their role models but also their mentors, and through them they gained recognition and promotion. Some worked under people who sponsored their promotions, i.e., superiors who recommended them for special projects. Where sponsors—influential figures in the organisation who help by speaking up for the sponsored—are necessary for men, they are *absolutely* necessary for women . . . by being associated with the sponsors they experienced a sense of reflected power or visibility. (Low, 1993, p. 35)

Percentage targets for female participation on university committees would also not find favor in Singapore because "it would divide the sexes" and wasn't necessary in a meritocratic system where, "if women have the skills, the education, and the will," success and achievement are guaranteed, regardless of sex:

- "Affirmative action is no good in the sense that it turns around and hits the women because the woman gets to the top, she feels diminished because she is up there, she got a job through affirmative action, not merit."
- "Yes, so it is a problem, and people say, "Yeah, you have got it because of your sex," and that doesn't do good for women."
- "Once you institutionalize something . . . you lose, women lose."
- "When you start getting too assertive, push things as women, it turns off a lot of people."

When I asked if, instead of formalized programs, perhaps informal support systems might be useful to enable dialogue among women, this too was considered inappropriate:

- "If you say 'dialogue' among women, it turns off a lot of women."
- "Once you say it is a meeting for women to discuss women's issue, it turns off men, it turns off women."

Women prefer to work behind the scenes. One woman recalled a recent effort to form a woman's group and "as soon as you say we must get power," the response is: "no, no, we prefer to work behind the scenes. We can do it in our own quiet way." Rather than "getting too assertive, push things in as women," the "Asian way" is a lot more subtle. It's about "talking over lunch, over meals, having meals together; it's a very cultural thing." A few women acknowledged that what is widely considered the Asian or feminine way of getting things done, asserting influence, or lobbying for change is in fact a model of political and organizational conduct prescribed and modeled by the government:

- "I think the government would prefer it if you did it in a gentler way."
- "That very traditional way of thinking comes right from the top down, from government right down."

At the close of the interviews, I gave all the women my own university's annual report on equity achievements and brochures on our Gender Equity Unit's functions, strategic goals, and range of programs for women and other equity target groups. I detected only marginal interest in this material or in considering such institutionalized support structures as relevant for Singaporean women. Despite their acknowledgment of glass ceilings, women's underrepresentation in senior management across the public and private sectors, women's various structural disadvantages under current law, gender equity initiatives under the mantle of any kind of affirmative action or equal opportunity legislation seemed "too political" and divisive for the women.

CONCLUDING REMARKS

Drawing on Bourdieu's (1988) work on academic power and capital in the French university system, Heward (1996) has argued that "any understanding of women in the academic profession has to examine the interaction of *structure* and *process*. There is no single barrier or 'glass ceiling' that can be shattered" (p. 17) [emphasis added].

The glass ceilings that women experience in Singapore are shaped by place-specific sociopolitical, economic, and cultural factors that are framed within a specific postcolonial legacy and do not fit neatly into the one-dimensional western conceptualization of glass ceilings as solely enacted by men or by a generalized patriarchy. And it is not only men, as the women revealed, who collude "to keep women down," who down-grade women or take credit for their ideas and work. Men *and* women enact career impediments. As the women testified, if "its women-women, it's more ugly" and often "worse." Over the years, many of my women friends and colleagues have shared similar stories but always in private. Yet western research on women and organizational cultures has been largely silent on tensions and conflicts among women (Itzin, 1994). This, I believe, has one-dimensionalized the concept of glass ceiling and, per-haps unintentionally, constructed a victim narrative around subjugated women and perpetrator men. Women's complicity in glass-ceiling politics seems to be a taboo subject. On this issue, however, the women in this study were candid and forthright, explaining why women self-select out at more junior ranks, and how senior women can misuse power and be just as divisive and unsupportive of women as men can be.

Western feminist studies on women and management consider men-toring and networking as crucial in facilitating women's career success. However, as the women in this study have shown, mentoring means dif-ferent things in different cultural contexts. Singaporean organizational culture and practices, while unmistakably male according to the women, is inflected with "the Confucian bind," with specific "Asian" values and ways of doing things. Thus, culturally specific expectations of women's conduct mediate academic women's conduct and relationships in the workplace and in public.

Career advancement for women (and men) is achieved through infor-mal patronage and successor grooming, which incur relationships built on dependency bonds of loyalty and obligation. The politics of loyalty and obligation further reinforce status and power differentiations between superior and subordinate which, when overlaid with the gender politics of "the so-called Asian traditional relationship of male superiority" (Koh, 1996, p. 30), suggests a very different, much more relational and histori-cally shaped, concept of career, career development, and aspirations. That is, it suggests a career trajectory strongly mediated by the need to craft and nurture relationships *over time* with potential and influential patrons. However, as the women explained, demonstrating long-term loyalty and self-sacrifice to one's senior is no guarantee of promotion. Yet once a posi-tion of power is attained, loyalty to one's sponsor and obligations for hav-ing been groomed remain powerful influences on future conduct, performance, and management decisions, because cultural norms and expectations require a retrospective "payback" of sorts: a demonstration of one's worthiness of patronage and consequent status attainment. The suspicions that arise from colleagues when women do achieve senior positions can further divide and isolate women.

In response to drafts of my paper that I sent all the women in this study, two replied saying they were "deeply saddened" to read what the women had said about the divisive state of affairs among women in academics. Some women still send me articles and booklets on feminist or higher-education issues. We meet at conferences in the region and in Australia, and continue to meet for lunch or dinner whenever I am in Singapore.

8

Hong Kong

Population	6.7 million
Languages English, Cantonese, Mandarin	
1998 UN Gender Empowerment Index ranking (out of 174)	25
Female combined primary-, secondary-, and tertiary-level gross enrollment ratio (1995)*	69.9%
Number of tertiary-level students (male and female) per 100,000 inhabitants (1996)	not available
Public universities—UGC funded†	8
Non-UGC-funded higher-education institutions	4
Gross enrollments (male and female, all levels), all UGC-funded higher education (1997–98)	150,000
Total full-time academic staff (male and female), all UGC-funded higher education (1997–98)	17,000
Public expenditure on education as percentage of GNP (1996)	2.9%

continued

*Expressed as a percentage of the population age group corresponding to the national regulations for these levels of education.

†University Grants Committee (UGC) is the funding body for public universities. Includes Open University of Hong Kong, Shue Yan College, Chu Hai College, Hang Seng School of Commerce. Excludes Hong Kong Academy for the Performing Arts, and Catholic and Christian theological universities and colleges.

Sources: University Grants Committee (1999), UNESCO Human Development Index (1998), UNESCO Statistical Yearbook (1998).

CONTEXT

The Hong Kong study was undertaken in September 1997, six weeks following the historic handover—or "return," from China's perspective—of rule from Britain to the People's Republic of China (PRC). Six weeks after this epochal event, people still seemed euphoric and somewhat invincible. That is, despite many comments tinged with concern and distrust of Beijing, people seemed convinced that Hong Kong's international stature, wealth, and strong economic base would weather any future political or economic storms. People readily talked politics, including the women in this study: from identity politics and Chinese "authenticity" to the "1997 question" and people's sense of place in a new order.

In the months leading up to the July 30th handover, the global media had given prominent coverage of many of Hong Kong's most senior public women, most notably Chief Administration Secretary Anson Chan and Secretary for Justice Elsie Leung. Other key women in the civil service to receive media attention included Secretary for Health and Welfare Katherine Fok, Secretary for Trade and Industry Denise Yue, Director of Immigration Regina Ip, and Chief Commissioner of the Independent Commission Against Corruption Lily Yam. Global networks such as CNN, BBC, ABN (Asia Business News, now CNBC) repeatedly profiled what one network called "the handbag brigade"—the upper female elite of the most senior officers in the new Special Administrative Region. The women I interviewed also consistently referred to these women as exemplars and evidence of the lack of glass ceilings in Hong Kong: "We do have large numbers of women leaders in the civil service; it demonstrates that women can get through those difficult parts." Several women gave me newspaper and magazine clippings they had saved for me featuring profiles of these senior female civil servants. But half a dozen high-profile women in a population of 6.7 million do not constitute overwhelming evidence to support arguments about the lack of glass-ceiling politics.

In Hong Kong, as in Singapore, Australia, or the United States, women have high rates of educational participation and outcomes and are making substantial inroads into high visibility, high-status positions in the private and public service sectors. Women's participation in Hong Kong higher education has been numerically equal to men since the postwar period, although "gender stereotypes are still reflected in enrolments for further and tertiary education courses" (Morris & Sweeting, 1995, p. 67). This has resulted in a persistent pattern of tertiary participation and outcomes that remain skewed along traditional gender lines: Women dominate enrollments in the arts and humanities, nursing, and education and remain underrepresented in the more traditional male fields of study, namely, medicine, engineering, science, and technology. Pipeline theories, therefore, may explain the lack of women in senior management in traditional male fields but fail to explain the dearth of women in senior positions in those disciplinary fields where women historically have dominated enrollments.

Women's domestic and family responsibilities are the most commonly cited career impediments, and double-day and dual-career conflicts are generally seen to subordinate women's career aspirations to a partner's career path. However, not all women are married and/or have children. Moreover, in Hong Kong as in Singapore, live-in domestic service is inexpensive and widely available. In the words of one dean, "it's common practice even among women who are only secretaries." Moreover, the cultural values placed on the care and integration of elderly kin into the family (deLeon & Ho, 1994) means that relatives and parents are expected to provide a fair share of child care. Arguably, household and family responsibilities cannot explain the dearth of women in senior positions in a context where live-in domestic help is affordable and widely used, and given that many women in middle and senior management are either single, widowed, divorced, or married without children.

"Asian" family structures and networks combine with the "residue of ancient root origins," which are blended with the legacies of diverse systems of colonial rule across Asia before, during, and after World War II (Yee, 1995). Although Asian traditions are not and never have been uniform across Buddhist, Confucian, Muslim, Christian, communist, and postcommunist Southeast Asia, today, especially in nation-states like Singapore and Hong Kong, they have combined with the sociopolitical ideologies and values of fast capitalism. Hence, western free-market notions of competitive individualism and meritocratic equality are woven within residual traditionally Confucian emphases on entrepreneurial familism (deLeon & Ho, 1994), utilitarian familism (Lau, 1997), and authoritarian paternalism (Yee, 1995). Yet Hong Kong's history as a British colony has circumvented the kinds of repressive governmentality and nationalist and nation-building ideological fervor that characterizes postcolonial states such as Singapore and Malaysia.

Over 150 years of British colonial rule have shaped such a distinctly British model of Hong Kong education that it is difficult to excavate whatever "original" or traditional Chinese values that might make Hong Kong education "culture specific" (Lau, 1997; Sweeting, 1993; 1995). What is culture specific to Hong Kong is its historically unique identity as a cultural hybrid. In terms of education, Chinese and British traditions have converged in a shared reverence for the educated person, and "in both cultures university status is the ultimate goal of education" (Yee, 1995, p. 47). Both cultures have historically placed high social and cultural value on the scholar-philosopher, but it appears that an academic profession today is not seen as a lucrative or high-prestige career choice.

Most of the women in this study, for instance, passed through the higher-education sector, first as students and later as junior staff, in an era when women's options were narrower than they are today. Their academic career success, and the impediments they encountered, must therefore be viewed in generational terms. The younger, 30-something women in this cohort face a very different mix of postfeminist choices and options in conjunction with residual traditional gender values. According to some of these women, the older generation of women who now hold senior positions embody many of those traditional values that are often said to be at the core of tensions among women. The career path struggles encountered by women who today are in their 50s and 60s are very different from what women in their 30s encounter in their ascent up the mobility ladder. However, across generations, academic women do face similar issues, such as the inescapable fact of biology and childbearing, cultural constructs that tie women to child care and childrearing, and women's position within enduring rules and practices of patriarchal power relations, institutional hierarchies, and academic cultures.

I had organized interviews with 13 women, of which 11 were able to see me at the time of my visit. All the women were ethnic Chinese and held positions as deans (one associate dean) and professorial department heads in faculties of science, medicine, accounting, social sciences, arts, and continuing education. They were located at the University of Hong Kong, The Chinese University of Hong Kong, Hong Kong Baptist University, City University of Hong Kong, and Hong Kong Polytechnic University. The youngest woman was 34 and the oldest 67; four women were in their 40s and five in their 50s. Eight women were married and three were single (two unmarried and one widowed). The two youngest women were unmarried and had no children. All the married women had children; seven women had school-aged and adult children living with them. The children's ages ranged from 6 to 24. All children over 21 were either attending or had completed tertiary education. Ten women listed Ph.D.'s as their highest degrees (most from the United Kingdom), and one had an MD. Eight women had full-time live-in maid service, two had regular part-time help, and only one had no hired help.

I began by asking about the disparity between the relatively large number of high-ranking women in public office and the lack of women in senior management positions in higher education. Was there a particularly pernicious set of glass ceilings in universities that restricted women's academic mobility? Considering the kind of affordable domestic help available in Hong Kong—a support system women in the west would envy—why has that not translated into enabling conditions to enhance women's career aspirations and mobility? Why have women's high educational achievement levels not produced more women in executive levels in the university sector? I found the concept of glass ceilings an appropriate entry point into conversations, because it was a widely understood concept about which women had very strong feelings. All the women had studied and some had worked overseas for extended periods, and all were familiar with the concept of glass ceilings, western debates about affirmative action and equal opportunity, and with versions of western feminism.

PIPELINE TRICKLE:
THE COMPETING PRIVATE SECTOR

All the women's initial responses invoked the pipeline theory: There are not enough qualified women coming through the system. Although I was familiar with the history of Hong Kong education, most of the women gave me a thumbnail history sketch as a prelude to their pipeline explanations. Generational differences figured prominently in all the women's observations. For example: "Back in the '50s, a lot of the girls' schools did not teach science or did not teach it well, and for admission into medicine you need science. . . . In my days, there were so few ladies [in university] and we were treated 'ladies first,' that sort of thing, even in clinical settings."

The generation of women now in their late 40s and 50s, who had gone through higher education and postgraduate studies in the 1960s (one woman in the 1950s), comprised in their day an elite group of privileged women. One woman sums up what many told me:

> If you look back, in Hong Kong and China, if there is a choice, because of limited resources, they only send the son to get an education and the girls always stay home to take care. So education was always more male dominated. Later, there were few females got into higher education. They're from families that are very much open and westernized and well-to-do. Women in the 1930s, '40s, '50s, their parents or grandparents may have had outside influences, so the girls of that generation got the equal opportunity to go into universities.

However, when I challenged their pipeline theory by pointing out women's long-standing educational achievement rates in Hong Kong (Suen, 1995), they readily granted that Hong Kong indeed has a long British tradition of meritocratic schooling, that women for several decades now have graduated with higher degrees at virtually the same rate as men across most faculties (except traditional feminine fields such as arts, humanities, nursing, and education), and that women by and large are better students than men: "You know, women always do work better." But why then don't they pursue a career in higher education? Two women alluded to a "diverted pipeline" of qualified women as part of the "brain drain" exodus related to the 1997 question. In higher education and the private sector, change had been underway "since 1984, and after that many people emigrated—a brain drain you call it" but "we now get the reverse brain drain. We get a lot of Chinese returning from North America, from the U.K." Another woman in her 30s explained the lack of senior women as part of the brain drain, a missing generation of women:

> A lot of people have left the university because of 1997. Most of our administrators, quite a lot of senior ones who are women, they have all left. Where is this generation? We don't see them—women in their 40s. That was the generation that has been most impacted by the 1997 question, and a lot of them actually left. So there is actually a very small pool of available and qualified women.

Similar to comments made by women I interviewed in Singapore, most of the Hong Kong women saw the private sector as a more lucrative career choice for today's young women graduates. Women, I was told, can make a lot more money going into business or industry: "The Hong Kong ethos is, after all, to make money." As one dean put it, "Women tend not to spend so many years in preparing for a career. You need only a first degree to join the private sector and the public sector." Further, Hong Kong men make "big money," which means that

> Women don't all need to work. They will work for a while to have some money to shop and travel; many have boyfriends who they will probably marry and who are already making a lot of money, or they will have very good incomes in a few years. So the women, they don't look at careers too seriously. I mean they want careers but not for the long haul.

Another woman said that "the young women, they want to be DINKs [double income, no kids], and for those incomes you have to go into business, not education." Because parents often still feel ambivalent about daughters continuing past undergraduate education, "a lot just don't go into it, and that's why you have a small pool of women at this level. A lot of women at my age are out in the private sector." The notion of a diverted pipeline into the private sector accounts, in part, for the limited flow of qualified women into higher-education administration and management. But for graduate women who do stay the course in academics, there are other reasons why they experience difficulties breaking down closed doors and opportunities.

ISOLATION

Isolation, long hours for relatively few rewards other than intrinsic job satisfaction, lack of female role models and support systems, and pressures to postpone marriage or children, were reasons the women repeatedly noted. Isolation had a lot do with women finding themselves as the only woman, or among only a small number of women, at senior levels: "Men are not used to having the only woman. In my time I was the only senior woman in the university." Once a senior position is reached and "you are the only woman on a committee where there has never been a woman before, you feel a lot of pressure. What will she say, how will she act, can we trust her?" Another woman felt that "if you are the first one in that position, a lot of people suddenly don't treat you like an old colleague, but they speak formal and friendly with you, not like before, and so you feel isolated because you never know if they are saying what they really mean." Stereotyped expectations of female behaviors can also make women feel isolated:

> Because I'm a woman, and the first one to hold this position, I think many men expect me to act in a certain way, but that's not me. They know I am outspoken, but now in this position, it is expected that I act more like a good Chinese girl, like their wives, their secretaries, or their daughters.

Several women also claimed that, although they did not feel any formal exclusion from the old boys' club, there were things such as talk about sports or "coarse language" that were part of a male code and made them feel excluded and isolated. "It's there all the time. You notice it but try to ignore it, but because it's there all the time in the way they joke and talk, you sort of sit there and think, 'Yes, it's hard to get into the boys' club, but who wants in?'" Male attention to women's appearance rather than intellect is another strategy that isolates and trivializes women, and makes them feel devalued and visible for all the wrong reasons. One woman explains in detail:

> If you ask the males in this university, they would tell you that there is no discrimination. It is this unconscious situation that allows them to have a [glass] ceiling . . . so they unconsciously discriminate [against] you. They refer to the secretaries about how they dress and you are the only senior woman in the room! I consider it quite rude that they tell jokes about other women, and when they approach you, they don't respect you as their colleague. They say, "Oh, you dress very nice today," which has nothing to do with me coming to the meeting. You can be in a meeting, giving the same kinds of proposals and ideas, but if it is coming from you, they don't consider it much. But if the colleague is a man, then everybody thinks it is a good idea.

Several women felt that they had to work twice as hard as men to gain respect, recognition, and approval.

- "I think it's because they don't know how to judge me now that I'm no longer simply an assistant dean, or in charge of postgraduate students, or something like that. And they don't know how to show approval or respect like they do with each other. I mean, they don't come and ask me to come for a drink or something like that. They can't slap me on the back, but they do it to each other."

- "Although it hasn't happened to me, I think men notice each other more as equals, but they notice women more for being nice, or attractive, or smart *and* attractive. It's difficult to be noticed as an intellectual equal, and if you are, men can feel more threatened by it. So you don't get noticed and appreciated, or rewarded in the same way, and so you work even harder."

Women's sense of invisibility, the lack of recognition and appreciation for what they perceived as doing twice the work of their male counterparts, was a common theme. Another woman had this to say:

For years I stayed late to do the paperwork, and I know my male colleagues just got their secretaries to do their jobs. Me, I did all the work myself. I think women do that: pay attention to all the detail. But I often thought I work much harder and longer hours but the men somehow get the better positions offered first; like important committee posts or things like that which later get you the big promotions.

But women's sense of isolation within a predominantly male institutional culture is only one, albeit common, form of isolation women can experience. Differences in cultural and linguistic backgrounds can also dislocate women (and undoubtedly men as well). For example, two Taiwanese women alluded to occasional feelings of social dislocation and isolation: not being able to fully and fluently participate in Cantonese conversations although "I understand what is being said"; being fluent in Mandarin, which is "good for doing [academic] business in China" yet not being considered as "authentic" Hong Kong Chinese therefore to represent the institution. In the cultural-historical context of Hong Kong, where the "majority of the population has always been Chinese but brought up under a colonial regime," issues of "authenticity"—who is really Chinese?—have been brought into new relief with the 1997 question. It is tied up with the ideological downgrading of Cantonese, with shifts in perceptions and cultural valuation of a foreign education, and with subtle changes in the hierarchical ordering of authenticity among the Chinese diaspora of the region as Hong Kong's political and cultural status slips from British to PRC rule. In one woman's view, "right now I think there is some confusion, some fear and anxiety of the mainland—of the politics and cultural influence—and how we should make our identity. It is complicated."

FAMILY

All the women saw marriage and children as the most important career-impediment and career-choice issues facing women. Women talked about having "to space the children out carefully," and "to fit the different things in at different times in your life; men don't have to do that." As one woman put it, "The 7-day week, 8 a.m. to 9 p.m., I can only do it now because my children are grown up." One woman in her late 40s with a six-year-old child had postponed having her first child, which was a "career-based decision." Unlike private sector careers, in academics "you have to go through 10 or more years of studying after you leave school, then you start from a lecturer position and slowly move your way up. It is a difficult choice to give that up and stop to raise a family." For women in medicine, the road is even longer:

> A medical degree will take you five years, then you are 23, one-year internship is 24, and specialty training at least three years after you pass the first examination, which would make 26, 27. If you don't pass the first examination, add more years. By the time you finish, you are almost 30 years old. Then you need to devote time to getting established in your first posting. Most medical women marry after 30 and have children even later, some in their early 40s. Medical women are better paid so they can have more than one Filipina maid and that helps.

On the other hand, as several women commented

- "Raising children is not a must today."
- "Women can choose not to have children."
- "Women today have choice, unlike the previous generation."

Several women saw women's opportunities and career aspirations in generational terms. The older generation, women in their 40s and 50s, came of age and through the academic system at a time when higher education was seen to diminish women's marriage opportunities: "For that generation, you go to university, then you have to work first, you have to get a master's degree, and all that would in some ways damage your marriage prospects as you get older, more educated, but less 'marriageable.'" One woman, part of the new generation, mentioned that her "mother refused to speak to me for six months when I decided to do a Ph.D. because she was concerned about me finding a husband." For the older generation, according to two of the youngest women in this group, a different kind of patronage system operated to channel women through the system. In that culture,

> your intelligence and appearance mattered a great deal. A lot had to do with looks. Women climbed up because they belonged to a patronage system which is run by men; they all graduated together, and that generation of men they prefer women like a nice-looking secretary, starting with a tea-maker. And then you climb up, so there is a lot of that in the traditional hierarchy where looks count. The adornment factor. For academic women, it's been that. Thankfully, that has changed.

That generation produced what one woman called "academic tai-tais"— academic "society ladies" who climbed the academic and social ladder through "old networks of my parents' generation'" who "dressed up," and sat on all the "right charity boards, went to all the right social functions. Oh they can be ruthless." Although "thankfully, that has changed," there are enduring cultural factors that maintain strong gender divisions of labor and roles, and what some called "a very Asian thing," "traditional values."

CULTURAL MINDSETS

Feminists in the west often denigrate women who choose to stay at home, to raise a family, to manage a household. However, in "Asian societies, it is considered a luxury, it is respected because it shows you are dedicated to the ideals of being a wife and mother, and it shows your husband can afford it. It is the poor women who go to work." One woman said, "I don't think there is as much pressure here as in the U.S., where there is a lot more pressure for women to become professionals, to work, and for those that don't, there is a certain guilt. But here they don't think that way." However, the cultural and ideological values associated with women and work and women as homemakers, are clearly class-based issues:

> It's a poverty issue in terms of whether women work and what work they do. It's a luxury to stay home if you have a wealthy husband; it's a luxury if you get a degree and work for a few years, and then marry and stay at home. But that's the upper and middle classes. Work and raising families is not a choice for poor women, but it is a choice for women from affluent backgrounds. So, it's different. The roles are different, the choices are different.

Others simply felt that

- "Hong Kong is still very much a male-dominated society, especially in the household."
- "It would be very unusual in Hong Kong for men to go home and help with the housework."
- "There are many traditional roles played by women in the middle-income level, and they still have to be much more submissive."

Repeatedly, however, women acknowledged the powerful cultural values that circumscribe women's role in the family in "Asian" or "Chinese" society. I will let one woman speak at length on this issue, for the issues she raised summarized many similar comments from the other women:

> For the eastern family, the Chinese society, there are lots of things to take care of by women: the relatives on the husband's side, or on the wife's side. You have to do a lot of things to show that you are polite, and respectful to the elderly. If it's the men or boys, people don't dare to criticize them or scold them, or not be too demanding of them. If you are a male, if you haven't paid too much attention to your mother's birthday or forgot someone else in the family, it's more acceptable than if you were a woman and forgot. If you have a wife, she should cater for everything, remember everything, note this or that. It's her job and it's a full-time job.

Culturally, "women's responsibility to have children, to raise them, to look after the parents, that is very important in Asian, particularly Chinese, culture." Parents still "want their married children to give them grandchildren, to carry the family name even if it's just symbolic and not about passing on wealth or property. But then even today, inheritance, especially in Hong Kong, is still a big thing." Producing a male heir remains an indirect pressure on women: "Having a boy used to be important in Chinese families. It is very important in China. Today we say it is not important in Hong Kong, but for many people it is still an issue. So that pressure is there indirectly for women." And despite the support of live-in help, women still "pay the price" of mothering:

> Most women still want to have children. It's important in Chinese society. And that means that you have to give up something. For women, it's the job. Even with maids, you still have to have the time to care for the

children, especially when they're young. Maids can cook, clean, take the children for walks or school, but only mothers can give the love, the nurturing. So, you have to walk away from your career for a while and then you miss out. You pay a price. If you choose not have children, you pay a price. If you have children, you pay a price.

Several women felt that rather than "any structural inequalities," which had long been eliminated in universities, the biggest impediments to women's academic career mobility were women's "mindset" and "the culture":

- "It's not the system. It's the mindset and also the culture because women are expected to care much more for the home and children. In academics, promotion depends very much on research, not teaching. And to do good research, you have to stay at the edge, go on sabbatical, go to conferences, network, and women find it very difficult to leave the family behind to go on sabbatical."
- "In Asian society, expectations of daughters are hardly as demanding as of a son. Then when they go into the workforce, they are not as competitive; I mean, they don't have the drive to be competitive. I think it's cultural."
- "Women's devotion to the family—it's very important in Chinese culture."

Although many traditional expectations for women seem to be changing for the current generation, particularly among the middle and upper classes, the "cultural mindset" continues to reproduce cross-generationally, as one woman noted:

I think the cultural part probably is what nurtures a woman's ambition. Women are not expected to rise high, in the cultural sense, in a family sense. Even I was surprised by my colleague talking about his daughter. He said "I don't want her to get into a too demanding job. She will find a good husband and she will be fine."

One Taiwanese-born and raised dean, who had worked in the United States for decades and had only recently moved to Hong Kong, made a similar observation: "I don't think I, or people of my background, would bring up a daughter and say, 'You go find a good husband and you will be settled for life.' But I see that more here." After our interview, we went to lunch where we talked for almost another two hours, sharing stories about places we knew in the United States and Canada. Evident in her comments was a profound sense of nostalgia for the times and a place called home in the United States. I detected a fair bit of frustration with what she perceived to be her lack of cultural fit into Hong Kong society and academic culture. On the surface, she was a Chinese woman/academic in Chinese society and yet, as diasporic subject, she was caught in a range of dissonant cultural values. At the time of preparing this book for publication, she was returning to the United States.

DOUBLE-DAY AND DUAL CAREERS

The consequences for women becoming mothers and managing the double-day—despite what one woman called a veritable "army of servants," from "drivers, gardeners, several maids" to "time-management consultants"—are that "their research production falls for a few years so there's a period when they don't get promotions." One single woman, recently retired from a term as pro vice chancellor, reflected on the plight of her female colleagues:

> I see it in my female colleagues: They had children later, and they are in their 40s with young children. The university provides housing so they live nearby, near the hospital. So I actually see my colleagues getting very sick because they have to go back and forth and look after the children all the time. We all go for lunch, we rest, but they have to do a lot of things during lunchtime, things for the family or household or children—check on maids, look in on sick children. They refuse to go on sabbatical, or to conferences.

Dual-career conflicts also impinge on women's professional aspirations and opportunities. Professional women tend to be married to professional men, but despite comparable professional status and commitments, it is commonly women who give up or interrupt their careers to follow partners' relocations. As one woman explained, "I was willing to give up my career to move with my husband; there are many women in that situation in Hong Kong. Of course, there are also men who give up their career for their wives, but less." Speaking of colleagues, two women explained:

- "She just got married, and now she's resigned because after marriage she moved from Hong Kong to Kowloon, to his apartment, and she had to

leave very early for work and come home very late because now she has
to be home to do the cooking and marketing and it was just too much."

- "She was a senior lecturer with us. Then she emigrated with her partner
  to Canada, and then she came back and had to start again at lecturer."

Women who had spent considerable time abroad studying and/or working
provided comparative analyses of Asian and European men. Asian men—
except, of course, their own husbands—were generally considered more
traditional:

- "They don't really help at home."
- "[They are] spoiled and sometimes arrogant, but then that's how they
  were raised by their mothers, and that's of a different generation."

The women considered European and American men, to be more "easy
going with helping at home," "pushing prams on the street," "pushing
trolleys in the supermarkets, that's a very American thing, all the men do
it." All the married women claimed that their husbands were extremely
supportive of their career choices and helped with the children at home,
although, "when the children are sick, I still have to take a day off, not
him." Despite the rhetoric of equality, especially in negotiated house-
holds, all the women with "extremely supportive husbands" acknowledged that women remain tied to domestic and child care responsibilities:
"He does what he can, but he's just not home as much as I am; he's away
in China or overseas a lot."

> When you wake up in the morning, the child is sick, who stays home?
> When you have a supportive husband, there is room for negotiation. But
> who has a day or half-day that you can cancel? Most likely the woman,
> even if she is a professional. The support in principle, the rational sup-
> port, it is not the same as the actual support.

It seems then that the choices educated women can make are structurally
available—"women can do whatever they want today, there are no
restrictions, it's up to women to work their way up"—but they are ideologically and subjectively circumscribed. "All the women I know who
become professors, they either married late or they have no children. If
they have children late in life, it's usually one, two at most." Cultural
expectations and gender-differentiated socialization still map out different expectations and opportunities for men and women. Subjectively, the

professional and personal choices women make, such as whether and when to raise a family, come at what many called a "cost" or "price":

- "You pay a price. If you chose not have children you pay a price. If you have children you pay a price."
- "Yes, I planned to have a child rather late, but I almost waited too long. I wanted to get my career established and then there was always something else. It is a price you pay."
- "Well, everything is trade-offs. If women have ability, they have choice. If you pursue a career, there are trade-offs and costs. If you have children, even with full-time help, and want to stay in your profession, there is a price to pay."
- "You can't do it all—have a career, a social life, and a family. Something has to go. For me, I let my social life go."

Until I worked closely with the transcripts in the course of my analysis, I was unaware of the prevalent use of terms such as *pay-off, price*, and *cost*. They appear in virtually every woman's transcript but are not mentioned at all by the Thai women, and only mentioned twice by the Singapore women. Metaphors are culture and place specific. Perhaps Hong Kong's entrepreneurial ethos has trickled its way into the discourse of everyday life where "costing" one's choices and decisions on a balance sheet of trade-offs seemed quite natural to the women in this group.

WOMEN'S SUPPORT:
"OH THEY CAN BE VICIOUS"

I asked all the women whom they considered most influential and supportive in their career development. Some said that the support of their husbands had been most invaluable. For others, mostly the older women who had been trained and had worked in traditional male fields such as medicine, mathematics, and the physical sciences, there had been no women in the departments and laboratories they trained in 20 to 30 years ago and eventually would work in as academics. One woman, was the first female "back in 1974" appointed to the Senate, and it caused quite an uproar:

The males objected to it. They were saying, this woman, not even a professor and never been in administration! They had a good point. I was fully untested. I wasn't even a professor at that time and after me, there were no more women until I became an PVC [pro-vice chancellor], and then there were a few more.

One woman explained that she could not comment on support or lack of support by other women because she had been the only female in her department for years, and had been "the only one in my [university] class." But what she had to say in terms of men as colleagues, as research collaborators, was instructive in light of both the cultural propriety surrounding the politics of gender relationships and the often lonely and isolated road academics can be for women:

> I can understand the case for a male colleague if he needs some partners to do things—it would be more convenient for him to get a male partner. That simplifies a lot of things, including unnecessary explanations between him and his wife, or even between him and his colleagues. They will not take the initiative to look for me as a collaborator. They are more used to getting along with males, so they feel a bit uneasy. They would ask, "With so many male colleagues there, why would he choose that one?"

Repeatedly, women told variations of the same narrative: "most of the help, it came from male colleagues"; "I was the only female for most part of my career." Although the women agreed that a lack of female role models might be one barrier to women's career aspirations in higher education, several women went further to comment on women's lack of support for each other:

> No, there are no or few role models. But women, even in middle management as I was coming up the ranks, don't support each other. They don't really talk to each other. They are not helpful to other women. So who wants those women as role models? The people who helped me most were men.

Some women made veiled allusions to having had bad encounters with other women. A few women were very explicit about women's lack of support for each other, in some instances characterized as open warfare and "very vicious." Tensions and jealousies between women can be "worse, much worse . . . such as that I may lose my job":

- "Women are most unsupportive, most unkind. They oppose other women. There are so few women and when they get in power, they are certainly not helpful to other women."
- "[Women] don't need a reason, maybe just that they don't like your looks, you are younger, taller, you are perceived as academically threatening, it could be as irrational as that, but these are the things that matter to women, especially those in a very traditional mold. And certainly women in my generation suffer a lot of that."
- "Men envy in a competitive sense; men envy other men because they are more intelligent whereas women envy because they are better looking."

One woman department head had been invited to apply for a deanship in an older, well-established university but was eventually turned down, despite much encouragement and support from senior male academics across the university. She gave a long and complicated account of this incident, which had obviously caused her much grief and stress. After submitting her application, she was told by the university's most senior officer, "Well, if you don't get it, you can always apply for associate deanship." Shortly after her interview, the chairman of the board said, "'Well, we feel that you are our candidate; however, we think that we would like you to serve as an acting dean.' A slap in the face!" Following her probation period, "they said, 'We want to observe you one more year'!" In the end, the senior executives gave her a litany of reasons to support their decision against her. As it turned out later, "the person who made all these comments about me was a woman. She was the incumbent exiting the position."

Women's lack of support for each other and the apparently common subversive and oppositional stance toward other women is something women don't readily talk about. The multilayered issues and tensions among women in professional contexts have not been addressed in scholarly literature. Yet my own experience and the many conversations I have had with women in the course of this study suggest that it is an issue that many women experience, and one that generates substantial anger, stress, and strong emotions. Among the women in this group, I sensed far more outrage, disappointment, and anger at the behaviors of other academic women than at the patriarchal culture and behaviors of men. It may be that women ascending the career ladder unconsciously expect the tacit support of senior women. On the other hand, women in senior positions who have made it through the system without female mentorship or support may feel that overt support and advice to aspirant women lower down the system may be seen as granting unfair and unprofessional favors (King, 1997).

Perhaps some, but certainly not all, successful academic women feel protective of hard-won positions and status and may feel threatened by the increasing competition of younger women. Women themselves may hold unconscious stereotypes of women as maternal nurturers, as "naturally" more caring and supportive than men. When those expectations fail to materialize, women may feel more disappointed and let down. It is possible, therefore, that women interpret other women's behaviors in more negative terms than they do the behaviors of men, from whom women may have learned to expect equally stereotyped behaviors associated with an overgeneralized notion of patriarchy. The "professional sabotage" (Spurling, 1997, p. 30) of and by women commonly attributed to men within patriarchal systems of institutional power and control, thus, must be reconsidered in light of the changing gender composition of institutional management and the cultural dimensions of the politics of interpretation.

GENDERED MANAGEMENT STYLES

Toward the end of our conversations, I asked if women bring different understandings and styles to senior management positions. Although most of the women claimed that "we cannot generalize: this sex does it that way, this one another way," the women did have experiences and interpretations of women's managerial and leadership styles that they viewed as different from men. The institutional position of women in relation to "centers of power" was seen to influence how women manage and relate to others:

> It's all linked with the issue of power. If you don't have that much power, you have to work your way around it, and that requires a much more indirect, interpersonal, more negotiating style. But that doesn't necessarily mean that all women adopt a different approach. I mean, different approaches have a context which has to do with hierarchy, and the way things have been.

In addition to women's structural positions in relation to power as one factor mediating their management style, women are also seen to use power differently: "Women see themselves as powerful when they say yes. Like, when women can say 'yes, I let you do it.' But men tend to see themselves as powerful when they say no. They deny you—that's being powerful. But women, they see it as confirming you." Most noted differences that match those identified in the literature:

- "Women can handle human relationships better than men."
- "Women do bring something different than men to a relationship, to a committee. I think because they understand life experiences differently."
- "[Women are] more inclusive and more careful about hurting others' feelings. They are less prone to use rough language. They don't use foul words, men do. In that sense, we are more careful about the way we carry ourselves."

One woman, with the longest record of serving academic and senior management among this group of women had this to say:

They [women] are better in interpersonal skills and they are more charming. There are two types of women: The majority try to rule by consensus, by consultation and they carry the rest of the committee. The other type of woman tries to take over from the men by being too aggressive. Some women try to compensate by shouting by behaving too aggressively. We have to strike a medium. Women have to stand firm, no matter how charming you are. Women have to be aggressive, but quietly aggressive.

On balance, the women in this group felt that both men and women can be domineering and aggressive in traditional masculine ways, and yet also manage in consensual and team-building ways:

- "You can't stereotype; it's the individual really."
- "We can't generalize—I find some women who are more like men. I think it's the individual person."

But underneath assumptions of individual style and personality, and despite many harsh comments about the lack of support from other women, some consensus emerged about women's different life experiences and their structural relation to institutional power, both of which tend to develop better negotiation, communication, and interpersonal skills.

CONCLUDING REMARKS

All the women I interviewed had worked hard to get to the positions they held. Women in their late 40s and 50s had virtually no management training and were, in some ways, self-taught:

- "I got to where I am by my own strength."
- "The university, it is a business now, you have a very high profit margin and need to know how to manage money. They don't teach you that."
- "Nobody knew how to do it [financial management] at that time. I felt scared because I had never done accounting. I asked this person in the university, 'Can you give me some help, advice.' He wouldn't give it to me, he wouldn't even help me. So I decided to get a traditional accounting book, and I worked it out myself."

Work is all consuming, and as noted earlier, most of the women were well aware of the price they had paid for professional mobility and success:

- "I seem to come in earlier and earlier. And weekends I always work."
- "It's a very long day, so less time with family."
- "There's other things that come with the job: the social commitments; then you become president of the society, vice president of that society, the meetings on weekends, and so on."
- "We have liaisons with universities in China, and we'll be taking the contingent to Beijing, and next year to Shanghai. A lot of that takes time, and when one has this position, one wants to enhance the standing of the university with international links of this kind.

Women in their 50s and 60s were looking forward to retirement and had no further career aspirations: "I have my reading, my orchids, travel. I'm looking forward to it. I think it's easier for women to retire than men because women have other interests. Men just have their work." Women in their 40s with a good part of their career still ahead of them had further career aspirations, which included professorial chairs, deanships, and "yes, maybe PVC, but that is a long way off." The older generation of women had been trailblazers: often the first women in senior positions or appointed to prestigious committees. Many had been the only women during their university student days, and the first or only women in departments where they first took junior lecturing positions. Some of the younger women talked about generational differences that positioned older women as having climbed "social" academic ladders in traditional "patronage" networks of their parents' generation. But the cultural and patriarchal values and attitudes those women confronted were undoubtedly different but perhaps no less difficult to surmount in an era in which women's professional aspirations were the exception rather than the rule. Women in their 30s and early 40s, by contrast, passed through higher education in Hong Kong and overseas, and subsequently into the academic system, at a time when women's options were greater and more varied.

However, their personal and professional struggles up the academic hierarchy are with other women as much as they are with the patriarchal culture of academia. Glass-ceiling politics, therefore, must be viewed in generational terms and reframed to include women as implicated in the complex visible and invisible barriers that academic women face. All the women had been trained in and seemed to have bought into the ideology of meritocratic equality. However, on closer probing, many narratives emerged that revealed different institutional and collegial treatment, and cultural expectations, on the basis of gender.

All the women alluded to personal and professional costs of having children and getting married, and several had delayed marriage and having children to accommodate career plans. Despite domestic help, women remain tied to family, domestic, and childrearing responsibilities. Women have worked hard to gain entry into the public sphere, the professions, and to break through old stereotypes and seniority barriers—in short, they have worked hard to earn the right to work the double-day. Conversely, it's apparent that men have not demolished old stereotypes and have not struggled to gain entry into the private household sphere where they might support women's double-day workload of professional commitments plus domestic and child care duties.

Given Hong Kong's exceptional record of gender-balanced educational outcomes at all levels, pipeline explanations for women's underrepresentation in senior higher-education management do not hold. Rather, the women in this study felt that the private sector lures many graduate women into more lucrative careers, that women don't plan careers "for the long haul," and that parents may still be an impediment to encouraging women to continue beyond an undergraduate education. Moreover, according to several women, the historical and sociopolitical context leading up to 1997 had diverted the pipeline into an overseas exodus of qualified women (and men)—a "missing generation"—in anticipation of 1997. As with glass-ceiling explanations, the pipeline concept must be contextualized in generational, historical, economic, and political terms.

Without wishing to make sweeping generalizations, the overall message was clear: Women loved their work, their teaching and research, and even their managerial roles, despite the many complex work- and family-related strategies they had to devise to achieve their goals. They were well aware of the professional and personal costs of their choices, yet they were prepared to put in the effort. The older women had stayed the distance during a time when women's presence in higher-education administration was largely confined to secretarial roles. The younger women were also intent on staying in academics for the long haul, committed to their work and academic career goals. The lure of private sector careers had not detracted these women from what I interpreted as their dedication to and love of their chosen disciplinary and research areas. Given the still persistent cultural values placed on "women's responsibility to have children, to raise them, to look after the parents, that is very important in Asian, particularly Chinese culture," the women had made some hard personal decisions about remaining childless, postponing children, or giving up their social life in efforts to pursue professional careers.

Malaysia

Population	Malay (56%), Chinese (34%), Indian (9%)	22.7 million
Languages	Bahasa Malay, English, Chinese dialects, Tamil	
1998 UN Gender Empowerment Index ranking (out of 174)		60
Female combined primary-, secondary-, and tertiary-level gross enrollment ratio (1995)[*]		61%
Number of tertiary-level students (male and female) per 100,000 inhabitants (1996)		not available
Public universities		10
Colleges, institutes, teacher training, polytechnics[†]		23
Gross enrollments (male and female, all levels), all higher education (1998)		—
Total full-time academic staff (male and female), all higher education (1998)		not available
Public expenditure on education as percentage of GNP (1996)		5.2%

[*]Expressed as a percentage of the population age group corresponding to the national regulations for these levels of education.

[†]Preservice professional training, certificate-, and diploma-granting institutions.

Sources: Department of Statistics Malaysia (1999), UNESCO Human Development Index (1998), UNESCO Statistical Yearbook (1998), World of Learning (1997).

CONTEXT

In late 1998, I spent two weeks in Malaysia interviewing senior academic women on higher-education and career mobility issues. It was a time of considerable political turmoil. "Reformasi" demonstrations had been sporadic following the imprisonment earlier in the year of dismissed Deputy Prime Minister and Minister of Finance Anwar Ibrahim. Anwar's trial had been suspended during the Asia-Pacific Economic Cooperation (APEC) summit meeting held in Kuala Lumpur, which received global media attention because of U.S. Vice President Al Gore's "culturally insensitive" comments encouraging prodemocracy demands by "the brave people of Malaysia." Gore's comment, which included the term *doi moi*, Vietnamese for economic liberalization, was seen as both a conceptual and linguistic *faux pas* and open to the usual criticisms by regional leaders as "foreign meddling into internal affairs." At the time of my visit, Anwar's trial had resumed, and Gore's APEC gaffe was still fresh in people's minds. Public demonstrations in the CBD and on university campuses received heavy western media coverage by CNN, the BBC, and Australian networks. Analogies were drawn between Indonesia's civil meltdown and the contagion effect now pulling Malaysia into the regional melee of civil unrest, anti-IMF sentiments, and popular disenchantment with autocratic and military regimes. It was my impression at the time that the events of 1998 had heightened a sense of political awareness and debate, at least among the educated elite. The word *politics* permeated discussion everywhere: over lunch, in interviews, during taxi rides, or in off-the-record small talk. Nearly all the women I spoke with readily talked about gender politics; the politics of authority, power, knowledge; the potential for political change; and how these issues tie in with women's role and status in Malaysian society. In many ways, the historical moment and context of this research politicized our dialogues: References to "universal social justice," "reform," "accountability," "transparency," and so forth permeated what women had to say.

As with my previous case studies of Thailand, Singapore, and Hong Kong, my aim in this study was to investigate a range of factors that can restrict women's equal opportunities and participation in higher education, as both students and senior managers. My overall analysis, therefore, focused on historically situated social, cultural, and political differences as well as patterns of similarities. One important structural, political difference that distinguishes Malaysian higher education from my other case studies, as well as most western countries, is that senior executive positions are political appointments, not advertised and filled through open and international competition vetted by independent and representative selection committees and accountability mechanisms (Lim, 1995; Omar, 1993). Another significant difference are social policies that confer educational and employment advantages, including access to and promotion within higher education, on *bumiputera* (indigenous) Malays, policies that have generated substantial discontent among Chinese and Indian Malaysians. Chinese and Indian women generally don't get past acting or deputy dean positions, although there are a few exceptions. As one Malay dean told me, "Basically the top management personnel are either men or Malays. Very few non-Malay Chinese or Indians ever get to the top." A Chinese dean confirmed, "I am a double minority in terms of gender, in terms of ethnicity. Ethnicity is also a factor in appointment of senior positions. As you know, they are all appointed, deans and all. There is a tendency to appoint Malays."

A third difference is a Muslim inflection on "Asian values" and Asian femininity that has implications for women's social conduct and self-representation, and for gender relations. These, in turn, form part of glass-ceiling politics among Muslim Malay women, and between Malay and non-Malay women.

SAMPLE

Women for this study were identified through my own academic and social network, and through identification on university Web sites. As with my other case studies, postal and e-mail correspondence initiated contact, which included a research brief of my project, participation requirements, and a questionnaire. With the help of Malaysian colleagues, several items relevant to the Malaysian context were added to the questionnaire. The items sought information about the extent to which race and religion factor into women's appointment and promotional opportunities and to what extent patronage figures into career mobility.

Not all the 17 women originally scheduled were available at the time of my visit due to unforeseen commitments. As some women dropped out others "snowballed" into group, and I eventually interviewed 14 women, most individually but some in groups. The women were located in four universities in and around the country's capital of Kuala Lumpur, at the University of Malaya, Universiti Putra Malaya, Universiti Kebangsaan Malaysia, and the Muslim-only Institut Teknologi Mara. I also interviewed women in Penang at the Universiti Sains Malaysia, a one-hour flight north of Kuala Lumpur. The women ranged from 41 to 58 years of age and held positions as deans, deputy deans, research center directors, and department heads, spread across faculties of medicine, architecture, law, and the natural and social sciences. Ethnic backgrounds consisted of Chinese (3), Indian (1), and Malay (10). In addition, I spoke with 5 women (2 Chinese, 2 Malay, and 1 Indian) who did not hold administrative posts and whose job classifications were at lecturer, senior lecturer, and associate professor levels. Again, as with my other studies, these more informal conversations attempted to gauge career aspirations and interpretations of potential opportunities or impediments among women in nonmanagement posts. The comments from this group alternately confirmed and contradicted what the more senior women had to say, but they also shed some light on how women perceive other women's management and leadership styles.

All the women were keen to find out what other women I had seen and what they had told me about the issues I was investigating. As is the case in small academic communities such as Hong and Singapore, or even in Australia, in Malaysia everyone knows everyone else within the disciplines. A few wanted to know if so-and-so was still wearing western dress or how they were wearing their headscarves, a practice growing in popularity among Muslim Malay women. Others in Kuala Lumpur were surprised when I mentioned that some of the women at the Universiti Sains Malaysia in Penang were openly wearing the white ribbon signifying "universal justice." This was considered a bold and courageous move, something "you wouldn't see in KL." But then, Penang has a progressive reputation: The university had just relaxed the rule requiring Malay women to conceal their necks when entering the library. Full facial veiling is prohibited on campus, and one veiled student, I was told, had recently been asked to remove the veil or leave campus. Issues of dress, related to the politics of enacting a "proper" Malay femininity came up frequently in conversations.

CONCRETE CEILINGS

The metaphor of the glass ceiling refers to transparent cultural, organizational, and attitudinal barriers that maintain invisible career limits for women. Women look up the career ladder and can see the top rungs, but they cannot always identify why and where they will encounter invisible impediments. Men, on the other hand, "can look down [the ladder] and ask why women are not achieving and, seeing no barrier, can only surmise a lack of talent, commitment or energy" (King, 1997). In Malaysian higher education, however, there is nothing hidden or transparent about women's inability to reach the most senior ranks of university management, because all senior executive positions in the sector are political appointments.

In a 1993 UNESCO report, *Women and Higher Education Management* (Dines, 1993), educational scholar Asmah Omar observed that although women's participation in higher education as undergraduate and postgraduate students and as academic staff had risen significantly over the last few decades, women remained relatively invisible in the top managerial ranks. Throughout the 1980s, lower-level administrative posts such as bursar and registrar were increasingly filled by women, and women's rise to professorial levels also increased, yet female participation in senior management remained low (pp. 123–126). Omar notes two reasons for this. First, and most significant, is a structural disadvantage for women because senior appointments are political appointments, not embedded in a meritocratic system of open competition and accountability. Omar writes:

> The appointment of the Vice-Chancellor [who subsequently appoints deans] is made by the Prime Minister's Office at the recommendation of the Minister of Education. The qualities that are looked for are the candidates' stature as academics, their expertise in management and their ability to lead . . . there is also the requirement that they have to be aware of and render their support to the ideology and aspirations of the government of the time. (p. 128)

She goes on to say that

> the reason for not considering women as Vice-Chancellors and Deputy Vice-Chancellors has never been made known. One can only conjecture that there is still a prejudice towards having women in the very top positions . . . It may [also] be that the women themselves are still subservient to the idea that those important posts should only be held by men. This may be related to the acceptance of the superiority of men which, as said earlier, is culturally ingrained in them. (p. 129)

Omar's second reason is the pipeline theory, which argues that the flow of qualified women has been negligible given women's low participation in "the early days of university education in Malaysia" (p. 126). However, those early days were over three decades ago. The sharp rise of women's participation in higher education in the last 30 years, therefore, challenges the alleged lack of qualified and credentialed female flow. Ariffin (1994) notes that female undergraduate enrollments in the 1980s jumped from 38.8% in 1983 to 41.2% in 1987, although women's enrollments remained concentrated in traditional female areas of study. In 1990, women comprised 45% of all tertiary enrollments, 28% at the Ph.D. level, and 34% at the master's level (Sidin, 1996). And, as I noted in Chapter 5, women today are outnumbering men in medicine and law. Malaysian women's increased participation in higher education suggests that pipeline arguments cannot explain women's underrepresentation at more senior levels. As Sidin puts it, "by 1990 in the eight universities there were over 2,100 women faculty members, constituting about 40% of the faculty. Despite their increase in number, however, few women are in decision-making positions" (p. 136).

These observations were reflected in many of the comments made to me by women nearly a decade after the UNESCO report was published. For example, deans from three different universities had this to say:

- "The statistics show that when it comes to top jobs, even in professions which are women's professions like teaching, it is the men who hold the top positions; Ministry of Education and so on. We have had one Director-General of Education, but she retired a couple of years ago, and after her, there were only three men. No woman has gone up yet and there's no women in line."
- "Yes, top down, especially the top post comes from there; there's not many women up there, only the men get picked for posts like that. In the whole university, there are about 26 schools, faculties, and there are only, what, two lady deans."
- "None of the women have been appointed vice chancellors. The dean is the highest so far. They are all men at the moment, throughout Malaysia, all the universities. Even for women deans, it's quite rare—here there are only two faculties with female deans . . . and in this university there are more female than male students."

A study of women in management at the University of Malaysia (UM) (Hashim, 1997) found that promotion on meritocratic principles applies to professorial promotions but not to managerial level appointments where "the basis for appointment is more subjective and may have elements of favoritism" (p. 3). At UM, partly because of corporate restructuring, the male/female ratio for deanships has increased from 3:1 to 7:1 throughout the 1990s, marked by an all-time low of 15:1 in 1994–95. Gender distribution of departmental and school headships has remained static throughout the 1990s: Men outnumbered women between 5:1 and 3:1 throughout the decade. Although women's representation as heads has "not improved in favor of the female group . . . compared to the Deanship, a woman Head of Department is more 'acceptable'" (Hashim, 1997, p. 2). In fact, in attempts to explain that women had indeed come a long way, the women repeatedly mentioned female heads as evidence of women's ascendancy to senior ranks. However, heads are more along the line of what Omar describes as "middle management," mid-level "paper-shuffling" administrators who do not have the power or authority over policy or finance that deputy vice chancellors or executive deans have. Relatedly, the Malay women frequently referred to the handful of non-Malay heads and the even smaller number of deans and deputy deans as evidence of the lack of glass ceilings for ethnic Chinese and Indian women. In all, as Hashim notes, female headships seem more acceptable to men and women, although here too women remain a minority.

In an institutional system where the senior executives of vice chancellors, deputy vice chancellors, and deans are political appointments, the notion of the glass ceiling is less ambiguous and transparent, with a more defined and visible "concrete ceiling." All the women I interviewed had come of age, as it were, in an academic system where the top rungs of the academic ladder had always been closed to them. Even when women reach professorial levels, they easily internalize the limits of their aspirations: "There are few women professors here. My friend, for instance, she has been professor for a long time and she's very capable but she will never get up." In another dean's view, "There is a general acceptance on both sides of the rules of the game. And there is never any need for those who appoint people in these positions to reckon with the fact that there are no women . . . there is a great deal of women in a very quiet way, letting this go." Two department heads commented that

- "So much of it is contributed by the male-dominated bureaucracy, and much of it is contributed by the women themselves, by acquiescing and leaving the status quo as it is."
- "These positions are politically biased and politically selected. It is the culture that we have been accustomed to, whether right or wrong . . . for whatever justification they have, then that is our glass ceiling."

In other words, women know the limits of their career aspirations, and they experience these lessons again and again in careers often spanning 20 to 30 years. Two deans explain:

- "Men have many ways of cutting women [down]. I mean look at our country, we are not taking the women to be vice chancellors. If the academic VCs are not thinking of programs for generating income, then we will take people from the corporate world so that's one way of saying, 'Well, we will put in men.' If they have competition from the academic women, alright, let's keep that aside—we'll take the men."
- "Like the registrar, when he retired you would think that because the ones below him were all women and they were first class, we thought that one of them would come up. No, they brought somebody from outside because, you see, he has to complement the top. And then even the bursar, the deputy bursar below was a woman, so you have to take from the outside."

Women resent the fact that they are excluded from even having the opportunity to compete at more senior levels. As one dean put it:

We have never had a lady Vice Chancellor. That is where the stop has been. There has been one, a DVC, at the University of Malaysia, but I think she served hardly one term. If there was [open competition] I think I would have possibly had the chance. Not that I would have, but I would have considered it. The principle of it!

Perhaps what women find most difficult to accept is that the political machinations and criteria for senior appointments are invisible and beyond reproach:

- "It is very difficult to see who are those more qualified for a certain position. So sometimes you feel there is this injustice where you have people being put into place where they are not really good, but just because the person is a male he is heading a certain unit."
- "We don't really know how these people have been chosen or whether these people really applied for this post. They were just selected by some top-ranking people, and sometimes these people who are chosen may not really be interested in that area."

Women are aware and skeptical of the nepotism or favoritism (Hashim, 1997) that underlies the politics of senior appointments. Although they may not be privy to insider politics of why certain men are selected for posts, they are fully aware that a gendered double standard exists, one that is embedded in a cultural milieu of male bonding, networking, visibility, and privilege. This, then, is one aspect of a subtle glass ceiling, one level below the concrete ceiling, that effectively keeps women out.

> Deans are appointed by the VC, and I guess one of the ways in which Deans get appointed is visibility, and certain people are more visible, and if you are part of the network, then of course you get appointed. That is never stated anywhere or told. Women don't get that opportunity—they are not so visible.

DOUBLE-DAY

The issue of women's double-day of professional and domestic responsibility was seen by all women as perhaps the most difficult impediment to overcome. This view has been shared by all women in my case studies and is well documented in the literature (Brooks, 1997; Davies, Lubelska, & Quinn, 1994; Eggins, 1997; Heward, 1996; Morley & Walsh, 1996). All the married women with children agreed that, unlike men, women do indeed work a double–day:

- "Women have to work triple hard. They have to work very hard at the home front, they have to work very hard in the office, and they have to work very hard to get recognized, and they have to work very hard to be visible. It is more than the double-day."
- "It is very difficult. Women are doing a lot more than double the work that the men are doing. And this happens at all levels, including you know, if you are holding a top post."

Guilt over the personal price women pay for pursuing professional careers was another common theme, as one deputy dean explains:

> Men don't feel guilty. For us, yes. When you go out you make preparations. Sometimes you even cook and then freeze. Okay, on certain days you can eat out. But you have to plan, make sure that the house is in order. Sometimes if I am in a good mood it is okay, but if I am not, you know, I feel the blame: you know, do this and that—that kind of thing.

Rather than taking credit for their own hard work and success, almost all the women attributed the success of their careers to the encouragement and support of husbands and families:

- "I grew up with a father who believed so much in academia . . . and I was just very lucky I found a man who had that kind of vision as a husband. And I had in-laws who were educated and whose expectations of the daughter-in-law was very, very different from a traditional north Indian family."
- "I am lucky my husband is supportive."

However, comments from some married and divorced women suggest that not all husbands are supportive of their wives' professional choices and obligations:

- "My husband, he doesn't like me to go out after office hours. He is still very conservative. He thinks I should spend time in the home, so I always reject all the evening events."
- "I am divorced. When I was deputy dean, then I have a lot of work to do every day, I have to sacrifice my sleep, weekends, which he was not very happy about. He always said people don't take home the office work. Because of that he started going around with other women perhaps. I have tried my very best and I expected some kind of understanding on his part—he just refused."

Nonetheless, for most, the day-to-day routine of child care remains women's work:

- "When I was doing my Ph.D., my child was one year old and then I had another one—two kids and doing a Ph.D., and work, and teaching as well. Oh, it's hard. Put the children to bed at 10 and then you start to work, writing, from 10 to 2. You have to be very focused."
- "I just have to find more time to be with my children. It's very difficult, but men always tell us ladies that we should manage time better, but I think we are managing time better, but it is just that there is not enough time I guess."

Domestic and child care duties, and constraints on women's mobility to enhance their visibility or to build and maintain influential networks, combine to put women into disadvantageous positions in terms of career mobility. "Not being in the informal network, not being visible, women themselves not being able to come forward because of their own double duties and things like that. So I think these three factors actually hold women back."

Particularly in academics, where at least a decade of full-time study is usually required to complete the requisite three-degree entry-level credentials, the start of women's professional careers almost always coincides with the cultural pressures and women's choices to start families. Early career years, then, are often filled with pressures to teach, research, do the committee work, as well as raise young children. In the view of one dean, this converging set of demands often puts research productivity on the back burner, which, in turn, can disadvantage women in later years as they seek professorial or managerial promotions.

> When a woman gets into academics here, she will have just started a family. Most Malaysian women would have started a family, and there's a pull to set up home, their children, and at the same time being productive in the academic field. So there's an automatic channeling of energies for immediate things like home and telling yourself, "I will come to research later." They don't get involved in research.

MALE CULTURE AND ATTITUDES

The feminist and management literature has long pointed to the notion of the old boys' club as indicative of larger patriarchal forms of power and control across all sectors of public, and indeed private, life. Despite variations in cultural and religious ideologies, male authority rules home and work, law and scripture. Male attitudes toward women share many universal stereotypes—women as gossips, too talkative and emotional, and so on—although they are always embedded in the cultural-religious particularities of local and historical contexts. The women in this study agreed that male cultures exist in Malaysian higher education, and that they can exert considerable influence over women's opportunities, if only by keeping them out of the informal networks of male-bonding and information sharing: "Being a woman, now that I am in this position, it's not all that easy because of the networking. It's much easier if you are a man." Women also felt that men held stereotyped perceptions of women's inferiority and fragile emotional state:

- "There is still the perception that ladies cannot go up. And they say it is because women are more emotional than men."
- "Some men, not all, still feel that women are inferior in terms of all sorts of things. Men are still superior. Especially when dealing with the Malay Muslim, because in Islam the woman has to be second compared to men."
- "There is that hidden discrimination, that perception that women are inferior and that they are not mentally stable. Men will say, 'Women normally bring their problems to the office,' but then I say 'Not all, even men do the same thing.'"
- "There's still this idea that women are a different category. There's jokes [about women], there's laughter, and if you say it all the time, it gets perpetuated and perpetuated. Sometimes, when I listen to some of the deans, I don't think they have moved out of old ideas about how problematic women are, how much they talk, and so on."

On one hand, men are seen to devalue women's alleged attributes and behaviors, and yet they would not approve of women assuming male-typified behaviors of assertion or aggression.

- "I feel very comfortable with men, and yet I do believe that there is the men's culture, yes. But the men don't want the ladies, the women administrators, to have their kind of behavior. I think I would go further by being a woman than to ape a man."
- "Perhaps they don't like aggressive women. They want women to be subdued, and they won't take orders from women. I think they feel slighted perhaps, if they get orders from women."
- "Once a man said to me, 'Why don't you be more lady-like?' Because I was a little bit aggressive. Yes, I was not ready to be subdued, you see. And sometimes they just won't recognize what you have produced, and they will belittle you. And not in little ways, but very outspoken, meant to insult very directly."

In a predominantly male-defined and governed society, "men still prefer men." As women's roles change and they become more visible in public life during times of rapid social, cultural, and not least, economic change brought about by a range of global influences, it is easier to "stick to old values":

- "Like engineers, you know, men still prefer men. In the office, yes we think women are suitable, but then if you need to go to a site to look at the projects, big projects, they still prefer men."
- "It could be a little bit of prejudice. Maybe men have not really discovered those women who would be able to hold such posts and perhaps they are not confident in working with women, so maybe they trust men more. They stick to old values."

Old boys' club networking is an important source of insider information trading, of male bonding, of being visible in contexts and with people who "count" and who may provide influence and patronage in subsequent career moves. Structurally and strategically, weekend retreats or after hours social events, tennis or golf games easily exclude women because of their domestic duties and, as we have heard earlier, some husbands disapprove of wives' after-hour work:

- "[Men] go and play golf. Rub shoulders with others. That's how they get to know themselves and they get all these connections but which we women don't."
- "I think a lot goes on between their golf swings, and many of them play golf you know. Informal networks are formed out of common interests, and women after office hours, we have our home to take care of, and it's not very convenient to just take off and play golf on our own."

On a smaller, tactical scale, women's presence in mixed-sex settings can be ignored in a number of demeaning and marginalizing ways:

- "The informal network is still a very masculine thing. I go to meetings and it is 90% male, and you don't feel very comfortable. For instance, at a Higher Studies Board meeting it is written on a paper that 'student cannot finish because of maternity problem.' So I insist, you know, 'Please don't put problem next to child-birth.' Then they go 'umm,' you know, that kind of condescending response."
- "I can call fellow deputy deans to ask them for help since I am quite new at this, but when they meet together there is always this segregation, men and women. Women on the other side and men on another. We don't really get to integrate, to talk to each other much. Boys and old boys' network."

- "At a dinner, you know things like that, the whole table is men, and you don't feel so comfortable, and the things they talk of are kind of alien to you. They just go on with their talk, and I just eat, you know. It's not very comfortable, but these are the networks in which they form the cliques and they consult each other, and so you get left out."

The invisibility women can feel in relation to the way even the most basic structural aspects of the university reflect exclusively male assumptions is exemplified by one woman's comment about deans' offices. Her comment may seem trivial, but it is no less real in symbolic and material terms than the silent lessons women learn about women's place in public life and gendered pathways to the upper echelons of institutional power and authority: "You want to change the place, but a lot of things depend on upstairs. I tell you, my toilet here, they are men's toilet because they are planned for men to be the dean. Never anyone thinks of making it a multi-purpose toilet. It is for men." Related to this not so insignificant comment are many other structural, textual, and even technological dimensions of everyday life in the university that represent men's assumptions and visions, and that make women invisible. For example, lapel mikes are designed to fit on men's shirt pockets, not women's clothes; fixed micro-phones are set at levels suitable for male speakers; and the persistent use of the male pronoun *he* in policy documents and student handbooks is supposed to refer to all students and all staff, but it linguistically excludes women.

"ASIAN VALUES"

The women in this study, like the women I interviewed in Thailand, Sin-gapore, and Hong Kong, had more or less the same things to say about the cultural expectations of women's role and conduct in Asian societies. In the words of one dean: "In our culture, we have this saying that 'you do not put yourself in a basket and carry it yourself.' So I think self-promo-tion is really not our culture." Despite religious-cultural differences across the four countries of my study, references to "Asian values" or "Asian cul-ture" are a persistent theme in explanations about women's participation in public life, their tendency to "work quietly" or "work behind the scenes," and their discomfort with self-promoting their abilities and potential. In Singapore and Hong Kong, women spoke about constructs of a "proper femininity" and "Asian family values" within the "Confucian value system" (cf., PuruShotam, 1998). Some women considered this not only as part of Chinese cultural heritage but also as government rhetoric and ideological constructs in the name of nation-state and identity building. In Thailand, women made similar references to Buddhist and Asian values to explain women's role in society. And in Malaysia, women commented about eastern culture, Muslim culture, and expectations of women within those cultural value systems.

As one dean noted earlier, men don't like women to imitate men's behaviors. Yet assertive, self-promotional strategies have worked well for men, whereas traditional feminine reluctance "to be pushy" or to market her "academic capital" (Bourdieu, 1988) has not apparently worked in women's favor:

- "And the thing is that many of us, Malaysian women or maybe Malays in general, want to get ahead, but you don't really unless other people accept you. And then you feel that if someone says you are good, okay, fine but I don't go around saying, you know, I'm good, I should get this. I think many of us eastern women are like that."
- "You would have to show off yourself so other people can remember. For me, I don't like to do it. It's easy for men."
- "You have to be pushy and sometimes do things that you don't like to get what you want. It's difficult. It is our culture. We just cannot do it. It is not us. Not appropriate for women, not here."

Several women, however, saw the need for women to overcome their inhibitions and to become more assertive, "more forward":

Women speak when it is necessary to speak. The assertive thing is important actually. I think a lot of Malay women, or for that matter all Malaysian women in administration, should be more forward. You know, we are too withdrawn. I think we should learn to say more often the things that we think should be said.

The western literature has strongly advocated that, to break through glass ceilings, women should be more proactive in self-advocating their aspirations, abilities, and potential. In short, to make themselves heard and visible, to assert their career goals, to speak up and demonstrate leadership abilities, to demonstrate rhetorical abilities such as arguing on principle (rather than anecdote) in public forums, to lead a team and also be a team-player, and so forth. Clearly, such individualist and competitive strategies of self-promotion are inappropriate in cultural contexts where women are socialized to enact a more "subdued," "quiet," invisible, and family-oriented femininity:

- "Women are not so visible, being culturally women in Malaysia, in Asia, I think we are more subdued. They do their work quietly. They don't talk so much. They don't join the informal group so they are less visible than the men."
- "I think there are a lot of cultural factors. Women, Asian women, prefer to work quietly and to achieve, to work. I'm not [supposed] to scream and shout about it, you know, so it takes quite a change in one's upbringing actually. Women are brought up that way."
- "Women who are seen to be aggressively selling themselves are few and far between, because something is telling them not to do it. I can't think of any women here who I can pick out and say this is one of those forward women."

Household and family are powerful signifiers of femininity and identity markers in women's lives that can exert professional costs by impeding academic productivity and development. Two deans explain:

- "I think women in Malaysia, I don't know about Chinese, but as Muslims, even though we hold top posts or any post at work, we are still a humble housewife when we go back [home] and we are a humble wife to our husband. That has worked very well with a lot of, especially Muslim, women."
- "Malay women, I know them pretty well because I am one of them; the priorities with appearing to have a good home, looking after the husband and family, are so important. You can't put this aside. And so basically it's the demands of domestic life in the early period of the academician's life that somehow starts their development later. Demands of family slow women's academic productivity."

The politics of Asian values and femininity raise questions about how women can best succeed professionally in a nonwestern, so-called Asian and Muslim cultural context but within a hierarchical institution that is essentially built on a western model of university education (Altbach, 1989). The generic bureaucratic structure of the university, the system of competitive examinations and grading, the dominance of western scientific paradigms, research and publishing cultures, and the intellectual division of disciplines are not historically eastern, Asian, or Malaysian but European. Malaysian higher education is a cultural hybrid of sorts: a post-colonial readaptation of British colonialism and high modernism. How can women proceed in this cultural confluence? Women do agree that they need to become more assertive about their abilities, aspirations, and leadership potential, that they need to become more visible and develop their own networks or break into existing influential networks. The complexity for Malaysian feminists, as Maznah Mohamad (1994) observes, is that their struggle is as much with resisting western patriarchal and feminist discourses as it is with challenging local, indigenous masculinist narratives and practices. In her words, feminists need to face head-on the "non-white male, non-rationalist discourse which is increasingly becoming the authoritative voice outside the western hemisphere articulating the new metanarrative of the anti-west movement" (p. 127).

DOUBLE STANDARDS: GENDER RELATIONS

Related to issues of cultural value systems that construct roles and expectation of women that may not be conducive to career mobility within certain labor market sectors are cultural attitudes toward gender relationships. We heard how women describe the difficulties they have breaking into the inner circles of influential male networks—the social-academic "clubs" where information and connections circulate. Several of the married and divorced women also spoke of the difficulties that can arise when women attempt to network with male colleagues, and of the suspicions surrounding even ordinary collegial encounters between men and women:

- "In the beginning it's [difficult] breaking in. Now they will listen, but there's always that barrier. I think it is culturally, especially with Malays, like me. Then men and women don't really work together. If they do, people's perception is that there is something going on, something like that, which is not very nice."
- "Yes, especially with Muslims you see—it is kind of very difficult for me to be seen with other men and things like that. I don't do all those kinds of things."

Historically and cross-culturally, compliance with social rules of decorum in gender relations almost always applies more harshly to and reflects on the conduct of women. In that regard, women may well pay a higher price for breaking social taboos, whereas men's conduct with and among women is usually less sanctioned. As was the case for women in Singapore, fears among women of being seen in the wrong light adds another constraint to career mobility opportunities. However, there are exceptions, such as age and ethnicity:

- "If they are much older than me, in their 50s, then okay, I can talk to them. There's very little barrier. But with the young ones . . . what would people think if that person and me who are not working together . . . it is difficult."
- "I'm not sure about elsewhere but here—I used to call it a small village— they have the village mentality. If you happen to walk more than once with somebody, I mean just because you want to discuss something, and people start talking, looking . . . I don't feel it so much, say, if I go out with a non-Malay man to discuss something. But should it be another Malay man, even though he is my colleague, there's always that—I don't know what it is. I have to watch myself. Not to be too friendly. People might think what's going on even though there's nothing."

One dean spoke of the impropriety of "crossing the path" of the gender divide. This suggests an apt metaphor for describing yet another barrier, another subtle and invisible line of women's confinement. Containment in a zone of feminine propriety denies women access to the social encounters and practices men take for granted: "We don't go out with men for lunch or for, you know, talk or golf or things like that. Women don't do that with their colleagues you see because it is simply beyond our cultural values for women to cross that path." One related aspect of perceived glass ceilings that straddles issues of gender relations, cultural values, feminine identity and "propriety," and generational differences is the issue of attire. Women's choice of dress seems a contentious issue, the historical and doctrinal politics of which cannot be pursued here. However, the women's comments do raise issues about the politics of feminine representation and how these affect women's career mobility. Several of the western-dressed Muslim Malay women told me of the substantial pressure they felt by being among a remaining handful in their institutions not complying with the wearing of *tudong* (headscarf) and *baju kurung* (tunic and long skirt). They claimed that this pressure would eventually wear them down and they would have to give in:

You see me, I don't wear the scarf. I don't wear it because I was raised
not wearing it. My mother didn't. I find it very difficult to start wearing
it, but if I don't, the pressure is greater for me now to wear it because
almost everybody on campus is wearing it and I think the networking is
better. It's better if you do. I think it would be easier for some of the men
to accept me as a leader if I were to wear it.

Some women claimed that their mothers' lives and their own childhoods
were unencumbered by the cultural pressures to wear the headscarf, tunic,
and long skirt:

My mother's generation, they didn't wear scarves. When I was a student
about 20 years ago I was not wearing any scarves, but I do get some
remarks from males, even female friends who say, "Why don't you wear
scarves?" You know, it is against Islam and that kind of thing. But now I
think people just accept it, even if you are not wearing it. People think
one day maybe she will change, she will wear it.

Two women provided detailed explanations of the principles of gender
equality embedded in the Q'uran, how Islamic precepts protect and
develop the "true" nature of women and political and doctrinal aspects of
the current debate in the Islamic world among Muslim feminists over *ijti-
had*, the reinterpretation of Islamic doctrine. Women's personal alignments with these debates are highly political. It is a sensitive topic for
outsiders, and the various ideological/feminist strands and political factions within what is clearly a global Islamic project are too complex to
map out here (cf., Bloul, 1998). Nevertheless, what became apparent in
these conversations is that women who support the Malay version of *hijab*
and those still resistant are aware of the cultural pressures on Muslim
women to conform, at least to *tudung*. Those who refuse may find things
"uneasy" for they "are surrounded" and have some difficulty networking:

- "If you notice in the private sector, there are not many women wearing
  scarves. You go to public sector, almost everybody. For those not wearing scarves, it's like it's uneasy. They are surrounded. But a lot of professionals, now they are wearing scarves. How you wear it is up to you."
- "I know I have to wear it. To get ahead and to conform. Because everybody else does. And I think the men, if I want to network, and I think
  because their wives also wear it so it would be a lot easier for me."

Of her experience at another university, one western-dressed deputy dean had this to say: "I have been told right to my face by one of my colleagues [at another university] that I would never be accepted there . . . .I think it is because of the men lecturers who were there. They feel comfortable if a lady is covered. They don't say it to me here, but I can feel it sometimes." She also spoke of some women allies in her faculty who are not "about to give in," and a vice chancellor who is supportive of her choice: "There are two other [Muslim Malay] lecturers in my faculty. One had her education in Australia, and she's not about to give in. . . . Luckily, the VC hasn't got any preferences." As I discuss later in this chapter, ethnic differences create what several non-Muslim, non-*bumiputera* women termed "ethnic concrete ceilings." In the women's comments about *tudung*, however, another intracultural ceiling emerges that apparently limits women's opportunities around issues of self-signification and cultural representation.

CAREER ASPIRATIONS

I asked all the women about their early career and current aspirations. Would they like to push on to more senior positions? How do women manage their career ambitions? Most claimed not to have had any managerial ambitions at the start of their careers. As with my other case studies, women got into higher education because they loved teaching and some enjoyed research. Since most of the women in this study were in their late 40s and early 50s, few had further career ambitions. This comment was typical: "Yes I would like to see more women in higher positions. Myself no. My aspirations are not that high. I never aspired Vice Chancellor, or even Dean. When I was younger, it's because of the kids and now I say not, I don't want the bother." For many, retirement was a goal to be realized in the near future, and most looked forward to it, although there was some ambivalence about such life changes: "Half of me wants to stay home and look after my husband properly because I have been neglecting him. But half of me cannot imagine not getting excited about presenting papers, about reading up on something or other. It's terrible!" Several women commented about what they perceived to be a lack of aspirations and motivation among women:

- "Well a large number of lecturers here have been pushed to apply for associate professor. They just give up. Some of them just couldn't be bothered."

- "I think in general women are little bit more inward in the sense that they don't show off or they don't boost themselves up, compared to the men."
- "We, the women, seem to be quite content in carrying on just where they are. Not terribly ambitious to go up."
- "Women are more likely to take lower-paying jobs. Women are more likely to follow their hearts in terms of what they want to do. So they don't get up."

However, in the view of one dean, the younger generation seems more driven to succeed, more ambitious, career focused, and competitive:

> They do quarrel amongst themselves; there's a lot of friction, which never happened before because we were all very nonthreatening to another, but now they are more ambitious and they see rivalry and that's no good. And they are always asking things like, you know sort of saying, what's in it for me. Now everything is noted, everything done is in their personal files, whereas I think of when I was younger, more junior, I never bothered about these things. Whatever I did was lost. There was no record to show for it.

A few women in their early and mid-40s had promotional aspirations all the way to vice chancellor (VC) or deputy vice chancellor (DVC) positions. Despite reservations about the chances of a woman being appointed at that level, one dean felt she might have a chance, convinced that "one day there will be one":

> If I do very well, then who knows, they might pick me as the VC or DVC, but it is not likely to be a VC because, simply, I don't think they will pick a woman. But even though there has never been in all the nine universities that we have in Malaysia any DVC lady, one day there will be one.

Other women had dreams of opening their own school, coffee shops, or bookshops:

- "I would like to work independently—an educational institution or a training center. I don't like this pressure looming over me: I am really sandwiched from the top and from below. I have got to take orders from the top, and sometimes they are not well taken up by the grassroots. So I am really caught in between. So I like to work in a place where I feel free. I don't feel free that I am pressured from all quarters."

- "I have visions of anything ranging from opening a school for young kids . . . to opening a restaurant. Especially a restaurant in a bookshop. Like a coffee place."

GENDERED CONCEPTS
OF CAREER AND SUCCESS

Men do tend to overestimate their abilities and their importance, whereas women are much more self-critical and often self-denigrating of their abilities and achievements. In the words of one associate professor, "Men feel they are better than they really are. Women feel that they are not as good as they really are. Never good enough, you know." Tied to gender-differentiated self-concepts and professional aspirations are gendered concepts of career and success. Again, feminine identity and socially sanctioned measures of female achievement and success are more closely linked with women as good homemakers, wives, and mothers. Whereas women see men's visions of career as extremely focused, women are seen to have a more multidimensional focus:

- "For a man, his priority seems very clear-cut. Career—extremely focused. He gets the support from the family. The woman, she places the family, her husband's success, as the first priority. I suspect that some women would not want to make the choice that I have made."
- "Men's equation of success is very different from a woman's. You see a woman's satisfaction and her equation of success is very multidimensional, and I think basically that is why women are not there. They see the benefits [of career] as lower than the cost that you pay for. And it is this multidimensionality in women which I think keeps them away."

For many women, career options are limited because family and child care responsibilities restrict their mobility if positions require extensive travel or even job relocations:

There was a post vacant and . . . I was considered for the job. The new VC, he thinks well of women, he thinks they can do the job, and he was thinking of a woman . . . who can move around a lot . . . .I can't take that job because it means leaving my family a lot more because this post involves a lot of traveling and meeting people. I am not ready for that . . . because of my young family.

On the other hand, generational changes have brought about a shift in women's "equation of success." Unlike their mothers, women are no longer able to rely solely on marriage as a lifetime career move. Women today have various options, but they also lack guaranteed financial and emotional security of married life:

> In the 50s, we had a different kind of equation of success, and more fac-
> tors. It isn't like the times of my mother, when you married you married
> for life. Women now tend to say well, half the time the marriages don't
> work anyway. In Islamic marriages, too, the security in a marriage is
> very questionable. I do find so many academics, you know, after a while
> the men do have second wives or things like that. So that security, that
> equation, has been taken away from some of the younger women today.

All the women had much to say about generational changes: from the way Chinese and Indian women perceived historical changes in race relations, to women's perceptions of differences in seniority and youth with regard to levels of respect from colleagues, and women's lack of institutional support and/or motivation to "break into administration" in the early 1980s.

GENERATIONAL CHANGE

Since most of the women in this study were in their late 40s and 50s, they had experienced a number of generational shifts and had a good sense of how social relations change in tandem with institutional seniority. Some attributed respect for older women to "eastern" cultural values that, unlike those of the west, place a high premium on family cohesion and intergenerational and kinship ties through the notion of filial piety and respect of elders:

- "We retire at 55, so I'm one of the oldest. I am one of the earlier professors . . . [and] the yet younger men, even the DVC, they do have that, that sense of respect—that's eastern culture, you know, in the men, they do respect age to a certain extent."

- "And I think being a senior woman helped. There is this culture of respecting older women."

Gender and age can work against women: young women are taken less seriously, and young men seem more acceptable in positions of authority than young women:

- "Gender and age both don't help me that much when I want to network with other deputy deans, unless they are about my age. It is somewhat easier . . . if my counterparts are about my age. If they are a bit older, then it's a bit different."
- "People are more accepting of younger men than of younger women. So women have got double disadvantage: the gender and the age."

Looking back over a long career, one dean regretted those early years "when I was younger, more junior, I never bothered about these things. Whatever I did was lost. There was no record to show for it." The possibility of "breaking in" or keeping track of teaching and research productivity was not part of the mindset of women in those years. Today, however, more senior women make efforts to encourage the upcoming generation to set their career sights higher and to pursue those goals with single-minded dedication:

- "In the early '80s, the thought of breaking in didn't even occur to us; . . . we were so dumb, you know, we were so complacent about the whole thing and we were not unhappy. We enjoyed the work, but administration was far, far away."
- "I notice there is a younger group of Malaysian women so committed to developing themselves . . . [and] I do think we watch out for them: telling them to publish, don't be slow, get confirmed [tenured]."

The Indian and Chinese women I spoke with, now in their 50s, perceived generational changes in the ways race factored into institutional life and career opportunities for non-Malay women. Several felt that a sense of racial tolerance was more evident in the 1960s and 1970s than it is today. In one Indian dean's view:

I went to university in the '60s. I didn't feel the racial element was inhibiting. Probably because at that time it was more an open system.

Senior administrators in that era were very open. When I was promoted from a Deputy to a Dean, I actually questioned the Vice Chancellor; I said, "Look, I have two negatives—I am not a *bumiputera* and
I am not a man." I was the only woman Dean in the university and I
told him, "No one would accept me," and he said, "No, I have full confidence in you."

In historical retrospect, this dean also felt that the younger generation of
Malay graduates who are now coming up through the administrative ranks
have had less exposure to cultural/racial difference and therefore might be
less tolerant:

Some have come from schools that have been purely residential for one
ethnic group. So I think they probably don't understand what it is like to
have an open competition. In a sense, it's a kind of shielding and gives
them the impression that they don't evaluate somebody else's background. There's the ethnic element that comes in. I see that. It is a different generation: The level of tolerance is different, and underlying the
cloak of nationalism is the ethnicity cohort. It's like yes, we are
Malaysian, but what we are doing is for our own kind.

Issues of ethnicity came up in a variety of conversational contexts with
Malay and non-Malay women, and it is to the question of ethnicity and
"concrete" ceilings that I turn to next.

ETHNIC CONCRETE CEILINGS

The questionnaire asked all the women to what extent they considered
ethnicity and/or religious background to be an important factor in shaping
career opportunities in Malaysian higher education. On a four-point Likert
scale, all Malay women responded that it was "not at all important,"
whereas every Chinese and Indian woman responded that it was
"extremely important." Such an ethnic-differentiated response suggests
that, by and large, the Malay women were not aware that decades of pro-
Malay social policies were, in fact, read as problematic by non-Malay
women. As one Chinese dean said, "To them [Malays] the ethnic glass
ceiling doesn't exist. They don't know that it exists." Conversely, the
Indian and Chinese women expressed very strong feelings about the kind

of race-based privileges accorded to Malays and the disadvantages they
perceived for their children and themselves:

- "I am a double minority. I am a minority in terms of gender. I am a
  minority in terms of ethnicity. In meetings, I am always the minority. I
  think ethnicity is also a factor in appointment of senior positions, you
  know. As you know, they are all appointed, deans and all." (Chinese
  deputy dean)
- "Basically the top management personnel are either men or Malays.
  Very few non-Malay Chinese or Indians ever get to the top. The posts
  and assistants are all political. And that would depend on the Prime Minister, at the recommendation of the Minister of Education. But I like to
  think this university is changing all that. We have Heads of Departments
  who are non-Malays now [and] a Deputy Dean is not Malay." (Malay
  dean)

When I asked the Malay women if they were aware that for many Chinese
and Indians the ethnic glass ceiling is seen as an unfair disadvantage, a
social justice and equity issue that many saw as a problem, the Malay
women often referred to the handful of non-Malays serving as deans or
heads, or else explained how most non-Malays are happy to move into the
business or private college sector:

- "I have heard about it but I don't know. I don't feel that it is quite true.
  Here one of the Deputy Deans is Chinese. We have non-Malays as
  Heads of Departments." (Malay head)
- "Chinese, Indian—they achieve, they attempt to achieve but in a different sphere, in the international sphere. In WHO, or UNESCO, world
  mangrove swamp experts, and so on. At least you are somebody internationally. This is where you find your outlet and your satisfaction. But at
  the same time it is important that there is representation from other ethnic groups, because if everybody looks outside and finds their satisfaction outside, there is no one to represent the group internally." (Chinese
  deputy dean)
- "Non-Malays, they already understand the situation, and they have
  adjusted very well. And if they feel that they cannot do well here, then
  they can do well somewhere else; they are doing very well in business
  side." (Malay dean)
- "That's why you see a lot of non-Malay in the private sector because
  there you can go up. You can be CEO and things like that in the private

sector. The private sector is very non-*bumi* . . .. It reinforces the whole cycle. All my friends are CEOs somewhere, making big money." (Chinese deputy dean)

Related to ethnic concrete ceilings are student intake quotas, which further complicate politics among academic staff:

- "Well at the University of Malaysia there are probably more non-Malays. But here probably more Malays. In terms of student intake, the policy states that you cannot take more than 50% of certain ratios because the number of Malays are more, so we have to give a certain percentage to the Malays, the non-Malays, the Indians, and Chinese." (Malay deputy dean)
- "There are many issues that involve ethnicity. The number of students who fail, who graduate, who get the top grades. If you look at the numbers of students who fail, at the bottom, a lot of them are Malays and the top are Chinese, so issues like that are being discussed, and I think they feel more comfortable talking to heads who are of similar kind, you know." (Chinese deputy dean)

In addition to having internalized the concrete ceilings of political appointments and cultural attitudes that limit women's access to senior decision-making positions, non-Malay women have also learned to internalize another set of limitations constructed around ethnic identity and race-based policies:

- "There is a constitution whereby we have to abide by, not just gender in that sense, but racial. So you see, all those holding top posts are not Chinese, not Indians but all Malays. So, being a Chinese, however good you are, you will never get a [chance] . . . the chances will be slim to be picked to be a dean." (Malay dean)
- "[My relative] she's in a very senior position in the university. She actually mentioned to me 'I am always the Dean of the School whenever it is *Hari Raya* because that is the long break and everybody takes a break, and she's made Dean for five days." (Chinese deputy dean)

In hours of off-the-record conversations, the Chinese women repeatedly raised their discontent. Conversations about women's views on the educational opportunities denied their children were not recorded. I therefore have no transcript evidence in support of their repeated expressions of dismay over the effects of legislated *bumiputera* privileges: from scholarships to enrollment quotas, grade distribution, and what one woman termed a "racist meritocracy." Although they admitted that, as a community, they do well in the private, corporate sector, not every Chinese wants to pursue a life in business. Many felt disheartened and embittered. In the words of one Chinese deputy dean:

> Efforts from the best brains are directed outside. It's a glass ceiling. Ethnic glass ceiling you know. You are not getting recognized and you are not going to be appointed to any senior position. You know, so why knock your head against that ceiling. So this [position] is as far as I go.

Malay women gave me "the facts" of race-based hiring and promotional policies. None talked too much about race as a career impediment for Chinese and Indian Malaysians, and none saw racial discrimination as a blatant flaw in popular meritocratic rhetoric about equal opportunity. However, one Malay dean cautiously alluded to race as a possible factor in curtailing Chinese and Indian academics' promotional prospects, thereby creating "disillusioned academics":

> Chances are authorities at the top will look for a Malay first, whether a female or a man, and then you go to the next level. I am not sure how bad it is but you hear stories of disillusioned academics where one wonders whether because they are Indians or Chinese or because there are other reasons for them not to have a chance.

Thirty of years of feminist scholarship has argued that, if women want to step out of the shadows of patriarchal dominance and rule and take their rightful place in partnerships with men in public life and civic affairs, women must act as a group, as a collective force for social change. Despite women's innumerable differences of race, class, sexuality, religion, and cultural backgrounds, the notion of coalition building across differences has been an integral component of feminist agendas and initiatives across the globe (e.g., NGOs, five UN conferences on women, UNESCO literacy campaigns for girls and women, rape and domestic violence shelters, etc). The point is that divisions among women are counterproductive for the advancement of all women. Strategies of divide and rule have always served patriarchy well, and they have served men particularly well in isolating and fragmenting women.

The sense of alienation, resignation, and disappointment I detected among the Chinese and Indian women, and the general lack of awareness about this issue among the Malay women, reveal a substantial gap among women (as well as families and communities). Such a gap—in opportunity, perceptions, understanding—is an artifact of history and politics. As a construct, it has no "essential," ahistorical, or inalienable biological features, and as such, it can be reversed and changed. Such change is possible if women work collaboratively to build that critical mass of women as change agents. Collectively, women are already demonstrating their intellectual, leadership, and managerial abilities that are equal to, if not sometimes better than, men. Indeed, as women in my other case studies noted, women's management and leadership styles embody the very features being promoted today as the hallmarks of the new postmodern managerialism and corporatist ethos.

GENDERED LEADERSHIP STYLES

I asked all the women if they saw any difference between female and male managerial and leadership styles. Their responses corroborate findings in the management literature and parallel responses from women in my other case studies. Women are seen as more perceptive, subtle, tolerant, meticulous, fair, and open-minded:

- "You can't generalize, but maybe some women are more meticulous."
- "We have our subtleties. Women rule more with that human touch. We are more instinctive."
- "I think they are very caring. Women tend to be more perceptive of a situation when they handle it. I think it is probably the maternal instinct. They handle things differently. Women are more consensual. More negotiating style. It's the style that women use in trying to get somebody to help them or to assist them. It's not autocratic. I think I see that."
- "I think women try very hard to be fair, to be transparent. There is more negotiation. I think we try sometimes to our disadvantage, to be more democratic. I think we talk more. We get people to come to talk to us more. Before we make decisions, we try to get a cross-section. And I think we are not as prejudiced as the men are towards women staff."
- "Detailed about a lot of things, fussy about small details. But that is typical of women, I suppose."

Generalizations are dangerous. However, the women made some insightful comparisons between male and female management styles that highlight the very distinctions raised in the literature between men's more self-centered and often autocratic approaches and women's focus on the task at hand, rather than on herself:

- "I think women in general, especially in academia, we have more—how do you say—depth, you know. It's more like a mission, you want to do it right, the right thing, a commitment. As for the men, it's more like, they do something that is not right, they'd try to cover it up . . . and then become defensive."

- "My goal is to make this faculty the best. Doesn't matter if it is me or not. Probably the man would say to make this faculty the best with 'me' on top."

- "I've got a man boss. I've never had a chance to work for a woman. Being there myself now, I noticed the difference between the two of us. I know he cares, but he leaves the details to other people. I make sure things are done because that is how I work. I don't know, many women are like that from what I know. They get things done. We spend time at each task compared to men."

Women have a sense of their own multidimensional orientation, for they frequently explained gender differences in management style by referring to women's multiple roles as professionals, household managers, accountants, logistics experts, wives, and mothers:

- "Women are more tolerant and they are more open-minded. And they are more rational. Most women have been mothers, so they would know how to look after the young . . . how to minister justly . . . so they would be tolerant . . . they would have to be fair. Men have always considered themselves as being the sole breadwinner. So they are the boss, so they always have that sort of attitude whereas the ladies, I think they have been taking various roles, from the subordinate to breadwinners."

- "A lot of negotiation that goes on in the household is unseen. Negotiations with your children, your husband. Negotiate at home, then you negotiate with students, with the bosses, staff. When the children are sick you have to be responsible, see what my time is like. You have got to negotiate all the time."

- "I believe women can become better leaders than men . . . because I think they listen more than they try to impose. They are more sympathetic. And they are more organized in their work, especially if you are a wife, mother, you have to manage your home. You manage everything, you can take stress better than men because you are used to handling a lot of work."

On the other hand, women's mothering and nurturing tendencies tend to reemerge in the workplace where they perform "mom work" or "smile work" (Tierney & Bensimon, 1996). As one woman said, "Wherever they are, you know, women mother, even in the office they still tend to play the same role—motherly instincts. I do not mean to say that men don't care, but women bring a different experience into their work."

All the women said that they were "thrown into the deep end" and learned by "trial and error." They relied on their intuition, on administrative skills they had learned at more junior levels as heads or deputy deans, and many relied on former deans and trusted colleagues to help out:

- "We never had any management courses. We were just thrown into the deep end and once we were there, I think we didn't do too badly."
- "Well I learned by trial and error. We are not given training. I think once or twice—quite by accident—they called us a few times just have some workshop how to handle management and all that, that's all."
- "There was no specific training to tell me what to do. If I want something, I have to ask people, previous Deputy Deans. It's a long process. It was a difficult one in the beginning. Now it is not so bad that I know what I am supposed to do."

In short, the women brought skills and attitudes to their positions for which they did not receive the kind of training seen as so essential to the new managerialism. However, all felt that they could benefit from some form of training in issues related specifically to women in management: how to manage upward and downward, how to negotiate one's role and agendas within a predominantly male managerial structure, how to cope with time management (work and home), feelings of isolation, managing male staff, and so forth. They also felt a need for training in financial management, policy implementation, and particularly, in the new bureaucratic administration of Malaysia's ISO 9000 quality assurance mechanisms and processes. Unfortunately, training specifically for women managers is not a university priority:

- "Recently there was a workshop for the women managers at Langkawi, but the university wasn't sponsoring anyone and nobody's able it to go. It costs money."
- "Priorities are different 'upstairs.' If there's a seminar on, let's say, total quality management, one of those key words today, then they would send someone, but if it's a seminar on training women managers, oh, then they say they have no money. They are not putting any priority on those things."

One might argue that the lack of institutional support for enhancing women's leadership and managerial repertoires is shortsighted because it ignores and devalues the huge pool of ability that lies dormant among women across the university sector. Moreover, from the point of view of the new corporatism and the push for total quality management (TQM) input and outcome measures, the failure to implement systems specifically designed to support a class of new recruits—namely, women managers—effectively reduces the potential for enhanced quality and productivity at both ends: input and outcome. Drawing on my own experience of quality assurance implementation that I outlined in Chapter 3, I explained to the women how discourses of TQM can be used to support the push for greater gender balance by using the principles of accountability, transparency, and quality in women's own interests and as a quality enhancement issue for the university.

WAYS FORWARD

In closing our conversations, I asked each woman if she thought the gender equity programs common in the west would be useful for women in Malaysia. Since all the women had studied overseas for at least one postgraduate degree, and most regularly traveled internationally for conferences, professional business, or sabbaticals, they were familiar with a range of equity programs and issues prevalent western universities:

It [equity programs] doesn't work here because the culture is different. Over there I do feel that they have taken up the gender issues; they give priority to a lot of things, lot of opportunity. Being a pregnant woman—you are given a lot of care and sympathy. The men are quite understanding.

Equity is not the same as a quota system typical of American-style affirmative action. Rather, it is about proportional benchmarking to achieve an incremental gender balance through provisions of systemic support. These can include adequate on-campus child care, mentoring programs, seminars to address the specific needs of female staff, management training, sexual harassment policies and procedures, policies for the nonsexist use of language in all university documents, inclusion in annual university reports of sex distribution across job classifications, promotion, tenure, and appointment rates, equity targets, and so forth. Equal opportunity legislation in Australia, for instance, requires all universities (and all companies of 100 or more employees) to report annually to the federal government on equity targets, systems, and outcomes for identified equity groups, which include persons with disabilities, indigenous and migrant groups, and women, among others. Many of the women felt that such an approach would not work in Malaysian higher education. Some felt that women had to lobby and build coalitions among themselves because they could not rely on men for unconditional support:

- "I don't think we have that awareness here yet (of equity programs). It has to start with the women themselves. Women must support women, that's important because if we have squabbles, if there is no cooperation among women, then we can't move forward "
- "We must support our own group because you can't depend on support from the men. It is difficult to break that sort of barrier."

Understandably, there are many other pressing issues that women struggle for besides securing more equitable opportunities for senior women academics. Moreover, in times of rapid social and economic change and instability, fighting for a "feminist cause" in what many may consider the elite sector of higher education may seem a bourgeois privilege with which few could sympathize. As one dean put it, "Just so many things we have to fight for. We are trying for the Women's Studies Unit, for a program for working women."

In one university, several women lauded their vice chancellor for his support of women. As much as change for women will invariably come from women organizing among themselves, a new generation of men "at the top" may help pave the way: "Our new VC, I mean he saw somebody who can do the work and he felt a lady would do the job better. He went ahead. I thought, well, why not. I mean some of the men are not going to be happy with that."

Relatedly, all the women saw the new corporate ethos in ambivalent terms. On one hand, they saw it as the introduction of yet another layer of bureaucratic reporting. On the other hand, all expressed various levels of dissatisfaction with existing top-down politics and felt that the gradual move towards decentralization and devolution might create greater autonomy for the sector, which may also open up more opportunities for women:

> The policymakers up there, they decide who will become who—this is the politics that comes down. I don't think it is a good thing. Hopefully, in a few years, when we are fully corporatized and we are free from the government's subsidy, you know, then we can do our own thing. We can be more autonomous. Academics would like to be free from the influence of the politics because the politics dictates what we have to do, what we can and can't do. We are not quite free to, you know, be academicians.

Yet to transform gendered attitudes and orientations, which are at the heart of gender and sexual politics in any society, is a much larger task. It is the task of parents at home and teachers and textbooks in schools, which still retain control over the primary and secondary socialization of the young. In one dean's view:

> [Change] has to come from the way we bring up our children and during schooling time, and how we perceive their roles. We have to offer jobs like typing for men so that they feel that, "Oh okay, men can also do this typing job, it's not only for women." Being a secretary, it doesn't always have to be a lady. Specification for jobs has to be more open in that sense.

Finally, in the words of one dean, the most significant target for change may be men themselves: "The target should be men now. We should educate them to understand that we women have tried to come out from our shell. Now, the men have to change." Clearly, this is not a short-term option. Women have changed, adapted, and worked hard to earn the right to leave the kitchen. Their struggles have resulted in their right to work the double-day. Yet have men struggled to gain greater access to the domestic sphere, to greater participation in childrearing, housework, or the emotional work of caring for family and kin? The target for change, then, must include men (and boys) if women envision a future for themselves and their daughters, where they will no longer see themselves as second-class citizens, passed over in favor of men, worried about being seen with male colleagues, or unable to attend after-hours work functions because husbands veto their mobility.

CONCLUDING REMARKS

Many of the women's experiences and interpretations in this study, and those reported in previous chapters, resonate with research on women in higher education in western and nonwestern societies. Women universally claim that the double-day of professional responsibilities and child care and household duties is a difficult balancing act. For many women, childbearing and rearing often occurs in the early years of their careers, which can impede the development of research productivity. Women also agree that there are gendered differences in career aspirations and opportunities, and that the culture of the academy is shaped around masculinist values and ways of doing academic business. Most, although not all, women are aware of old boys' clubs in their institutions that are generally closed to women. Exclusion from powerful senior networks limits women's visibility and access to crucial information, influential alliances, and promotional prospects.

Across the four case studies I have conducted in Southeast Asia, women all seem to agree that Asian values or Asian culture espouse a specific concept of femininity. Whether in Islamic Malaysia (Bloul, 1998; Stivens, 2000), Buddhist Thailand (Limanonda, 2000; Unger, 1998) or Confucian Singapore (Chan, 2000; Hill & Lian, 1995) and Hong Kong (Lau, 1997; Tang, Au, Chung, & Ngo, 2000), women's roles and conduct in public life are framed by cultural expectations that place a premium on women as wives, mothers, and homemakers, and on women's conduct as "subdued," "quiet," and "withdrawn." Collegial relations between men and women, even women well into their 50s, raise eyebrows and are seen with suspicion. Cultural codes of conduct infuse gender relationships that restrain women and impede social and career mobility. In such a cultural milieu, it can be argued that western solutions to reversing the gender imbalance in higher-education management by advocating a more individualist and self-promotional approach to breaking the glass ceiling are seen by women as inappropriate. Yet there is also the perception that generational change is underway as a new generation of academic women are coming up the ranks and are more career oriented, competitive, and ambitious.

In generational terms, then, it is important to acknowledge that many of the women I interviewed in Malaysia, as well as those in Thailand, Singapore, and Hong Kong, had already silently broken through rigid and long-established barriers and pursued goals not commonplace among the majority of young women in their day. That is, some 20 or more years ago, women now in their late 40s and 50s, made the choice to undertake the rigors of Ph.D. study, often with young children in tow. They worked their way up through junior lectureships into mid-level administration, all the while raising young families and some, eventually, ending up as single parents following divorce. Few women had any management training and yet most could claim that "we didn't do too badly."

Postscript

The women who have spoken here have given us insights into how women's career trajectories and opportunities are shaped by the intersections of historically situated cultural values and structures, and place-specific sociopolitical and economic factors. This network of intersections is framed within colonial and postcolonial legacies that do not neatly fit into single-theory explanations or one-dimensional western conceptualizations of glass ceilings or a generalized patriarchy. Whatever the actual impediments described in the concept of glass ceiling may or may not be, one thing is certain: They can only be made intelligible by reference to local sites, sociopolitical and cultural contexts and histories. We need to look at the politics of place—that is, historically contingent and shifting cultural and political discourses, structures, and processes—to understand how women shape and are shaped by the social enactment of personal and professional relations, career aspirations and mobility, and concepts of career.

Like all research, feminist or otherwise, this study is partial, incomplete, the product of my interpretive viewpoints and blind spots. It is both enabled and limited by the situated contexts of these case studies. Arguably, the insights of a dozen women in each of four countries cannot be taken as representative. And yet they do tell us something about the way local cultural and gender ideologies blend within larger global discourses circulating throughout higher-education sectors. Family and child care responsibilities appear to be similar for Southeast Asian and western women. And yet women's position in relation to family in the west is far less tied to notions of filial responsibility to parents and elderly kin. So-called Asian values—whether contemporary interpretations of Islamic, Confucian, or Buddhist ideologies—infuse Southeast Asian women's sense of social conduct in ways described by the women as a "tendency to understate, to hide"—a sense of public decorum characterized by restraint and working quietly behind the scenes.

No comparable values constrain western women's public and work-place conduct in quite the same way. Instead, we are encouraged to self-promote, to make our achievements and aspirations heard and visible, to learn how to compete on an uneven playing field. Through western eyes, Asian women appear bound to a self-effacing feminine propriety. Through Asian eyes, we appear unseemingly forward, often loud, individualist and competitive, neither familial nor communal.

I began this project with a very simple question: How do local contexts frame academic women's career paths and opportunities? I began with the notion that academic glass ceilings would be much the same everywhere, particularly since the university is indeed a global institution in bureaucratic and program structure, function, forms of labor, and educational requirements for staff. My interest was to go beyond the antici-pated similarities of women's experiences of glass ceilings impediments to investigate how local political and cultural narratives dovetail with more global structural issues endemic to women's workforce participation in general but characteristic especially of academia.

Women's family and child care responsibilities mediate women's workforce participation everywhere, in every occupation. This compli-cates matters for women in ways it does not for men. In academics, women, like men, face the obligatory three-degree route that often takes well over a decade to complete. But for women, this usually coincides with the time in their lives when they are either raising young children or planning to start families. Time out for childbearing and rearing reduces research productivity, interrupts the building of seniority and promotional prospects, stagnates established networks, and so forth. Alternatively, women delay having children, which can extract heavy personal and social costs.

Much academic work occurs outside the normal 38-hour workweek. Doing research, writing papers, getting published, securing grants, and the endless round of marking and grading are hugely time-consuming activities for which extra work on weekends, holidays, and evenings are hardly sufficient. Work intensification is a global issue for academic women and men. But it is women who hold up not half but almost all of the domestic sky. Moreover, the "delayed gratification" and reward of, say, a publication two years after initial manuscript or book submission, a successful tender or grant application 10 or 12 months after a submission deadline, or the academic promotion years after the painstaking accumulation of academic capital—these all render academic labor profoundly different in kind from most other professions. There is no paid overtime for weekend or evening work. And it is the nature of this kind of work—writing, marking papers, or doing e-mail early in the mornings before the kids get up, working holidays and weekends, and then some more during sabbaticals—that sets the academic profession apart and which extracts a different toll from women than from men. These are universal issues academic women everywhere contend with, including women who can afford the luxury of "an army of servants."

Globalization, particularly in the higher-education sector, has forged new circuits that many academic women regularly travel. Women everywhere are familiar with gender equity issues, with western-style women's liberation and feminism and its popular face through affirmative action. Yet most reject special consideration or initiatives for women in academics or girls in schooling, arguing that women in their countries achieve on principles of merit. Yet the skewed gender imbalance in higher education in these four countries and, indeed, globally, underscores the fraudulence of meritocracy. Moreover, beliefs in the efficacy of gender- and race-blind principles of merit do not sit well in cultural-political contexts that legislate racial preferences and are ruled by patronage systems, whether political, familial, or academic.

Despite the global reach of an increasingly standardized university system and universal forms of academic labor, it is local histories, politics, and the cultural ground to which global products, systems, or flows attach. These ultimately shape and fill in rather than "empty out" the local "real"ization of globalization. The women's commentaries in this study, I believe, are testimonies to the variable but enduring resilience of locally embedded cultural values and structures and, importantly, the capacity of the state to enshrine them in legal-juridical systems. Contrary to popular claims of the death of the nation-state, Malaysia and Singapore are powerful counterexamples that illustrate the persistence of nation-state sovereignty over discourses of national identity and forms of nationalism grounded in cultural and ethnic essentialisms.

Networked on global electronic, publication, and conference trails, displaying cosmopolitan and westernized dispositions, the women in this study nonetheless also embody and enact, translate and renegotiate the cultural imperatives of "home." That is not to suggest an originary cultural residue or anthropological notion of tradition, place, and home. Rather it points to contemporary cultural reworkings, to governmental and, not least, academic narrativizations of the confluence among so-called Asian values, Asian femininity, and local interpretations of modernization, globalization, and capitalism.

The dynamics of globalization are typically discussed in spatial and temporal terms. Despite conceptual acknowledgements of uneven and disjointed effects and counterflows, the dominant imagery of globalization remains tied to the spatial dynamics of center-to-periphery rollout, a leveling or flattening out of all that comes before it. In temporal, syntagmatic terms, history always remains the empirical and discursive precursor of development, modernization, and globalization. Local histories and cultural boundaries, contours and differences thus are *in situ* and precede and predate variable infiltrations of globalizing forces: precolonial predates colonial predates postcolonial, and so on. Together, in the time-space metaphor of globalization's spatial diffusion and local encounters, the local and global are argued to coconstitute, to blend, mix, and reterritorialize that "third space" of glocalization.

Arguably, what partially makes for uneven effects, disjunctive orders, and variable push-pull dynamics is the tenacity of local cultural imagery and memory and, importantly, the power of the state to select, recraft, and in many instances, to legislate cultural tradition and values. Singapore and Malaysia are cases in point. And since the power of the state is globally invested in ruling elites consisting principally of men who represent ruling racial and dominant class interests, the gender politics subtending national agendas and public discourses remain firmly entrenched—indeed, patriarchy as global form but locally inflected, encoded and enacted. And patriarchy isn't just about men—the politicians, generals, mullahs, academics, captains of industry or media—but is powerfully embodied in and enacted by hegemonized women. The resurrection of Asian and Islamic values is unquestionably the work of ruling patriarchs across the region. But women are as much its coauthor and supporter as its critic.

There are no easy or simple conclusions to draw from the issues the women in this study have spoken about. Gender inequality at the most senior ranks of higher education persists. And yet academic women (and men) hold steadfast to notions that women should not receive special treatment or exemptions, and that hard work allows anyone to achieve in their land of meritocratic opportunity. Senior academics circulate on global networks, engage in global-speak, and critique globalization, yet they display many of the characteristics of the new global cosmopolitan elite. They defend and romanticize the local as much as they retranslate it through western theoretical and analytic paradigms. They contest westernization in the symbolic shorthand of CNN or "McDonaldization" platitudes, yet they are its biggest consumer class in their countries. They argue strongly for the retention of local values, tradition, and schooling, yet they pride themselves on their overseas degrees and send their own children to prestigious overseas prep schools and universities.

From western theoretical perspectives, these women's lives and identities could be framed as contradictions in the classic Hegelian sense of opposing, incommensurate ideological positions or social practices. Yet, this isn't about a simple dichotomy, cultural clash, value or generational dissonance. Isn't it, instead, indicative of an endless heterogeneity of values, beliefs, and practices that are the very fabric of subjectivity and being in the world? These stories are about working out one's choices and courses of action within constraints and opportunities, within localities of place and histories, and within relationships here, there, and intergenerationally. Talking about identity formation, Hall argues for the continuous historical transformation of identity, "the continuous play of history, culture and power" that seeps through us and that we remake and replay. There is no pure local place or discursive space in which people enact singular, hermetically sealed cultural identities and practices.

People valorize home or the values of their generation and yet live and enact the symbols, practices, and aspirations of new times and new places. There is nothing extraordinary, contradictory, or "post" about romanticizing the local or the past while vigorously defending or critiquing the global or the historical present of new times. New times are trans-historical, a continuous infusion of change and transition that imperceptibly flows around and through us. We make ourselves within the old, the new, and the in-between, as much as within local situations and global forces. Islamic revivalism is as much a way forward for some as it is retro and a way backward for others. The man who tills the soil or the woman who weaves cloth and stops work for a Coke and a Marlboro surely isn't agonizing over contradiction but is merely having a break. Is it "living a lie" or a contradiction when immigrant families recreate home in a distant land and yet work hard to afford the lifestyle accoutrements of modernity or to provide a better, let alone western, education for their children?

It is my view, and one shared by all the women I have spoken to over the years, that women are eminently capable researchers and scholars, intellectuals, administrators, managers, and leaders. But they are also the social and emotional glue of any society: childbearers and rearers, carers of kin and the aged. We might ask then why women's multiple abilities, contributions, and pivotal role in any society are so routinely undervalued and their aspirations thwarted? To deny women the structural and ideological support that would enable their full and equal access, participation, and share of rewards in the professions of their choice is to deny and impoverish society as a whole. For women to take charge of their educational goals and professional aspirations may mean mounting a cohesive and collaborative effort across women's class or ethnic differences to lobby for and implement a culturally appropriate mix of the kinds of gender equity initiatives that have been institutionalized in the west. As one of the last remaining bastions of patriarchal privilege and power, higher education can only benefit from a greater gender balance over the control and administration of knowledge.

References

Abou-El-Haj, B. (1997). Language and models for cultural exchange. In A. King (Ed.), *Culture, globalization and the world-system* (pp. 139–144). Minneapolis: University of Minnesota Press.

Abraham, C. (1997). *Divide and rule: The roots of race relations in Malaysia.* Kuala Lumpur: INSAN.

Abu-Lughod, J. (1997). Going beyond global babble. In A. King (Ed.), *Culture, globalization and the world-system* (pp. 131–138). Minneapolis: University of Minnesota Press.

Acker, S. (1994). *Gendered education: Sociological reflections on women, teaching, and feminism.* Buckingham, UK: Open University Press.

Acker, S., & Feuerverger, G. (1996). Doing good and feeling bad: The work of women university teachers. *Cambridge Journal of Education, 26*(3), 401–422.

Adler, N., & Izraeli, D. (Eds.). (1994). *Competitive frontiers: Women managers in a global economy.* Massachusetts, MA: Blackwell Business.

Allen, F. (1994). Academic women in Australia: Progress real or imagined? In S. Lie, L. Malik, & D. Harris (Eds.), *The gender gap in higher education.* London: Kogan Page.

Allen, M. (1994). Casualisation and women workers in higher education. *NTEU Frontline, 1*(1), 13.

241

Altbach, P. (1989). Twisted roots: The western impact on Asian higher education. *Higher Education, 18*(1), 9–29.

Angel, D., & Savage, L. (1997). Globalization of R & D in the electronics industry: The recent experiences of Japan. In R. Lee & J. Wills (Eds.), *Geographies of economies* (pp. 209–218). London: Arnold.

Anzaldua, G. (1987). *Borderlands/La frontera.* San Francisco: Aunt Lute Books.

Appadurai, A. (1990). Disjuncture and difference in the global cultural economy. In M. Featherstone (Ed.), *Global culture* (pp. 295–310). London: Sage.

Ariffin, J. (1994). *Women and development in Malaysia.* Kuala Lumpur: Pendaluk Publications.

Arnot, M., & Weiner, G. (Eds.). (1987). *Gender and the politics of schooling.* London: Hutchinson.

Aspland, T. (1999). Struggling with ambivalence within supervisory relations. In A. Holbrook & S. Johnston (Eds.), *Supervision of postgraduate research in education* (pp. 95–111). Coldstream, Australia: Australian Association for Research in Education.

Aspland, T., & O'Donoghue, T. (1994). Quality in supervising overseas students. In O. Zuber-Skerritt & Y. Ryan (Eds.), *Quality in postgraduate education.* London: Kogan Page.

Bacchi, C. (1993). The brick wall: Why so few women become senior academics. *Australian Universities' Review, 36,* 36–39.

Badenoch, R., Brown, R., & Sebastian, A. (1999). Emotional and intellectual safety: A paradigm of successful learning in postgraduate study. In L. Cohen, A. Lee, J. Newman, A. M. Payne, H. Scheeres, L. Shoemark, & S. Tiffin (Eds.), *Winds of change: Women and the culture of universities* (pp. 714–723). Sydney: University of Technology Sydney Press.

Bannerji, H., Carty, L., Dehli, K., Heald, S., & McKenna, K. (1991). *Unsettling relations: The university as a site of feminist struggles.* Toronto: Women's Press.

Bartky, S. L. (1990). *Femininity and domination: Studies in the phenomenology of oppression.* New York: Routledge.

Bauman, Z. (1992). Love in adversity: On the state and the intellectuals, and the state of the intellectuals. *Thesis Eleven, 31,* 81–104.

Beauregard, G. (1999). Travelling stereotypes: "The Japanese tourist" in Canada. *Communal/Plural, 7*(1), 79–95.

Becher, T. (1989). *Academic tribes and territories: Intellectual enquiry and the cultures of disciplines.* Milton Keynes, UK: Society for Research into Higher Education, Open University Press.

Benhabib, S., Butler, J., Cornell, D., & Fraser, N. (1995). *Feminist contentions.* New York: Routledge.

Beyer, P. (1998). Globalizing systems, global cultural models and religion(s). *International Sociology, 13*(1), 95–116.

Bhabha, H. (1991). The third space: Interview with Homi Bhabha. In J. Rutherford (Ed.), *Identity: Community, culture, difference.* London: Lawrence Wishart.

Birch, D. (1999). Reading state communication as public culture. In P. Chew & A. Kramer-Dahl (Eds.), *Reading culture: Textual practices in Singapore* (pp. 19–36). Singapore: Times Academic Press.

Blackmore, J., & Kenway, J. (Eds.). (1988). *Gender issues in the theory and practice of educational administration and policy.* Geelong: Deakin University Press.

Bloul, R. (1998). Gender and the globalization of Islamic discourses: A case study. In J. Kahn (Ed.), *Southeast Asian identities* (pp. 146–167). Singapore: Institute of Southeast Asian Studies.

Bordo, S. (1990). Feminism, postmodernism, and gender-skepticism. In L. Nicholson (Ed.), *Feminism/postmodernism* (pp. 133–156). New York: Routledge.

Boukhari, S. (1998, September). Graduates for hire. *UNESCO Courier, 31*–33.

Bourdieu, P. (1988). *Homo academicus.* Cambridge: Polity Press.

Bowen, M. (1994). Mainstreaming equity activities in universities: The next challenge. *Australian Universities' Review, 27*(2), 19–23.

Brah, A. (1996). *Cartographies of diaspora.* New York: Routledge.

Brooks, A. (1997). *Academic women.* Buckingham, UK: Open University Press.

Brown, D. (2000). *Contemporary nationalisms: Civic, ethnocultural & multicultural politics.* New York/London: Routledge.

Bulbeck, C. (1998). Women's movements in the Asia-Pacific. In R. Maidment & C. Mackerras (Eds.), *Culture and society in the Asia-Pacific* (pp. 163–184). London: Routledge.

Bunch, C., & Pollack, S. (Eds.). (1983). *Learning our ways: Essays in feminist education.* New York: Crossing Press.

Burbules, N., & Torres, C. (Eds.). (2000). *Globalization and education: Critical perspectives.* New York: Routledge.

Burton, C. (1997). *Gender equity in Australian university staffing.* Canberra: Department of Employment, Education, Training and Youth Affairs.

Butler, J. (1995). Contingent foundations. In S. Benhabib, J. Butler, D. Cornell, & N. Fraser (Eds.), *Feminist contentions* (pp. 35–58). New York: Routledge.

Castells, M. (1996). *The rise of the network society.* Oxford: Blackwell.

Castles, S. (1998). New migration in the Asia-pacific region: A force for social change. *International Social Science Journal, 50*(2), 215–228.

Chan, J. (2000). The status of women in a patriarchal state: The case of Singapore. In L. Edwards & M. Roces (Eds.), *Women in Asia: Tradition, modernity and globalisation* (pp. 39–58). Sydney: Allen & Unwin.

Cheah, P. (1998). The cosmopolitical—today. In P. Cheah & B. Robbins (Eds.), *Cosmopolitics: Thinking and feeling beyond the nation* (pp. 20–44). Minneapolis: University of Minnesota Press.

Cheah, P., & Robbins, B. (Eds.). (1998). *Cosmopolitics: Thinking and feeling beyond the nation.* Minneapolis: University of Minnesota Press.

Cheng, L., & Katz, M. (1998). Migration and the diaspora communities. In R. Maidment & C. Mackerras (Eds.), *Culture and society in the Asia-Pacific* (pp. 65–88). London: Routledge.

Chew, P. (1994). The Singapore council of women and the women's movement. *Journal of Southeast Asian Studies, 25*(1), 1–32.

Chow, R. (1993). *Writing diaspora: Tactics of intervention in contemporary cultural studies.* Bloomington: Indiana University Press.

Christian-Smith, L., & Kellor, K. (Eds.). (1999). *Everyday knowledge and uncommon truths: Women of the academy.* Boulder: Westview.

Chua, B. H. (1991). Not depoliticized but ideologically successful: The public housing programme in Singapore. *International Journal of Urban and Regional Research, 15*(1), 24–41.

Chua, B. H., & Tan, J. E. (1999). Singapore: Where the new middle class sets the standard. In M. Pinches (Ed.), *Culture and privilege in capitalist Asia* (pp. 137–158). London: Routledge.

Chua, B.-H. (Ed.). (2000a). *Consumption in Asia.* New York/London: Routledge.

Chua, B.-H. (2000b). Singaporeans ingesting McDonald's. In B.-H. Chua (Ed.), *Consumption in Asia: Lifestyles and identities* (pp. 183–201). New York/London: Routledge.

Chua, B.-H. (1998). Globalisation: Finding the appropriate words and levels. *Communal/Plural, 6*(1), 117–124.

Chutintaranond, S., & Cooparat, P. (1995). Comparative higher education: Burma and Thailand. In A. H. Yee (Ed.), *East Asian higher education* (pp. 55–68). Kidlington, UK: Pergamon/Elservier Science.

Clammer, J. (1995). Asian intellectuals and the university. *Pendidikan Tinggi— Higher Education, 2,* 31–47.

Clark, V., Garner, S., Higonnet, M., & Katrak, K. (Eds.). (1996). *Anti-feminism in the academy.* London: Routledge.

Cockburn, C. (1990). *In the way of women: Men's resistance to sex equality in organisatons.* London: Macmillan.

Cohen, D., Lee, A., Newman, J., Payne, A. M., Scheeres, H., Shoemark, L., & Tiffin, S. (1998). *Winds of change: Women and the culture of universities.* Sydney: University of Technology Sydney Press.

Committee on Quality Assurance in Higher Education. (1995). *Report on 1994 Quality Reviews.* (Vols. 1 & 2). Canberra: Australian Government Publishing Service.

Commonwealth Higher Education Management. (1998, December 16). *Single sex education? Representation by gender amongst staff at Commonwealth universities* [On-line]. Association for Commonwealth Universities. Available: http://www.acu.ac.uk/chems/surveys/women1.html.

Conway, J., & Bourque, S. (Eds.). (1993). *The politics of women's education: Perspectives from Asia, Africa, and Latin America.* Ann Arbor: University of Michigan Press.

Culley, M., & Portuges, C. (Eds.). (1985). *Gendered subjects: The dynamics of feminist teaching.* Boston: Routledge and Kegan Paul.

Davies, S., Lubelska, C., & Quinn, J. (Eds.). (1994). *Changing the subject: Women in higher education.* London: Taylor & Francis.

Dean, M. (1994). *Critical and effective histories.* New York: London.

Deleuze, G. (1986). *Foucault.* Minneapolis: University of Minnesota Press.

Derrida, J. (1987). Women in the beehive: A seminar. In A. Jardine & P. Smith (Eds.), *Men in feminism* (pp. 189–203). New York: Methuen.

DETYA. (1999). *Selected higher education staff statistics, 1998.* Canberra: Department of Employment, Education, Training, and Youth Affairs.

deLeon, C., & Ho, S.-C. (1994). The third identity of modern Chinese women: Women managers in Hong Kong. In N. Adler & D. Izraeli (Eds.), *Competitive frontiers: Women managers in a global economy* (pp. 43–56). London: Blackwell.

deWit, H. (Ed.). (1995). *Strategies for internationalisation of higher education: A comparative study of Australia, Canada, Europe and the United States of America.* Amsterdam: European Association for International Education.

Dicken, P., & Wai-Chung Yeung, H. (1999). Investing in the future: East and southeast Asian firms in the global economy. In K. Olds, P. Dicken, P. Kelly, L. Kong, & H. Wai-Chung Yeung (Eds.), *Globalization and the Asia-Pacific* (pp. 107–128). London: Routledge.

Dines, E. (Ed.). (1993). *Women in higher education management.* New York: UNESCO/Commonwealth Secretariat Publications.

Dirlik, A. (1996). The global in the local. In R. Wilson & W. Dissanayake (Eds.), *Global/local: Cultural production and the transnational imaginary* (pp. 197–221). Durham, NC: Duke University Press.

Edwards, L., & Roces, M. (Eds.). (2000). *Women in Asia: Tradition, modernity and globalisation.* Sydney: Allen & Unwin.

Eggins, H. (Ed.). (1997). *Women as leaders and managers in higher education.* Buckingham, UK: Open University Press.

Eisenstein, E. (1980). *The printing press as an agent of change* (Vols. 1 & 2). New York: Cambridge University Press.

Eisenstein, H. (1991). *Gender shock: Practicing feminism on two continents.* Sydney, NSW: Allen & Unwin.

Eisenstein, H. (1996). *Inside agitators: Australian femocrats and the state.* St. Leonards, NSW: Allen & Unwin.

Eisenstein, Z. (1988). *The female body and the law.* Berkeley: University of California Press.

Eisenstein, Z. (1994). *The color of gender: Reimaging democracy.* Berkeley: University of California Press.

Featherstone, M. (1995). Global and local cultures. In J. Bird, B. Curtis, T. Putnam, G. Robertson, & L. Tickner (Eds.), *Mapping the futures* (pp. 169–187). London: Routledge.

Featherstone, M. (1996). Localism, globalism, and cultural identity. In R. Wilson & W. Dissanayake (Eds.), *Global/local: Cultural production and the transnational imaginary* (pp. 46–77). Durham, NC: Duke University Press.

Featherstone, M., Lash, S., & Robertson, R. (Eds.). (1995). *Global modernities.* London: Sage.

Febvre, L., & Martin, H. J. (1976). *The coming of the book: The impact of printing 1450–1800.* Norfolk, UK: Lower & Brydone.

Foucault, M. (1977). *Discipline and punish: The birth of the prison.* New York: Pantheon.

Foucault, M. (1979). Governmentability. *Ideology and Consciousness, 6,* 5–22.

Foucault, M. (1983). Afterword: The subject and power. In H. L. Dreyfus & P. Rabinow (Eds.), *Michael Foucault: Beyond structuralism and hermeneutics* (pp. 208–226). Chicago: University of Chicago Press.

Foucault, M. (1989). *Foucault live: Interviews, 1966–1984* (J. Johnston, J., Trans.). New York: Columbia University/Semiotext(e).

Foucault, M., & Gordon, C. (1980). *Power/knowledge: Selected interviews and other writings, 1972–1977.* New York: Pantheon Books.

Fraser, N. (1995). False antithesis. In S. Benhabib, J. Butler, D. Cornell, & N. Fraser (Eds.), *Feminist contentions* (pp. 59–74). New York: Routledge.

Friedman, J. (1995). Global system, globalization and the parameters of modernity. In M. Featherstone, S. Lash, & R. Robertson (Eds.), *Global modernities* (pp. 69–90). London: Sage.

Friedman, J. (1997). Global crises, the struggle for cultural identity and intellectual porkbarrelling: Cosmopolitans versus locals, ethnics and nationals in an era of de-hegemonisation. In P. Werbner & T. Modood (Eds.), *Debating cultural hybridity* (pp. 70–89). London: Zed Books.

Fuss, D. J. (1989). *Essentially speaking: Feminism, nature & difference*. New York: Routledge.

Gallop, J. (1995). *Pedagogy: The question of impersonation*. Bloomington: Indiana University Press.

Gibbons, M. (1998). A commonwealth perspective on the globalization of higher education. In P. Scott (Ed.), *The globalization of higher education* (pp. 70–87). Buckingham, UK: Open University Press.

Gibson-Graham, J. K. (1996). *The end of capitalism (as we knew it)*. Oxford: Blackwell.

Gibson-Graham, J. K. (1997). Re-placing class in economic geographies: Possibilities for a new class politics. In R. Lee & J. Wills (Eds.), *Geographies of economies* (pp. 87–97). London/New York: Arnold.

Gilligan, C. (1982). *In a different voice*. Cambridge: Harvard University Press.

Girling, J. (1996). *Interpreting development: Capitalism, democracy, and the middle class in Thailand*. Ithaca, NY: Cornell University Press.

Glazer-Raymo, J. (1999). *Shattering the myths: Women in academe*. Baltimore: Johns Hopkins University Press.

Gore, J. (1993). The struggle for pedagogies. New York: Routledge.

Hacking, I. (1982). Biopower and the avalanche of printed numbers. *Humanities in Society, 5*(3 & 4), 279–295.

Hannerz, U. (1992). *Cultural complexity: Studies in the organization of meaning*. New York: Columbia University Press.

Hannerz, U. (1997). *Scenarios for peripheral cultures*. Minneapolis: University of Minnesota Press.

Haraway, D. J. (1988). Situated knowledges: The science question in feminism and the privilege of partial perspective. *Feminist Studies, 14*(Fall 1988), 575–599.

Haraway, D. J. (1992). *Primate visions: Gender, race, and nature in the world of modern science*. London: Verso.

Harvey, D. (1995). Globalization in question. *Rethinking Marxism, 8*(4), 1–17.

Hashim, R. (1997). Women in management in the University of Malaya: A brief update. Paper presented at the Women and Management in Higher Education Conference, Sri Lanka.

Hede, A. (1994). The glass ceiling metaphor: Towards a theory of managerial inequity. *Canberra Bulletin of Public Administration, 76*, 77–90.

Heelas, P., Lash, S., & Morris, P. (Eds.). (1996). *Detraditionalization*. Oxford: Blackwell.

Heng, G., & Devan, J. (1992). State fatherhood: The politics of nationalism, sexuality, and race in Singapore. In A. Parker, M. Russo, D. Sommer, & P.

Yaeger (Eds.), *Nationalisms and sexualities* (pp. 343-363). New York: Routledge.

Henry, M. (1994). Ivory towers and ebony women: The experiences of black women in higher education. In S. Davies, C. Lubelska, & J. Quinn (Eds.), *Changing the subject: Women in higher education* (pp. 42–57). London: Taylor & Francis.

Heryanto, A. (1999). The years of living luxuriously: Identity politics of Indonesia's new rich. In M. Pinches (Ed.), *Culture and privilege in capitalist Asia* (pp. 159–187). London: Routledge.

Heward, C. (1994). Academic snakes and merit ladders: Reconceptualising the "glass ceiling." *Gender and Education, 6*(3), 249–262.

Heward, C. (1996). Women and careers in higher education: What is the problem? In L. Morley & V. Walsh (Eds.), *Breaking boundaries: Women in higher education* (pp. 11–23). London: Taylor & Francis.

Heward, C., Taylor, P., & Vickers, R. (1997). Gender, race and career success in the academic profession. *Journal of Further and Higher Education, 21*(2), 205–218.

Hewison, K., & Rodan, G. (1996). The ebb and flow of civil society and the decline of the left in southeast Asia. In G. Rodan (Ed.), *Political oppositions in industrialising Asia* (pp. 40–71). London: Routledge.

Hill, M., & Lian, K. F. (1995). *The politics of nation building and citizenship in Singapore.* London: Routledge.

Holbrook, A., & Johnston, S. (Eds.). (19909). *Supervision of postgraduate research in education.* Lilydale, Australia: Australian Association for Research in Education/Commodore Press.

Hong Kong University Graduate Committee. (1999). *Staff and students* [Online]. Available: http://www.ugc.edu.hk.

Howell, J. D. (1998). Religion. In R. Maidment & C. Mackerras (Eds.), *Culture and society in the Asia-Pacific* (pp. 115–140). London: Routledge.

IDP Australia. (1999, June 10). *Australia's exports of education services* [Online]. IDP Education Australia. Available: http://www.idp.edu.au/research/International.

Itzin, C. (1994). The gender culture in organisations. In C. Itzin & J. Newman (Eds.), *Gender, culture, and organisational change* (pp. 11–29). London: Routledge.

Jones, K. (1991). The trouble with authority. *Differences, 5*(1), 104–127.

Kahn, J. (1995). *Culture, multiculture, postculture.* London: Sage.

Kahn, J. (1998). *Southeast Asian identities.* Singapore/London: Institute of Southeast Asian Studies.

Kaplan, C. (1994). The politics of location as transnational feminist critical practice. In I. Grewall & C. Kaplan (Eds.), *Scattered hegemonies* (pp. 132–146). Minneapolis: University of Minnesota Press.

Kaplan, E. A. (1997). Feminism, aging, and changing paradigms. In D. Looser & E. A. Kaplan (Eds.), *Generations: Academic feminists in dialogue* (pp. 13–30). Minneapolis: University of Minnesota Press.

King, A. (1995). The times and spaces of modernity (or who needs postmodernism?). In M. Featherstone, S. Lash, & S. Robertson (Eds.), *Global modernities* (pp. 108–123). London: Sage.

King, A. (Ed.). (1997). *Culture, globalization and the world-system.* Minneapolis: University of Minnesota Press.

King, C. (1997). Through the glass ceiling: Networking by women managers in higher education. In H. Eggins (Ed.), *Women as leaders and managers in higher education* (pp. 91–100). Buckingham, UK: Open University Press.

Knodel, J. (1997). The closing of the gender gap in schooling: The case of Thailand. *Comparative Education, 33*(1), 61–86.

Kojima, Y. (1995). *Women in development: Mongolia.* Bangkok: Asia Development Bank.

Koh, T. A. (1996). Wandering through the minefield: Leading who, where to and for what? *Awareness, 3*(1), 23–30.

Kong, L. (1999). Globalisation, transmigration and the renegotiation of ethnic identity. In K. Olds, P. Dicken, P. Kelly, L. Kong, & H. Wai-Chung Yeung (Eds.), *Globalisation and the Asia-Pacific* (pp. 219–237). New York: Routledge.

Kuo, E. C. Y. (1987). *Confucianism and the Chinese family in Singapore: Continuities and changes.* Singapore: National University of Singapore/Department of Sociology. Working Paper #83.

Lather, P. (1991). *Getting smart: Feminist research and pedagogy with/in the postmodern.* New York: Routledge.

Lau, C. K. (1997). *Hong Kong's colonial legacy.* Hong Kong: The Chinese University Press.

Ledwith, S., & Colgan, F. (Eds.). (1996). *Women in organisations: Challenging gender politics.* Basingstoke, UK: Macmillan.

Lee, J., Campbell, K., & Chia, A. (1999). *The three paradoxes: Working women in Singapore.* Singapore: Association of Women for Action and Research (AWARE).

Leitch, A. (1999). We are not all sisters: Illusions of equity in affirmative action. In L. Cohen, A. Lee, J. Newman, A. M. Payne, H. Scheeres, L. Shoemark, & S. Tiffin (Eds.), *Winds of change: Women and the culture of universities* (pp. 123–126). Sydney: University of Technology Sydney Press.

Lenn, M. P., & Campos, L. (Eds.). (1998). *Multinational discourse in professional accreditation, certification, and licensure: Bridges for the globalizing professions.* Washington, DC: Center for Quality Assurance in International Education.

Lewis, M. G. (1993). *Without a word: Teaching beyond women's silence.* New York: Routledge.

Lewis, M., & Simon, R. (1986). A discourse not intended for her: Learning and teaching within patriarchy. *Harvard Educational Review, 56*(4), 475–72.

Lewis, R. (1996). *Gendering orientalism: Race, femininity, representation.* London: Routledge.

Leyshon, A. (1997). Introduction: True stories? Global nightmares, global dreams and writing globalization. In R. Lee & J. Wills (Eds.), *Geographies of economies* (pp. 133–146). London: Arnold.

Lie, S., & O'Leary, V. (Eds.). (1990). *Storming the tower: Women in the academic world.* London: Kogan Page.

Lim, T. G. (1995). Malaysia and Singaporean higher education: Common roots but differing directions. In A. Yee (Ed.), *East Asian higher education* (pp. 69–83). Oxford: Pergamon.

Limanonda, B. (2000). Exploring women's status in contemporary Thailand. In L. Edwards & M. Roces (Eds.), *Women in Asia: Tradition, modernity and gobalisation* (pp. 247–264). Sydney: Allen & Unwin.

Low, G. T. (1997). Women, education and development in Singapore. In S. Gopinathan (Ed.), *Education in Singapore* (pp. 343–362). Singapore: Prentice-Hall.

Lui, H.-K., & Suen, W. (1993). The narrowing gender gap in Hong Kong: 1976–1986. *Asian Economic Journal, 7*(2), 167–180.

Luke, C. (1989). *Pedagogy, printing, and protestantism: The discourse on childhood.* Albany: State University of New York Press.

Luke, C. (1994). White women in interracial families: Reflections on hybridization, feminine identities, and racialized othering. *Feminist Issues, 14*(2), 49–72.

Luke, C. (1996). Feminist pedagogy theory: Reflections on power and authority. *Educational Theory, 46*(3), 283–302.

Luke, C. (1999, June). *Women's career mobility in higher education: Case studies in southeast Asia.* Association of Commonwealth Universities Bulletin of Current Documentation, 139.

Luke, C., & Carrington, V. (2000). Race matters. *Journal of Intercultural Studies, 21*(1), 5–24.

Luke, C., & Gore, J. (Eds.). (1992). *Feminism and critical pedagogy*. New York: Routledge.

Luke, C., & Luke, A. (1998). Interracial families: Difference within difference. *Ethnic and Racial Studies, 21*(4), 728–754.

Luke, C., & Luke, A. (1999). Theorising interracial families and hybrid identity: An Australian perspective. *Educational Theory, 49*(2), 223–249.

Lyotard, J. (1984). *The postmodern condition*. Manchester: Manchester University Press.

Maher, F. (1985). Pedagogies for the gender-balanced classroom. *Journal of Thought* [Special Issue: Feminist Education], *20*(3), 48–64.

Maher, F. A., & Tetreault, M. K. T. (1994). *The feminist classroom*. New York: Basic Books.

Mak, G. (Ed.). (1996). *Women, education, and development in Asia*. New York: Garland Publishing.

Malik, L., & Lie, S. (Eds.). (1994). *The gender gap in higher education*. London: Kogan Page.

Mallea, J. (1999). *International trade in professional and educational services: Implications for the professions and higher education*. Paris: Organisation for Economic Co-operation and Development/Centre for Educational Research and Innovation (CERI).

Marchand, M., & Parpart, J. (Eds.). (1995). *Feminism/postmodernism/development*. London: Routledge.

Marshall, C. (Ed.). (1994). *The new politics of race and gender*. London: Falmer Press.

Marshall, C. (Ed.). (1997). *Feminist critical policy analysis*. London: Falmer Press.

Marshall, J. (1995). *Women managers moving on*. New York: Routledge.

Mazumdar, V. (1993). A survey of gender issues and educational development in Asia. In J. Conway & S. Bourque (Eds.), *The politics of women's education: Perspectives from Asia, Africa, and Latin* (pp. 15–22). Ann Arbor: University of Michigan Press.

McDonald, M. (1995). *Women in development:* Vietnam. Bangkok: Asia Development Bank.

McNeely, C., & Cha, Y.-K. (1994). Worldwide educational convergence through international organizations: Avenues for research. *Education Policy Analysis Archives, 2*(14), 1–11.

Mees, W. (1998). National difference and global citizenship. In J. Kahn (Ed.), *Southeast Asian identities* (pp. 227–269). Singapore: Institute of Southeast Asian Studies.

Middleton, S. (1993). *Educating feminists: Life histories and pedagogy.* New York: Columbia University Press.

Ministry of Community Development. (1995). *Singapore—A pro-family society.* Singapore: Family Development Division, Ministry of Community Development.

Ministry of Community Development. (1996). *Singapore family values.* Singapore: Ministry of Community Development.

Ministry of University Affairs. (1998). *Fact and figures* [On-line]. Government of Thailand. Available: http://www.inter.mua.go.tha.

Mohamad, M., & Wong, S. K. (1994). Introduction: Malaysian critique and experience of feminism. *Kajian Malaysia: Journal of Malaysian Studies, 12*(1 & 2), i–xiii.

Mohamad, M. (1994). Poststructuralism, power and third world feminism. *Kajian Malaysia: Journal of Malaysian Studies, 12*(1 & 2), 119–143.

Mohanty, C. T., Russo, A., & Torres, L. (Eds.). (1991). *Third world women and the politics of feminism.* Bloomington: Indiana University Press.

Morley, L., & Walsh, V. (Eds.). (1996). *Breaking boundaries: Women in higher education.* London: Taylor & Francis.

Morris, P., & Sweeting, A. (1995). *Education and development in East Asia.* New York: Garland Press.

Mouffe, C. (1993). *The return of the political.* New York/London: Verso.

Murphy, P. (1993). Research policy, quality assurance and affirmative action. In A. Payne & L. Shoemark (Eds.), *Women, culture, and universities: A chilly climate?* (pp. 223–233). Sydney: University of Technology Sydney Press.

Narain, M. (1997). Shifting locations: Third world feminists and institutional apioras. In D. Looser & E. A. Kaplan (Eds.), *Generations: Academic feminists in dialogue* (pp. 151–164). Minneapolis: University of Minnesota Press.

Nicholls, J. (1994). Qualitiative judgements: Women and the quality fund. *NTEU Frontline, 1*(1), 6.

Nicholson, L. (Ed.). (1990). *Feminism/postmodernism.* New York: Routledge.

Noddings, N. (1984). *Caring: A feminine approach to ethics and moral education.* Berkeley: University of California Press.

Ockey, J. (1999). Creating the Thai middle class. In M. Pinches (Ed.), *Culture and privilege in capitalist Asia* (pp. 230–250). London: Routledge.

OECD. (1998). *International trade in professional services: Advancing liberalisation through regulatory reform.* Paris: OECD.

Oerton, S. (1996). *Beyond hierarchy: Gender, sexuality and the social economy.* London: Taylor & Francis.

Omar, A. H. (1993). Women managers in higher education in Malaysia. In E. Dines (Ed.), *Women in higher education management.* (pp. 121–133). New York: UNESCO/Commonwealth Secretariat Publications.

Ong, A. (1998). Flexible citizenship among Chinese cosmopolitans. In P. Cheah & B. Robbins (Eds.), *Cosmopolitics: Thinking and feeling beyond the nation* (pp. 135–162). Minneapolis: University of Minnesota Press.

Payne, A. M., & Shoemark, L. (Eds.). (1995). *Women, culture and universities: A chilly climate?* Sydney: University of Technology Sydney Press.

Peters, M. (1992). Performance and accountability in post-industrial societies: The crisis of British universities. *Studies in Higher Education, 17*(2), 123–139.

Perera, L. (1996). How men see women: The changing reality in today's Singapore. In A. E. Collective (Ed.), *The ties that bind: In search of the modern Singapore family* (pp. 168–189). Singapore: Armour Publishing.

Phongpaichit, P., & Baker, C. (1996). *Thailand's boom.* Sydney: Allen & Unwin.

Pieterse, J. (1995). Globalisation as hybridization. In M. Featherstone, S. Lash, & R. Robertson (Eds.), *Global modernities* (pp. 45–68). London: Sage.

Pinches, M. (1996). The Philippines. In R. Robison & D. Goodman (Eds.), *The new rich in Asia* (pp. 105–136). London: Routledge.

Pinches, M. (1999a). Cultural relations, class and the new rich in Asia. In M. Pinches (Ed.), *Culture and privilege in capitalist Asia* (pp. 1–55). London: Routledge.

Pinches, M. (1999b). Entrepreneurship, consumption, ethnicity and national identity and the making of the Philippines' new rich. In M. Pinches (Ed.), *Culture and privilege in capitalist Asia* (pp. 275–301). London: Routledge.

Pinches, M. (Ed.). (1999c). *Culture and privilege in capitalist Asia.* London: Routledge.

Poole, M. (1995). *Leaving the sticky floor and shattering the glass ceiling.* Paper presented at the Women in Education Conference, Sydney.

Probert, B. (1994). Women's working lives. In K. Pritchard-Hughes (Ed.), *Contemporary Australian feminism* (pp. 153–176). Melbourne: Longman Cheshire.

PuruShotam, N. (1998). Between compliance and resistance: Women and the middle-class way of life in Singapore. In K. Sen & M. Stevens (Eds.), *Gender and power in affluent Asia* (pp. 127–166). London: Routledge.

Rajan, R. (1997). The third world academic in other places; or, the postcolonial intellectual revisited. *Critical Inquiry, 23,* 596–616.

Raslan, K. (1998). *Ceritalah: Malaysia in transition.* Kuala Lumpur: Times Books International.

Reynolds, C. (1998). Globalization and cultural nationalism in modern Thailand. In J. Kahn (Ed.), *Southeast Asian identities* (pp. 115–145). Singapore: Institute of Southeast Asian Studies.

Rizvi, F. (2000). International education and the production of global imagination. In N. Burbules & C. Torres (Eds.), *Globalization and education: Critical perspectives* (pp. 205–226). New York: Routledge.

Robertson, R. (1992). *Globalization.* London: Sage.

Robertson, R. (1995). Glocalization: Time-space and homogeneity-heterogeneity. In M. Featherstone, S. Lash, & R. Robertson (Eds.), *Global modernities* (pp. 25–44). London: Sage.

Robertson, R. (1997). Social theory, cultural relativity and the problem of globality. In A. King (Ed.), *Culture, globalization and the world-system* (pp. 69–90). Minneapolis: University of Minnesota Press.

Robertson, R., & Khondker, H. (1998). Discourses of globalisation: Preliminary considerations. *International Sociology, 13*(1), 25–40.

Robison, R., Beeson, M., Jaysuriya, K., & Kim, J.-R. (Eds.). (2000). *Politics and markets in the wake of the Asian crisis.* New York/London: Routledge.

Robison, R., & Goodman, D. (Eds.). (1996). *The new rich in Asia.* London: Routledge.

Rodan, G. (Ed.). (1996). *Political oppositions in industrialising Asia.* London: Routledge.

Rojek, C., & Urry, J. (1997). Transformations of travel and theory. In C. Rojek & J. Urry (Eds.), *Touring cultures* (pp. 1–22). London: Routledge.

Rollison, K. (1999). "I never feel I'm different from the men. Never.". In L. Cohen, A. Lee, J. Newman, A. M. Payne, H. Scheeres, L. Shoemark, & S. Tiffin (Eds.), *Winds of change: Women and the cultures of universities* (pp. 246–259). Sydney: University of Technology Sydney Press.

Rose, G. (1993). *Feminism and geography.* Cambridge: Polity Press.

Ross, C. (1996). Struggling for inclusion: Black women in professional and management education. In L. Morley & V. Walsh (Eds.), *Breaking boundaries: Women in higher education* (pp. 90–101). London: Taylor & Francis.

Sadler, D. (1997). The role of supply chain management strategies in the "'Europeanization'" of the automobile production system. In R. Lee & J. Wills (Eds.), *Geographies of economies* (pp. 311–320). London: Arnold.

Scheurich, J. J. (1997). *Research method in the postmodern.* London: Falmer Press.

Schniedewind, N., & Maher, F. (Eds.). (1987). Feminist pedagogy [Special issue]. *Women's Studies Quarterly, 15*(3 & 4).

Scott, P. (1998a). Massification, internationalization and globalization. In P. Scott (Ed.), *The globalization of higher education* (pp. 108–129). Buckingham, UK: Open University Press.

Scott, P. (Ed.). (1998b). *The globalization of higher education.* Buckingham, UK: Open University Press.

Setiadarma, E. M. (1993). Indonesian women in higher education management. In E. Dines (Ed.), *Women in higher education management* (pp. 105–119). New York: UNESCO/Commonwealth Secretariat Publications.

Shamsul, A. B. (1999). From Orang Kaya Baru to Melayu Baru: Cultural construction of the Malay 'new rich'. In M. Pinches (Ed.), *Culture and privilege in capitalist Asia* (pp. 86–110). London: Routledge.

Sidin, R. (1996). Malaysia. In G. Mak (Ed.), *Women, education, and development in Asia* (pp. 119–142). New York: Garland Publishing.

Siengthai, S. L. O. (1994). Women in management in Thailand. In N. N. Adler & D. Izraeli (Eds.), *Competitive frontiers: Women managers in a global economy* (pp. 160–171). London: Blackwell.

Singh, J. (1997). Partnerships for sustainable educational development. *The Australian Educational Researcher, 24*(1), 27–48.

Smith, D. (1990). *The conceptual practices of power: A feminist sociology of knowledge.* Boston: Northeastern University Press.

Smock, A. (1981). *Women's education in the developing countries: Opportunities and outcomes.* New York: Praeger.

Soin, K. (1996). National policies: Their impact on women and the family. In A. E. Collective (Ed.), *The ties that bind: In search of the modern Singapore family* (pp. 190–208). Singapore: Armour Publishing.

Spain, D. (1992). *Gendered spaces.* Chapel Hill: University of North Carolina Press.

Spivak, G. C. (1993). *Outside in the teaching machine.* New York: Routledge.

Spurling, A. (1997). Women and change in higher education. In H. Eggins (Ed.), *Women as leaders and managers in higher education* (pp. 49–62). Buckingham: Open University Press.

Spring, J. H. (1998). *Education and the rise of the global economy.* Mahwah, NJ: Lawrence Erlbaum Associates.

Still, L. (1993). *Where to from here? The managerial woman in transition.* Sydney: Business and Professional Publishing.

Stivens, M. (1998). Sex, gender and the making of the new Malay middle classes. In K. Sen & M. Stivens (Eds.), *Gender and power in affluent Asia* (pp. 87–126). New York/London: Routledge.

Index

DATE DUE

DEMCO 38-296